They Have No Rights

Dred Scott

Harriet Scott

Eliza and Lizzie Scott

THEY HAVE NO RIGHTS

Dred Scott's Struggle for Freedom

Walter Ehrlich

Contributions in Legal Studies, Number 9

Greenwood Press
Westport, Connecticut • London, England

Library of Congress Cataloging in Publication Data

Ehrlich, Walter, 1921-
    They have no rights.

    (Contributions in legal studies ; no. 9 ISSN 0147-1074)
    Bibliography: p.
    Includes index.
    1. Scott, Dred. 2. Slavery in the United States--
Law. I. Title. II. Series.
KF 4545.S5E35   346'.73'013   78-22135
ISBN 0-313-20819-0

Library of Congress Catalog Card Number: 78-22135
ISBN: 0-313-20819-0
ISSN: 0147-1074

First published in 1979

Greenwood Press, Inc.
51 Riverside Avenue, Westport, Connecticut 06880

Printed in the United States of America

10 9 8 7 6 5 4 3 2

Shortly before completing this book I suffered a severe heart attack. I was fortunate to be "recalled to life," in the words of the immortal Charles Dickens. I humbly dedicate this book to all who contributed to that "recall," especially the skillful personnel of the Medical Intensive Care Unit of the Jewish Hospital of St. Louis, with sentiments of heartfelt appreciation and affection that no words can possibly express. I wish I could do more.

Contents

Illustrations

Preface

EXCEPT FOR *MARBURY* V. *MADISON,* probably more has been written about *Dred Scott* v. *John F. A. Sanford* than about any other litigation in the history of the United States Supreme Court. In what has been recorded as perhaps its most ill-advised and unfortunate action, the Court attempted in 1857 to solve a virtually unsolvable issue; instead it unleashed irreconcilable passions that merged with those already building inexorably to the outbreak of hostilities between North and South. At the very least the decision was a major factor contributing to the nation's calamitous plunge toward civil war; it may even have been the crucial "point of no return." True, the doctrine of popular sovereignty in the Kansas-Nebraska Act (1854) awakened what Professor Allan Nevins referred to as the "sleeping tiger" of sectional antagonisms. But Kansas-Nebraska only opened portions of the old Louisiana Purchase territory to slavery; *Dred Scott* seemed to give constitutional sanction to the "peculiar institution," placing Negro slavery in the same category with any other property protected by the nation's highest law. If that was not enough, many construed the Court's action as the vanguard of a movement to legalize slavery everywhere. (That is not, of course, what the Court did; what is important, though, is that many believed it was what the Court would do, given its logic in *Dred Scott.*)

This intrusion by the Court into the slavery issue created an unprecedented political dilemma. It appeared to compromise the Republican party, whose very *raison d'etre* now seemed undermined. Continued existence as a party demanded respect for law; but that existence also demanded the overturn of *Dred Scott* law. This meant attacking the Court, not the law, by focusing on an unwarranted *obiter dictum* charge and by exacerbating a supposed "Slave Power conspiracy."

Still, the political realities of the time offered little likelihood for a successful resolution of the Republicans' predicament. The newly elected Thirty-fifth Congress, controlled by Democrats and with proslave southerners in many key positions, certainly could not be expected to counteract the decision by legislation. Nor was there any foreseeable prospect that the Court would reverse itself. It would be at least four years before the electoral process might place in the White House and in Congress the necessary combination to make appropriate Supreme Court appointments, and even that was predicated upon vacancies or congressional legislation enlarging the Court. A constitutional amendment that might reconcile differences over *Dred Scott* also was out of the question, for it would require considerable legislative and popular support, neither of which existed in 1857.

Reversing a Supreme Court decision by any other way involved a hard new look at existing American institutions. To many in both North and South any compromise over slavery was now impossible. After *Dred Scott,* consequently, the attack on slavery was bound to involve action more radical than anything the democratic process had ever before experienced; and in like manner, the defense of slavery was destined to become equally inflexible. Indeed, once the Court had spoken in *Dred Scott,* the two sections, if they had not been so committed before, now were irrevocably moving down a road that could lead only to disaster. Even though some historians argue that the Civil War still might have been averted, events developed otherwise. As Lincoln predicted, the "house" no longer could remain divided. Many doubted whether the American political process could survive the struggle that loomed ominously ahead.

How those events unfolded has been told time and time again. So much has been written about the causes of the Civil War that one wonders what can be added. Certainly this is true of the *Dred Scott* decision; indeed, within the past few years Carl Brent Swisher, David M. Potter, and Don E. Fehrenbacher have authored excellent works on what the Court said and did. Scholars have repeatedly analyzed Chief Justice Roger Brooke Taney's Opinion of the Court as well as the concurring and dissenting opinions. They have interpreted and reinterpreted those opinions in light of both contemporary and later events and developments. Yet, except for the one attempt by Vincent Hopkins (*Dred Scott's Case* [New York, 1951]), the detailed morphology of the case itself—the intricate unfolding of the puzzling events and the perplexing involvements of the famous and not-so-famous people—has never been done.

I have written a history of the *Dred Scott* case, from its obscure inception in 1846 through the dramatic pronouncements in the Supreme Court on Friday and Saturday mornings, March 6 and 7, 1857. Earlier writers have been more concerned with the legal and political implications of the decision and have dealt only tangentially with the litigation itself. Even those who did attempt a more probing analysis encountered an especially difficult obstacle: they were unable to locate critical court documents long believed missing. I did locate them, and their contents clarified many misunderstandings about how this fascinating case evolved. I have analyzed heretofore unused lawyers' briefs to trace changes in arguments and issues that converted an insignificant local action into a national event of immense consequence. Furthermore, all analyses of this fateful decision have been based on the official Supreme Court version published in 19 Howard 393 (1857). Scholars have overlooked that that Opinion of the Court is significantly different in some places from what was read in open Court by Chief Justice Taney and reported in the press. For two months before the official decision was available, public attitudes and reactions, often firmly and intractably established, were based upon a press version of Taney's opinion that no scholar has examined critically. By using important materials heretofore unknown or overlooked, I have put together for the first time the full story of an important event that contributed so much to American history.

But does a knowledge of the details of this case really mean that much? Does it matter, as J. H. Plumb asks rhetorically in *The Death of the Past* (Boston, 1971), whether we know all that actually occurred? Is it not how we interpret the past that is important, rather than the details of those bygone years? What is there about the history of the *Dred Scott* "case" that warrants its telling rather than some novel interpretation of the *Dred Scott* "decision"?

One answer is that Professor Plumb's contentions are oversimplistically Baconian and anti-intellectually utilitarian. In an era characterized by unwarranted pressures upon historians for innovative interpretations, there is need to clarify what the historical craft is all about and to remind ourselves, as Professor William W. Freehling does, that "the historian's task is not to judge but to explain" ("The Founding Fathers and Slavery," *The American Historical Review* 78 [February 1972] : 82). But even those who want to judge must concede the obvious: one cannot judge without the facts.

In the specific instance of *Dred Scott*, reactions to that decision cannot be fully appreciated unless one comprehends what the Court said (and did not say) and the context in which those statements were rendered. Unfortunately, points out Professor Stanley I. Kutler (*Judicial Power and Reconstruction* [Chicago, 1968], p. 7), "more attention has been lavished on the political and public reaction to the decision . . . than on the actual opinions of the Supreme Court justices." This brings us directly to the engrossing litigative evolution of Dred Scott's struggle for freedom, for the controversial decision would not have occurred as it occurred had it not been for the unique character of the litigation itself. When it started there were no constitutional questions involved. But as it progressed through the courts, issues changed: from noncontroversial to controversial, from *pro forma* freedom under accepted state law to interstate comity to slavery in the territories to citizenship of blacks to the constitutionality of the Missouri Compromise. Furthermore, new issues were added by judges as well as by counsel.

Without these unique developments this case never would have reached the Supreme Court to become a *cause célèbre*. Thus the history of the litigation itself is important, because it was how and why and when the issues changed that created the monumental dilemma for Taney and his colleagues. The case came into the federal courts not to challenge any legislation that manumitted slaves who went into a free state or territory; that was long-accepted doctrine, although many in the South would have changed it. At issue was whether such admittedly emancipated persons could be remanded to bondage by returning to a slave state. Suddenly the whole focus changed when counsel introduced the radical concept that denied freedom in free territory in the first place. A study of the history of this case shows also that the opposition to the decision was not by "the North" or by "the northern press" as is commonly taught. Northern Democrats tended either to applaud the decision or to accept it begrudgingly as the voice of their highest tribunal, hoping such a judicial pronouncement finally might settle the divisive slavery issue. The Republican and abolitionist press, though, spewed billingsgate and vituperation upon the Court, distorting what Taney said into something even more nefarious than it was. The press, not the chief justice, was responsible for the phrase Negroes "have no rights" that white men were bound to respect. Furthermore, a careful reading of the decision shows that Taney's "Opinion of the Court" was not really that at all—it was his own reasoning and his own law, not an accurate reflection of what the majority maintained. An analysis of all nine opinions makes it abundantly clear that the *obiter dictum* accusation is without foundation, regardless of the substantive odium of that portion of the decision.

Last but not least, a knowledge of how this litigation unfolded shows how close both the Missouri and the United States supreme courts came to exercising judicial restraint and avoiding calumny. History easily could have sidestepped *Dred Scott*; it did not. That is another reason why the morphology of this case is so important. For in addition to inferring questions about the function of the historian and the responsibility of the press, this book also suggests questions about the role of the judiciary. Where should we draw the line between what the Court should decide and what should be determined instead by legislative processes? It is the same question posed by Raoul Berger (*Government by Judiciary* [Cambridge, 1977], p. 2) and others: Is the Supreme Court a "continuing constitutional convention"?

One final note. Since this is a history of the case and not of the decision, it is not possible in so brief a discussion to do justice to the exciting developments that followed March 6-7, 1857, and contributed to the polarization that resulted in civil conflagration. Others deal with those events; I hope I have given them due credit in footnote references. Furthermore, many scholars have written excellent analyses and interpretive essays about *Dred Scott,* either in journal articles or as portions of biographies or period studies. I have tried not to rehash their scholarship but rather to summarize and incorporate it in my unfolding narrative. I hope I have given them, too, their fully merited credit. If I have slighted anyone, I accept full responsibility and apologize unhesitatingly.

My sincerest thanks go to many who made this work possible. Librarians and archivists far too numerous to list have my deepest appreciation, but I would be remiss if I did not single out those at the Library of Congress, the National Archives, the Missouri Historical Society, and the St. Louis Public Library. I am equally indebted to many courteous and cooperative court officials in St. Louis, Jefferson City, New York, and Washington. Ralph P. Bieber and Elmer E. Hilpert, of the Washington University history department and law school respectively, were my original mentors in this enterprise. Along the way I received invaluable advice and assistance from Carl Brent Swisher, E. Merton Coulter, and William N. Chambers. Chief Justice Fred M. Vinson, Associate Justice Wiley B. Rutledge, and Clerk of

the Court Harold B. Willey made me feel right at home in the Supreme
Court of the United States. I owe much of my knowledge about the black
community of St. Louis to Ellis S. Outlaw. Stanley N. Katz and Don E.
Fehrenbacher read my manuscript in its entirety, and I am grateful for
their constructive criticisms and suggestions and especially for their support and encouragement. My sincerest thanks for their helpful observations on portions of my manuscript to Harold M. Hyman and William M.
Wiecek. Among my colleagues in the University of Missouri-St. Louis
history department, James N. Primm, James L. Roark, and Louis S.
Gerteis have been especially helpful. At various times I benefited from
scholarly observations by Stanley I. Kutler, Raoul Berger, Jack P. Mad-
dex, and Louis Filler. I thank them all. My department's clerical staff put
in endless hours typing numerous manuscript drafts; my appreciation
is extended to them. No publication is possible without proper editorial
assistance, and for this I am grateful to Paul L. Murphy and to Greenwood
Press's fine editorial staff, especially James T. Sabin, Nancy J. Clements,
and Mary A. De Vries. Last but certainly not least, there are no words
that can ever express my deepest feelings for a loving and understanding
wife and family who for years simply accepted Dred Scott as just another
member of the family. To all these people and more, my gratitude for
what is good about this book. I alone am responsible for anything negative.

They
Have No
Rights

Prologue

FRIDAY, MARCH 6, 1857. A capacity crowd filled the chamber of the Supreme Court of the United States, on the ground floor of the north wing of the Capitol building. The anxiously awaited decision in *Dred Scott v. John F. A. Sanford*[1] was about to be pronounced. Then, speaking in a tone that was very low and at times barely audible, Chief Justice Roger Brooke Taney addressed the hushed and attentive audience. What he said that morning was speedily and widely—and inaccurately—reported in newspapers throughout the country. In reacting to what was reported, the American people moved inexorably closer to the Civil War.

The *Dred Scott* decision dealt with highly emotional slavery issues that for years had been the focal point of bitter controversy. But now the Supreme Court seemingly had strengthened and legalized one side against the other. According to this decision, many believed, Negro slaves were a species of private property protected by the Constitution of the United States. Blacks were inferior people who could not be citizens of the United States. Furthermore, that portion of the Missouri Compromise Act of March 6, 1820, that had prohibited slavery in the Louisiana Purchase territory north of $36°30'$ was now declared to have been an unconstitutional assumption of power by Congress. Not only was that law null and void, but presumably prohibitions against slavery in Oregon and Washington territories now could be invalidated; and any future attempt by Congress to stem the spread of slavery in the territories would meet the same fate. Some even thought the inevitable next step would be the legalizing of slavery throughout the nation.[2]

Coming at a time when these issues were the subject of extremely bitter sectional and politically partisan debate, and the cause already for

violence and bloodshed in Kansas and elsewhere, the *Dred Scott* decision
and the resulting reaction added fuel to the fires of dissension burning
fiercely toward secession and civil war. The highly charged opposition to
the Supreme Court's decision became a vital factor in the resurgence of
the Republican party following the presidential election of 1856.[3] Furthermore, this decision was one of the main points of controversy between
Abraham Lincoln and Stephen A. Douglas in their hotly contested senatorial campaign in 1858; and it was during these famous debates, in an
attempt to reconcile the principles of the *Dred Scott* decision with the
theory of popular sovereignty, that Douglas enunciated his ill-fated Freeport Doctrine. One reaction to the Freeport Doctrine was the demand
by some southern leaders for a congressional slave code. The dispute over
this demand, resulting from differing interpretations of just what the Supreme Court had adjudicated, led to the North-South split at the Democratic national convention in Charleston in 1860. That paved the way for
the election of the Republican Lincoln, and the election of Lincoln led
immediately to the secession of South Carolina.

Of course the *Dred Scott* decision was not the sole cause for this
sequence of events, nor were these developments so simplistically isolated
from other factors that brought on secession. Nevertheless, the importance
of *Dred Scott* was more than minimal. Because it revolutionized the law
pertaining to slavery in the territories, it threatened to be a mortal blow
to the coalition that had just emerged as the new Republican party. If
that party was to remain a viable component of the American political
scene, *Dred Scott* had to be reversed or rescinded, for the only direction
the country could go as long as that decision prevailed was toward more
protection for slavery. In this sense, then, the *Dred Scott* decision was
the point of no return for antislavery forces. Once the law reached this
point, their only course of action, unless they were willing to accept it—
which they were not—was to force its reversal. That came finally with the
Fourteenth Amendment. But that, in turn, could never have occurred
when and how it did without the Civil War. If the bloody tragedy that
was triggered by Fort Sumter was to be avoided, at least one opportunity
disappeared with Chief Justice Taney's pronouncement on that fateful
Friday morning in March 1857.[4]

The *Dred Scott* decision played an important role in the pre-Civil
War period in still another way. Not only were individual Supreme Court
judges singled out for abuse and denunciation because of their legal opin-

ions, but the institution of the Supreme Court itself was assailed and degraded as a partisan political body no longer capable of rendering justice without bias in cases involving freedom and slavery. Perhaps never before in the history of the United States was there so much need for the stabilizing influence, the sobriety, and the sound guidance that a respected Court might have provided. That these attributes had been swept away by the stormy reactions to *Dred Scott* is evident from observations made by Jefferson Davis several decades later, as he reminisced on the attitudes of the time:

> . . . Instead of accepting the decision of this then august tribunal as conclusive of a controversy that had long disturbed the peace and was threatening the perpetuity of the Union, it was flouted, denounced, and utterly disregarded by the Northern agitators, and served only to stimulate the intensity of their sectional hostility.
>
> What resources for justice, what assurance of tranquility, what guarantee of safety, now remained for the South? No alternative remained except to seek, out of the Union, that security which they had vainly endeavored to obtain within it. The hope of our people may be stated in a sentence: it was to escape from injury and strife within the Union; to find prosperity and peace out of it.[5]

Repercussions to the *Dred Scott* decision were thus momentous. Many consider it the most important case ever decided by the Supreme Court.[6] Yet its origins were strikingly modest. The suit against John F. A. Sanford was instituted in 1853 in a circuit court of the United States; but it was the sequel to an earlier litigation instituted in 1846 in the state courts of Missouri by an obscure slave Dred Scott against his equally obscure mistress Mrs. Irene Emerson. Unpretentious and inconspicuous in its origins, this case experienced an unprecedented transition in both personnel and issues as it was drawn first into local and then national politics. The history of the federal case of *Dred Scott v. John F. A. Sanford* begins, then, with the history of the state case of *Dred Scott v. Irene Emerson.*[7] The history of *Dred Scott v. Irene Emerson* begins with the life of Dred Scott.

PART   I
BACKGROUND: TRAVELS OF DRED SCOTT

Dred Scott's Portrait, by an Unidentified Artist
(Courtesy of the New-York Historical Society, New York City)

Chapter 1

Before Dr. Emerson

DRED SCOTT WAS BORN in Virginia, of Negro slave parents, sometime in the last decade of the eighteenth or the first decade of the nineteenth century. The exact date is unknown, as evidently no record was made of it—not at all unusual in the case of slaves—but later estimates set the date between 1795 and 1809. He was the property of Peter Blow, but exactly when and how he became Blow's property is unknown.[1]

Peter Blow was born in 1771 in Southampton County in southeastern Virginia. Not much is known about his early life that affected the *Dred Scott* litigation. He grew up in Virginia, he owned and worked land there, he paid his taxes there.[2] In 1800 he married Elizabeth Taylor, a marriage productive of eleven children.[3] Blow served briefly during the War of 1812 as a lieutenant in the Sixty-fifth Virginia Militia and then returned to his farming.[4] Whether Scott was with Blow during the war and, if so, what he did are unknown.

The years following the War of 1812 were trying times for the Blow family, and like many others they turned westward. Selling their 860 acres in Virginia, in 1818 they moved to a cotton plantation near Huntsville, Alabama. In 1820 the family moved again, to Florence, Alabama, where they remained for ten years. But raising cotton still proved unprofitable, and once more Blow uprooted his family. This time the move was permanent; in 1830 the family settled in St. Louis.[5] Accompanying them was their slave Dred Scott.[6]

The move from rural Virginia and Alabama to the city environment of St. Louis brought a drastic change in the way of living for the Blow family. Founded in the winter of 1763-64 as a French trading post, St. Louis by 1830 was no longer a frontier village. It was a thriving and bustling town, with a population of almost 6,000, growing rapidly, and already referred to as the "gateway to the West." Steamboats plying up and down the Mississippi found it to have excellent port facilities. Commerce, trade, and manufacturing were expanding as mills, brickyards, and mercantile establishments grew and prospered. With growing children and slaves to feed and support, Peter and Elizabeth Blow had to start a new way of life in St. Louis. They rented a large home, paying twenty-five dollars a month, and opened a boarding house, calling it the Jefferson Hotel. Then tragedy struck; after a long and painful illness, Mrs. Blow died on July 24, 1831, at the age of forty-six.[7]

A number of events now occurred in the Blow family that influenced developments in the later litigation. The first was the marriage of Charlotte Taylor Blow, on November 8, 1831, to Joseph Charless, Jr. It was a most fortuitous event for the Blow family, for Charless was one of St. Louis's most eligible bachelors, a member of a family already prominent in local political, business, and cultural circles.[8]

In 1833 Peter Ethelred Blow, the oldest of the living Blow brothers, married Eugenie LaBeaume, daughter of Louis Tarteron LaBeaume by his second wife, Suzanne DuBreuil. Her oldest brother, Louis Alexander LaBeaume, became a prominent and wealthy businessman in St. Louis; among his most successful enterprises was a partnership organized in 1841, Peter E. Blow and Company. Another brother, Louis Tarteron LaBeaume, although not as financially successful, became sheriff of St. Louis County in the late 1840s and early 1850s. Still another brother, Charles Edmund LaBeaume, became a prosperous lawyer in St. Louis. All were to play important roles in Dred Scott's litigation.[9]

A third marriage by one of Peter Blow's children that was later to affect Dred Scott's case was the union in 1835 of the youngest daughter, Martha Ella, to Charles D. Drake, a lawyer recently arrived in St. Louis from Cincinnati. Martha Ella died in 1842, leaving the young widower to care for two small children. Sister-in-law Elizabeth Blow, who never married, helped look after them, and because of this Drake remained close to the Blow family.[10]

In addition to these marriages, brief mention must be made of the careers of Henry Taylor Blow and Taylor Blow. The former had aspirations for the law and even started apprenticing in a law office. But when Peter Blow died in 1832, young Henry Taylor Blow, only fifteen and with the family struggling financially, gave up the idea of law and became a clerk in the wholesale drug and paint store of his brother-in-law Charless.

By 1838 the firm that had been Charless and Company became Charless, Blow and Company, testimony undoubtedly to Henry Taylor Blow's business acumen. He went on to accumulate a fortune and to become one of the most distinguished business and civic leaders of pre-Civil War St. Louis and later also a congressman and minister to Venezuela and Brazil.[11] Younger brother Taylor Blow was also successful. He, too, started as a clerk in Charless and Company, and he, too, became a partner in the firm. In later years, as his older brother and brother-in-law concentrated on other business ventures, Taylor Blow ran the company and became a prominent member of the St. Louis business and civic community.[12]

Thus the children of Peter Blow eventually did very well for themselves, although the family faced a difficult situation when Mrs. Blow died in 1831. Peter Blow continued as proprietor of the Jefferson Hotel, apparently profitably, but on June 23, 1832, after a short illness, he died. He left the bulk of his estate to the two then unmarried daughters, Elizabeth and Martha Ella (also called Patsey), and to the two younger sons, Taylor and William Thomas; the two older sons, Peter Ethelred and Henry Taylor, were already self-supporting. Son-in-law Charless was named executor of the estate, and records in the St. Louis Probate Court indicate that he administered it capably.[13]

Meanwhile, exactly what Dred Scott was doing for the Blows during this time is not clear. In 1857, when he was liberated by Taylor Blow, Scott referred to his emancipator as one of "them boys" with whom he had been "raised," thereby intimating that he had been a companion of the young Blows as well as their slave.[14] Apparently, too, he was hired out to others. He was "assigned" to Elizabeth Blow, in her middle twenties and still unmarried, so whatever income he earned would go toward her support. Although there is no contemporary record of such hire, many years later, in 1907, the widow of the youngest of the Blow children, Mrs. William T. Blow, recalled that Scott was "a poor workman, lazy and inefficient. His mistress received little or no return for his labors, he was so worthless. He was often hired out to work on the steamboats going up and down the river." Unfortunately from this recollection it is not possible to determine how much, if any, of this work on steamboats was done while Scott was assigned to Elizabeth Blow or how much was done before or after.[15]

Sometime after the arrival of the Blows in St. Louis, but before December 1, 1833, Dred Scott was sold to Dr. John Emerson, a physician residing in that city. The exact date of the sale and the amount paid are unknown, as apparently no record was made or remains of the transaction. Nevertheless, this sale has always posed an intriguing puzzle to historians: Who sold Dred Scott to Emerson, and why? The answer to the "why" is not difficult. After he arrived in St. Louis, Peter Blow found himself "slave poor," as his daughter-in-law described it—that is, he had more slaves than he needed and he simply could not afford the upkeep. The only solution was to sell some.[16]

But as to *who* sold Dred Scott, the answer is far less certain. The earliest known statement about the sale was made more than a decade later, on April 6, 1846, by Scott himself, in the petition that instituted the suit for freedom: "That the said John Emerson purchased your petitioner in the city of St. Louis . . . from one Peter Blow now deceased." But in 1907, about seventy-five years after the sale, Mrs. William T. Blow recalled that "after his [Peter Blow's] death about 1831, the slave, Dred, was assigned as the property of Miss Elizabeth Blow" and that "about 1834 he was sold to Dr. John Emerson." In the same document, however, Mrs. Blow said a number of things about Scott that were contradicted by known facts. After these discrepancies were called to her attention, Mrs. Blow subsequently wrote: "I distinctly remember him among the family servants brought to St. Louis by his old master Mr. Peter E. [sic] Blow[;] later given over to Miss E. R. Blow for the small earnings he brought to this elder sister until passing into the possession of others." Unfortunately she did not identify the time of "until passing" as before or after Peter Blow's death. Nevertheless, beginning with Professor Frank Hodder in 1929, historians have concluded from Mrs. Blow's statements that it was Elizabeth Blow who sold Dred Scott from the estate of her deceased father.[17]

One writer, John A. Bryan, even identified Scott as a slave originally named "Sam" who was sold to Emerson for five hundred dollars. His conclusion is based upon probate records of the Peter Blow estate, even though there is no mention in those documents of a "Dred Scott." The inventory of the estate does list, in addition to a few household furnishings, the names of five slaves—Solomon, Hannah, William, Luke, and finally "Sam—sold for $500." This is the only indication of the sale of a slave; additional documents account for all others in the estate. Since Scott was sold from Blow's estate, and since the only slave sale referred to in the estate records was the sale of Sam, and since all other slaves were accounted for, Bryan concluded that it had to be Sam who was sold to Emerson, and that Sam's name later was changed to Dred Scott.[18]

Although this appears convincing, there is stronger evidence that Blow himself sold Scott to Emerson (and obviously before he died), and that therefore Scott never was a part of the estate in the first place. The first reason is based upon admittedly weak historical evidence, and yet it cannot be overlooked. Among the Peter Blow probate documents is a record of an account held by him with the company of Sproule and Buchanan, merchants in St. Louis. As of August 8, 1831, Blow owed Sproule and Buchanan $173.62. The next day, August 9, "Doct. J. Emerson" paid to Sproule and Buchanan $28.00, which was credited to Blow's account. There is no reason given why this payment was made or why it was credited to Blow, and specifically there was no indication whether it was in any way a partial payment by Emerson for Dred Scott. But if it was, the date August 9, 1831, is obviously significant. Nevertheless it should be reiterated that this is weak and speculative evidence if it must stand alone; all that can be said about it with any historical certainty is that it indicates some financial dealing between Blow and Emerson in August 1831.[19]

But the Sproule and Buchanan document acquires considerable significance when coupled with two other items of substantial historical authenticity. The first is the slave's own statement, made on April 6, 1846, that it was indeed Peter Blow who had sold him.[20] It is undoubtedly easy to challenge the accuracy of a statement made by an illiterate slave who probably could not discern any significant legal differentiation between being sold more than a decade earlier by Peter Blow or by Peter Blow's daughter or by the executor of an estate. On the other hand, the fact that Scott was illiterate does not mean *ipso facto* that he was insensitive to what transpired around him. He may have been an illiterate slave, but he was a human being. Having lived all his life in the Blow family, it is indeed plausible that Dred Scott was very much aware whether it was the head of the family while he still lived or his children after his death who sold him.

Adding considerable credence to Scott's statement is the corroborating assertion made by one of Peter Blow's own sons. On June 30, 1847, Henry Taylor Blow testified in court that his father, Peter Blow, had sold Dred Scott to Emerson.[21] True, young Blow was only about fifteen or sixteen at the time of the sale, and he made his statement about fifteen years after that. On the other hand, a young man of fifteen is aware of things happening around him, and Henry Taylor Blow was bright, alert, and intelligent. Furthermore, his statement was made under oath. He had no reason to lie or to hedge or to deceive. Had he said something else about the sale, it probably would have gone unchallenged anyway. But he did not say something else. He made the positive affirmation that it was his father who had sold Dred Scott to Emerson. All of this, then, is convincing evidence that Dred Scott was sold before Peter Blow's death and by Peter Blow himself.

But the fact that Peter Blow sold Dred Scott still does not necessarily mean that Dred Scott and Sam were two different slaves. There is nothing in the Peter Blow probate records to indicate *when* Sam was sold, only that he was sold for five hundred dollars and that the five hundred dollars was paid to the estate. Perhaps Peter Blow sold the slave *before* he died, but the payment was made to the estate *after* he died. If that is true, Dred Scott and Sam could have been the same person after all.

But if Sam and Dred Scott were the same person, how and when did the name change from Sam to Dred Scott? Bryan theorized that it occurred when the slave was with Emerson at Forts Armstrong and Snelling:

> The outstanding man in the United States Army . . . was General Winfield Scott, known as "The Great Pacificator" among his admirers, and to those not so fond of him as "Old Fuss and Feathers" or "Great Scott." . . . Sam or Dred was an illiterate and somewhat stupid Negro, but not mean nor sullen. He was quite fond of attention, and it is probable that the soldiers at Rock Island began calling him "Great Scott" in a teasing way. Likely this was more flattering than annoying to Sam, since General Scott was a fine-looking man, of powerful physique, and always well-dressed.
>
> Moreover, he was a Virginian, as was Sam. Anyone familiar with the dialect of the average Southern negro knows that "great" is pronounced "dret" in those circles, as "might" is "mout." It would have been easy for "Dret" to become "Dred" at the hands of newspaper reporters who were not familiar with the niceties of speech around slave cabins.[22]

This is interesting speculation, but there is absolutely no evidence to substantiate it. On the contrary, there is incontrovertible evidence that the slave definitely was called Dred Scott at least ten years before any newspaper reporters ever heard of him.[23] Furthermore, "Dred" was not an uncommon name among slaves anyway; Harriet Beecher Stowe even entitled one of her antislavery books *Dred: A Tale of the Great Dismal*

Swamp, and this was before Dred Scott became a famous personality.[24]

Yet another question about Sam and Dred Scott must be posed: If they were the same, why did not someone ever say anything about it? Certainly the Blows would have known. Those who later testified to Scott's presence at Forts Armstrong and Snelling where, according to Bryan, the change took place, would have known of it. After Scott became famous and many stories were written about him in the newspapers, certainly some reference might have been made to it. But there was never the slightest suggestion. Why? One reason is simply that no one ever bothered to mention it. But much more plausible is the equally simple observation that no one had reason to mention it in the first place— because Dred Scott had always been just that, Dred Scott, and nothing more. He was Dred Scott, and Sam was Sam, two completely different people.

In the last analysis, of course, the only absolutely accurate statement about the Dred Scott sale is that we do not have all the evidence. But based on existing data, and unless and until additional documentary proof is produced, this much can be concluded: that Dred Scott and Sam were two different people, that Dred Scott was sold to Dr. Emerson by Peter Blow, before the latter died, for a price unknown.

A number of legends developed concerning this sale. One is that Emerson purchased Scott out of compassion and at the latter's own request, after the slave had been severely beaten by his former master for gambling.[25] Another is that Scott so disliked Emerson that, when he learned of the sale, he ran away, hid among the various haunts of his fellow slaves in a place then called "Lucas Swamps," and managed to elude his pursuers for a few days before he was finally captured.[26] Lending some credence to the latter story is the existence in the Peter Blow probate records of a summons issued to Charlotte Charless and Peter E. Blow to appear in the County Court in St. Louis on August 10, 1833, to testify in a case in which "John Emerson" was plaintiff and "Peter Blow's administrator" was defendant.[27] Perhaps this was a suit related to the alleged attempt by Scott to flee. However, St. Louis court records show that no litigation ever materialized for adjudication; if there was any truth to the story, the case was dropped. Whatever substance there might be to any of these anecdotes, there is no question that Dred Scott did become the slave of Dr. John Emerson.

Chapter 2

With Dr. Emerson

IT WAS IN DR. EMERSON'S service that Dred Scott experienced the grounds upon which he later sued for freedom. Because of attitudes that existed toward slaves, little direct evidence exists concerning Scott's activities and whereabouts. However, if the activities of the master can be traced, one can have some inkling about where the slave went and perhaps what he did. Thus a narrative of Emerson's life and travels is essential to understanding the life and travels of his slave Dred Scott.

John Emerson was born in Pennsylvania, about 1802 or 1803.[1] Little is known of his early life. He earned his medical degree from the University of Pennsylvania in 1824, practiced medicine for a short time in Pittsburgh, then spent "several years" in a "southern climate." By August 1831 he settled in St. Louis and within a few years established himself as "an honorable man, of high standing in his profession." Among his friends and associates were prominent national and local figures such as Missouri's United States Senators Thomas Hart Benton and Alexander Buckner; Dr. William Carr Lane, the first mayor of St. Louis; William H. Ashley, fur trader and explorer and congressman from Missouri in the early 1830s; and several members of the Missouri state legislature.[2]

As early as September 1832 Emerson applied for an appointment as medical officer in the United States Army, but before his application was acted upon, he found an opportunity to serve in a civilian capacity. The army doctor stationed at Jefferson Barracks, south of St. Louis, became very ill, and the commanding general of the Western Department, Brigadier General Henry Atkinson, authorized the employment of a "citizen physician." Hired on September 28, 1832, for only one month, Emerson remained for more than eight months, until June 5, 1833, when he was duly replaced by an army doctor. On that occasion General Atkinson formally commended Emerson for the "manner in which the duty has been performed by him, since he has been employed in the public services."[3]

In the meantime, Emerson continued to push for a regular appointment. Medical officer appointments were in proportion to a state's representation in Congress, and the quota for Missouri was already filled. But since he had been born in Pennsylvania, Emerson succeeded in being designated as a candidate from that state, and subsequently, in the fall of 1833, he was summoned to New York to be examined by an Army Medical Board. Whether Dred Scott accompanied him is unknown. Had he done so, Scott could have included this excursion into free states in his freedom suit. But he did not. Either he just did not think of mentioning it later, or he did not make the trip. Of course, as indicated above, it is possible that Scott was not even Emerson's slave yet. Whichever is the case, there is no evidence either that he accompanied Emerson or where he remained in St. Louis if he stayed behind. For Emerson, though, the trip was worthwhile.[4]

On October 25, 1833, he was appointed assistant surgeon in the army of the United States, the appointment to take effect on December 1, 1833. Accompanying his letter of appointment were orders posting Emerson to Fort Armstrong, Illinois. On November 19, 1833, the day after he received his letter of appointment and his first orders, Emerson left St. Louis. This time, there is no doubt, he was accompanied by his slave Dred Scott.[5]

Emerson reported for duty at Fort Armstrong on December 1, 1833. Constructed as one of a series of forts along the western frontier after the War of 1812, Fort Armstrong was situated at the western end of Rock Island, in the Mississippi River but within the boundaries of the state of Illinois, where the city of Rock Island, Illinois, is now located. By water, along the Mississippi, the distance from St. Louis to Rock Island is about three hundred miles. Although one might assume that Emerson and his slave went upriver by steamboat, in view of later developments it should be noted that there is no evidence how they made the trip. Fort Armstrong was commanded by Lieutenant-Colonel William Davenport, First Infantry, and the troops stationed there were elements of Companies C, G, and K, First Infantry. The Black Hawk War having recently been concluded, their major concern, as with most troops in the upper Mississippi at this time, was peacekeeping operations with Indians.[6]

Living conditions at Fort Armstrong were difficult. The old log and timber buildings were in decrepit condition, in a constant state of rot and decay. Quarters of both enlisted men and officers leaked badly with every rain. The post hospital, just one small, damp, filthy room, was in such wretched condition that Emerson replaced it with tents. Cholera was an ever-present danger; correspondence from Emerson to the Surgeon General often mentioned this dreaded disease. If the soldiers lived under such conditions, one wonders what the living conditions of slaves—and particularly Dred Scott—might have been. Certainly they were no better. Yet all the time that Emerson was at Fort Armstrong, Scott remained there, "in service" to the doctor "as a slave and used by him as such."[7]

At any time while he was at Fort Armstrong, Scott might have sued for his freedom, for slavery was prohibited in the state of Illinois. That prohibition actually preceded the creation of the state. On July 13, 1787, the Congress of the Confederation had passed the so-called Northwest Ordinance, Article VI of which provided that neither slavery nor involuntary servitude should exist in the Northwest Territory, except as punishment for crimes. When the new United States government under the Constitution came into existence in 1789, one of its first acts was to renew the Northwest Ordinance. Subsequently, when Illinois was carved out of the Northwest Territory and admitted into the Union as a state in 1818, its constitution also prohibited slavery. This slavery prohibition was in effect during the entire period that Dred Scott was at Fort Armstrong, and based upon it he might have sued successfully for his freedom. But there is no evidence either that Scott was aware of that fact or, for that matter, that he showed any inclination toward securing his freedom.[8]

Military life was rigorous at Fort Armstrong. Once Emerson suffered the recurrence of a painful "syphiloid disease" he had contacted when he had gone to New York for his examination in 1833. For a while he enjoyed the diversity of treating civilians (military regulations forbade administering to civilian patients without special authorization). On one occasion he was arrested following an altercation with a fellow officer. But mostly life was routine, the main distractions resulting from the poor living conditions and the dreaded cholera.[9] Partly because of these deplorable conditions, but primarily because of the Indian situation along the frontier, in the spring of 1836 the War Department decided to abandon Fort Armstrong.[10]

At some time (or at various times) while Emerson was at Fort Armstrong, he acquired four plots of land nearby. Three, totalling over one hundred sixty acres, were located in Illinois; the fourth, a half-section claim, was on the west side of the Mississippi River, just opposite Rock Island, in what is now Bettendorf, a suburb of Davenport, Iowa. A part of the Black Hawk cession, this acreage had not yet been surveyed for formal sale, having been ceded to the United States government only on June 1, 1833, but Emerson joined others in preempting the land. Exactly what Emerson did with these lands is unknown, but he did at least build a log cabin on the Iowa side, near the river. A tradition in the area has it that when Emerson went to Fort Snelling in May 1836, he left Scott there for a short while to look after things. There is, however, no documented basis for this story; on the contrary, one of the soldiers later testified that Scott went to Fort Snelling along with Emerson and the rest of the troops. Were there any validity to the legend, it could have been another justification for the later freedom suit. That it was not referred to may indicate that it never occurred; on the other hand, it was minor enough to be easily overlooked. At any rate, when Emerson learned that he was leaving the Fort Armstrong area, he arranged for the care of his lands by giving the power of attorney over them to Antoine LeClaire, a close friend and one of the prominent earlier settlers of Davenport, Iowa.[11]

On May 4, 1836, the troops stationed at Fort Armstrong, including Dr. Emerson, evacuated that post and on May 8 arrived at Fort Snelling. Lieutenant-Colonel Davenport immediately assumed command at the new post, retaining it until August 30, 1837, when he was replaced by Major Joseph Plympton of the Fifth Infantry.[12]

Established in 1819 as Fort St. Anthony, Fort Snelling was located on the north bank of the St. Peter's (now the Minnesota) River, where it flows eastward into the Mississippi River, in what was then the newly created Wisconsin Territory. Being on the west bank of the Mississippi River, it was located in that portion of the Louisiana Purchase territory where slavery had been prohibited by the Missouri Compromise of 1820. Once again Dred Scott might have sued for freedom; but once again, as when he had been in Illinois, there is no evidence either that he was aware of that right or that he was even interested yet in becoming a free man. Instead, he remained with Emerson "as a slave and used by him as such."[13]

Although busy with his regular medical duties, Emerson managed to diversify his activities somewhat. He serviced many nearby Sioux, on one occasion vaccinating as many as three hundred. He was active in a mission school located at nearby Lake Harriet. Once he even found himself involved in a slapstick comedy episode, when several insubordinate and recalcitrant—but hungry—cows broke into the post vegetable gardens, stubbornly refusing to obey the orders of a sadly confused rookie sentinel charged with the awesome responsibility of protecting that vital piece of government real estate against unlawful four-legged nocturnal marauders.[14]

Sometime in 1836 or 1837 Dred Scott married a black woman, Harriet Robinson, the slave of Major Lawrence Taliaferro, agent of the St. Peter's Indian Agency near Fort Snelling. One of the most influential, and controversial, civil officials in the upper Mississippi region, Taliaferro (pronounced "Tolliver") frequently visited his native Virginia, bringing back with him slaves for use in the agency or to hire out at Fort Snelling.[15] Among them, brought up sometime between 1833 and 1835, was a young girl named Harriet Robinson. She was only in her middle teens at the time, considerably younger than Dred Scott, but the two became closely attached and shortly thereafter were married.[16]

The marriage of Dred Scott and Harriet Robinson merits several observations. First, there was an actual civil wedding ceremony, an event not often accorded to unfortunates held in bondage. Taliaferro felt very strongly that the many traders with growing Indian families should legitimize their children by marriage. As there were rarely any ministers in the area, and since in addition to other duties Taliaferro was also justice of the peace, he officiated at numerous wedding ceremonies, legally uniting many couples as husband and wife. Among them were Dred Scott and Harriet Robinson.[17]

Another interesting footnote about this wedding is that it was the second for Scott and the first and only for Harriet. This was disclosed later, in newspaper stories that appeared first in the *St. Louis Daily Evening News* (April 3, 1857) and in *Frank Leslie's Illustrated Newspaper* (June 27, 1857) and then were widely reprinted. Both stated that Scott had no children by his first marriage, but four by Harriet—two boys, both dead, and two girls, both living. As to the first wife, one newspaper indicated that she had been sold away from Scott; the other said nothing about this. Although there is no further contemporary evidence to corroborate either the first marriage or the two sons, there is little reason to doubt them, as this kind of data relating to slaves would be very rare. Besides, the information came directly from Dred and Harriet Scott themselves. What is not known, of course, is when Dred Scott was first married, to whom, for how long, and where—in Virginia, in Alabama, in St. Louis, or at Fort Armstrong—or what happened to his first wife. It is one of the countless genealogical threads so inhumanely torn asunder by the institution of human slavery.

Another interesting detail relates to the ownership of Harriet. Although a number of documents in the later court actions referred to Harriet as being "sold" by Taliaferro to Emerson, this is not what happened. In his autobiography, written in 1864, Taliaferro stated that he officiated at the "union of Dred Scott with Harriet Robinson—my servant girl which I *gave* him."[18] At about the same time, though, in a newspaper interview, Taliaferro referred to his "marrying the two and *giving the girl her freedom.*"[19] That is quite different. If he did indeed give Harriet her freedom, there is neither a record of that manumission nor any evidence of Harriet claiming to be a free person. On the contrary, she continued to be a slave, only now owned by Emerson rather than by Taliaferro. What plausibly appears to have happened was that the two slaves discussed their situation with their masters, the decision was agreed to (certainly by the two masters and probably also by the slaves) that there should be a legal marriage with a ceremony performed by Taliaferro, and then some sort of arrangement was made whereby both would belong to Emerson. But just what that "arrangement" was is not clear—a gift, a trade, or something else. Perhaps the most accurate description is that Taliaferro simply "transferred" his ownership of Harriet to Emerson; certainly he did not "sell" her in the conventional sense.

The exact date of the marriage is unknown, but it can be placed sometime between May 8, 1836, and September 14, 1837. The former date is obvious—that is when Emerson arrived at Fort Snelling, Dred Scott with him. It is reasonable to expect that at least several weeks or months elapsed before two erstwhile perfect strangers became man and wife. The latter date, September 14, 1837, is the date of the arrival at Fort Snelling of Lieutenant James L. Thompson, Fifth Infantry, and his wife. One of the first things they did was to hire Harriet *from Dr. Emerson,* whose slave she already was. Since Harriet had become Emerson's slave when she married Dred Scott, the wedding obviously had to have occurred before September 14, 1837.[20]

Now husband and wife, Dred and Harriet Scott not only worked for

Emerson but from time to time were hired out to others. For whom Dred worked is unknown, but Harriet was hired out to at least two employers. One, of course, was the Thompsons, who hired her immediately after their arrival at Fort Snelling for "some two or three months" in 1837. The other was Major Joseph Plymptom, who replaced Lieutenant-Colonel Davenport as post commander on August 20, 1837, but just when she worked for Plymptom is not clear. It was probably later, because Harriet was soon to leave Fort Snelling for a while.[21]

Throughout his military career Emerson repeatedly requested assignment in or near St. Louis. He finally got his wish. On October 20, 1837, he left Fort Snelling for St. Louis and Jefferson Barracks. At any other time this voyage probably would have been made by steamboat, but the upper Mississippi was already freezing and navigation was very precarious, and so Emerson had to travel down three hundred miles of the Mississippi by canoe. As a result he left behind most of his personal property, including his two slaves, Dred and Harriet Scott, who were hired out at Fort Snelling.[22] Since Emerson had no idea when or if he would return to Fort Snelling, he had to make some disposition of his slaves. He could have freed them. He could have sold them or even given them to someone, as Taliaferro had given Harriet to him. Instead, he left them temporarily with someone else, to send for them later. That he could do this indicates the readiness of the slaves to remain in that status even though they had an apparent opportunity to flee.

Dr. Emerson had hardly reached St. Louis when he was transferred again, to Fort Jesup, in Louisiana, where he reported on November 22, 1837.[23] But he was very dissatisfied there, constantly expressing unhappiness about the weather, his health, and his colleagues. Complaint followed complaint as he badgered the Surgeon General for reassignment.[24]

Life at Fort Jesup was not completely infelicitous, however. Also stationed there was Captain Henry Bainbridge of St. Louis, and with him was his wife, Mary. Visiting her from St. Louis was her sister Eliza Irene Sanford. On February 6, 1838, at Natchitoches, Louisiana, after what must have been a whirlwind courtship, Irene Sanford and John Emerson were married.[25]

Shortly after his marriage and some four months after having left them, Emerson sent for his slaves Dred and Harriet Scott, and in April 1838 they joined him in Fort Jesup. Thus, having lived in free territory for several

years where, had they known about the possibility, they might have sued
for freedom, both Dred and Harriet Scott voluntarily returned to slave
territory, still as slaves. When the freedom suits were brought later, this
Fort Jesup episode was totally ignored, even though Harriet mentioned it
in her petition and Mrs. Anderson in her testimony. Of course, the slaves
returned voluntarily and unaccompanied by their master; that might not
have helped their case. Also, the Scotts sued later under Missouri law
after returning to Missouri; this episode involved Louisiana. But whatever the reason, the fact that Dred and Harriet Scott went *twice* into
free territory and twice returned to slave territory was never considered
an issue in the case, nor has it even been noted by historians.[26]

Despite earlier failures, Emerson continued to press for a transfer
from Fort Jesup. He cited continued poor health, fears that he might
lose his land near Fort Armstrong, and even problems in St. Louis
where one of his slaves was suing him.[27] He asked to be stationed where
he would be near enough to attend to his private affairs and thereby have
a better mental attitude toward his duties as a medical officer. Evidently
this brought results, for by September 1838 he and his wife and their
slaves were on their way back to Fort Snelling. They reached St. Louis
on September 21, laid over for five days, departed on September 26,
and on October 21, 1838, the trip upriver slowed by low water, they
finally arrived at Fort Snelling. The voyage from St. Louis to Fort
Snelling was made on the steamer *Gipsey,* commanded by Captain Thomas
Gray.[28]

Dr. Emerson's second tour of duty at Fort Snelling lasted from October
1838 to May 1840. Aside from a few personal problems (petty disagreements with a fellow officer, concerns for his Iowa lands), perhaps his
most out-of-the-ordinary activity was being a signatory to a treaty with
the Chippewa. But generally things were fairly routine. The same was
true for his slaves Dred and Harriet Scott—they worked unobtrusively
either for Dr. and Mrs. Emerson or in the hire of others. Then after more
than six years of military service and continuous harping about his assign-
ments, Emerson inquired about a promotion. But before he could move
far on this, he was again transferred from Fort Snelling, this time to
Florida to the zone of military operations of the Seminole War.[29]

There now occurred one of the most misunderstood events in the unfolding narrative of Dred Scott. On his way to Florida, Emerson left his
wife and slaves in St. Louis for safekeeping. Even though this was cited

as the specific basis for the freedom suit—that is, the erstwhile free Negroes were now brought back into a slave state—nothing was said during the entire litigation in the state courts about this phase of Dred Scott's travels other than that he had returned from free territory to a slave state. Not until the case moved into the federal courts was there any reference to the birth of a child in free territory. It was in an agreed statement of facts that stated:

> Eliza is about 14 years old and was born on board the Steamboat Gipsey north of the north line of the State of Missouri & upon the River Mississippi.

The next sentence avowed that the Scotts' other daughter Lizzie was about seven years old and had been born at Jefferson Barracks in Missouri. Then the next paragraph stated:

> In the year 1838 [*sic*] said Dr. Emerson removed the plaintiff and said Harriet & their daughter Eliza from said Fort Snelling to the State of Missouri where they have ever since resided.[30]

Even though this agreed statement of facts does not say so, every account of the *Dred Scott* case has assumed from it that the Emersons and the Scotts traveled from Fort Snelling to St. Louis on the steamboat *Gipsey* and that it was en route but before the *Gipsey* reached the northern boundary of Missouri that baby Eliza was born.

That is not how it was. First, the *Gipsey* was not even at Fort Snelling at that time. Records of river traffic indicate that the *Gipsey* left St. Louis "for the Illinois River"—nowhere near Fort Snelling—on May 25 and returned to St. Louis "from the Illinois River" on June 1, seven days later. On June 9 the *Gipsey* departed once again "for the Illinois River" and did not return to St. Louis until well after Emerson had arrived in Florida.[31] Unless these records of river traffic were incorrect or incomplete—and there is no reason to suspect they were—the only time Emerson's party could possibly have arrived in St. Louis aboard the *Gipsey* was on June 1. But that could have happened only if the *Gipsey* had gone on May 25 all the way to Fort Snelling instead of only to the Illinois River (recall that Emerson left Fort Snelling on May 29) and had made the sixteen hundred-mile round trip in only seven days, getting back to St.

Louis on June 1. But that was impossible. Indeed, four years later, in 1844, the steamboat *Iowa* made a round-trip run between St. Louis and Galena, Illinois, in slightly less than *five* days, a *new speed record* on the upper Mississippi—and Galena was only half as far as Fort Snelling![32] The evidence is conclusive, therefore, that when Emerson and his party came down from Fort Snelling, it was not on the *Gipsey*.

Contributing to the *Gipsey* legend was the fact that its captain, Thomas Gray, was later summoned as a witness.[33] As things developed, he did not testify. But the fact that he had been summoned led to the assumption that he would have testified about this alleged voyage from Fort Snelling to St. Louis. However, as related above, the *Gipsey* was involved in Dred Scott's travels earlier in 1838, when the slave returned to Fort Snelling from Fort Jesup. Captain Gray was summoned to testify, then, not about the voyage downriver from Fort Snelling to St. Louis in 1840, when Dred and Harriet Scott returned from free territory to a slave state, but rather about the trip upriver in 1838, when they went from slave territory into free territory.[34]

But if Dred and Harriet Scott did not come down from Fort Snelling on the *Gipsey,* then where and when was Eliza born? There is no reason to believe anything other than what is in the agreed statement of facts, that she was indeed born on the *Gipsey.* But since that document says nothing about the time—that was all contrived by later writers—and since the only time Harriet can be placed on the *Gipsey* was in October 1838, on the way up to Fort Snelling, it must be concluded that that is when Eliza was born, on the *Gipsey* traveling northward, and, as the agreed statement of facts says, "north of the north line of the State of Missouri & upon the River Mississippi."

Recapitulating these events, then, Dr. Emerson left Fort Snelling on May 29, 1840, for Florida. Accompanying him were his wife and their slaves Dred and Harriet Scott and their eighteen-month-old daughter Eliza (named after their mistress Eliza Irene Emerson), born earlier in free territory north of the Missouri state line, on board the *Gipsey,* in October 1838, when they had returned to Fort Snelling from Fort Jesup. Presumably the party traveled now (in 1840) by steamboat from Fort Snelling to St. Louis, but on which steamboat is unknown. Emerson left his wife and slaves in St. Louis and proceeded to the zone of military operations, arriving at Cedar Keys, Florida, on June 27, 1840. There in Florida he remained for about two and one-half years, until November 1842, serving as a medical officer in the Seminole War.[35]

Chapter 3

After Dr. Emerson

WHILE HER HUSBAND WAS in Florida, Mrs. Emerson lived in St. Louis with her father, Alexander Sanford. The exact whereabouts of the slaves, on the other hand, is uncertain, because from time to time they were hired out to different people, sometimes separately and sometimes together. In February and March 1842 Emerson was back in St. Louis for a leave of absence, and when he returned to Florida his "family"—presumably this meant Mrs. Emerson—was with him briefly at Fort Pickens, near Pensacola, Florida. Whether Dred or Harriet accompanied her is not known. Certainly, though, in March 1846 both were in St. Louis in the employ of Mrs. Emerson's brother-in-law Captain Henry Bainbridge.[1]

One of the baffling episodes of Dred Scott's whereabouts is his reputed presence with Bainbridge on the Rio Grande at the outbreak of the Mexican War in 1846. Nothing in court records alludes to this; the story appeared much later in the newspapers.[2] Yet it could have happened. Bainbridge was in St. Louis in 1844 before extended frontier duty in Louisiana and Texas; Scott could have accompanied him then. The events that triggered the Mexican War occurred near Corpus Christi in March and April 1846. Bainbridge was at Corpus Christi from August 1845 until February 1846 and then at nearby Matamoras until September. During that time, though, he never left the area. Yet Scott was in St. Louis in March 1846. If he had been with Bainbridge, Scott must have returned to St. Louis alone or with someone else. That this may have happened is suggested in an article in the *Springfield* (Mass.) *Daily Republican* on the occasion of Mrs. Emerson's death in 1903: "The slaves were taken by Mrs. Emerson's brother-in-law Col. Henry Bainbridge, on the death of Dr. Emerson, *who kept them at army posts for four years, and then sent them back to St. Louis.*"[3] On the other hand, refuting the whole Texas story is the statement in one court document that the Scotts and their baby Eliza had been brought from Fort Snelling to Missouri "where they have ever since resided." If that statement was solicitously and circumspectly worded for accuracy, the Texas story is without basis. But if it was just a broad and general affirmation of the Scotts's presence in Missouri, intentionally disregarding other places not necessary for this litigation (note that there was also no mention of the Fort Jesup interlude), the Texas episode might be true.[4] As with other events in Dred Scott's life, this, too, remains an enigma because of inadequate evidence.

In March 1846, in St. Louis, Dred Scott and his wife were hired out to Samuel and Adeline Russell. By this time, too, there was another addition to the family, Lizzie, born at Jefferson Barracks.[5] This was their status the following month, April 1846, when Dred and Harriet Scott instituted their suit for freedom.

In the meantime, a great deal had happened to the Emerson family that was to affect the Scotts. The Seminole difficulties abating, the War Department reduced the number of doctors in the army, and among those honorably discharged, on August 26, 1842, was Dr. John Emerson. He wasted little time returning to St. Louis. But being so suddenly released from the service created problems. Because he had considerable seniority among assistant surgeons, he experienced inordinate embarrassment in having been summarily discharged, albeit honorably, rather than having voluntarily resigned, because it led some to question his professional ability. More serious were rumors that he had mishandled hospital funds, which cast doubts on his personal integrity.[6] Faced with these deprecations, he sought to reenter the service, but in vain. On July 1, 1843, after he had written numerous letters to the Surgeon General disclaiming the allegations, Emerson's application for reinstatement was rejected. His military career was over.[7]

While these events were developing with the army, Emerson also tried to establish himself as a civilian physician. Shortly after his return from Florida, he purchased a nineteen-acre tract of land in St. Louis County, not far from the then western city limits of St. Louis.[8] Then the rumors of his alleged military peculations began to affect his ability to make a living in St. Louis. So he went to Davenport, Iowa, where he owned land, and began a private practice there. During the spring and summer of 1843 he traveled between Davenport and St. Louis several times, and then, after he was turned down by the army, he decided to settle permanently in Davenport. His wife joined him there, and shortly thereafter Henrietta Sanford Emerson was born. Then, suddenly, on December 29, 1843, Emerson died, at the age of forty.[9]

Dr. Emerson must have realized the precarious state of his health, for only a few hours before he died he made out his last will and testament. The only property mentioned specifically in his will was his medical books, which he bequeathed to his brother Edward P. Emerson. "All the rest residue & remainder . . . & effects real & personal whatsoever & wheresoever & of what nature & kind soever" were left to Mrs. Emerson "for & during the term of her natural life." Upon the death of Mrs. Emerson, this property was to devolve upon her daughter Henrietta and to her heirs. The will also provided that Mrs. Emerson should educate the daughter and "maintain & support her until she reaches twenty-one years of age." Furthermore, Mrs. Emerson was empowered to sell "all or any part" of the "land and tenements," provided the proceeds of such sale were for "her own maintenance & support" or for "the education & support" of Henrietta. Nothing was said in the will about what should happen if Mrs. Emerson remarried. John F. A. Sanford and George L. Davenport were named as executors of the estate.[10]

Emerson's will was offered for probate at the Probate Court of Scott County, in Davenport, on February 28, 1844. The three witnesses to Dr. Emerson's signature were examined by Judge James Thorington, and they satisfied him that the deceased had been of full age and of sound mind and not under any coercion when the will was signed. Thereupon Judge Thorington ordered the will entered as an official record.[11]

He then took up nominations of Sanford and Davenport as executors of the estate. According to Iowa law, to be appointed executor of an estate a nominee had to appear personally before the probate court within twenty days after the will had been probated and he had been nominated. Davenport did appear and was duly appointed. But Sanford did not appear within that twenty-day period, and as a result he was never appointed by the probate court as executor.[12]

The Iowa court implemented the terms of Emerson's will and dispensed with his property in Iowa Territory; but ancillary legal action was necessary in Missouri where Emerson had left additional property. That resulted in the naming of Alexander Sanford (Mrs. Emerson's father) as administrator of the estate in Missouri. That estate was not large, as most of Emerson's property was in Iowa; it consisted of only a few items of furniture and the nineteen-acre plot that Emerson had bought shortly after returning from Florida. The inventory of the Missouri estate made no mention of any slaves, but why Dred Scott and his family were overlooked is not known. It may have been that they were not around to be noticed and accounted for. Where they were, as discussed above, is unknown; but it would seem that they were not working for Mrs. Emerson, where at least they would have been visible.[13] Interestingly enough, the inventory of the Iowa estate did list "several slaves"; but unfortunately that inventory has since disappeared. The only identification of any of these slaves is a reference to one of them as Emerson's "servant Nelson."[14] Whether any of the Scott family was ever in Iowa is unknown; certainly when the freedom suits were filed later, they were in St. Louis.[15]

Following her husband's death, Mrs. Emerson returned from Davenport to St. Louis, where she and her infant daughter lived with Mrs. Emerson's father. Nothing more is known of her activities for almost two years. In March 1846 Dred and Harriet Scott were in the service of Mrs. Emerson's brother-in-law Captain Henry Bainbridge. That was when Mrs. Emerson hired them out to Samuel Russell in St. Louis.[16] Then one month later Dred Scott and his wife Harriet sued for their freedom.

PART II
THE STATE COURTS: *DRED SCOTT* V. *IRENE EMERSON*

Chapter 4

Issues and Lawyers

ON APRIL 6, 1846, Dred and Harriet Scott filed suit against Irene Emerson, initiating litigation that lasted eleven years and culminated in the famous decision of the Supreme Court of the United States. It was to be widely assailed and bitterly denounced as the contrived chicanery of political partisans. Nothing could have been farther from the truth. The case originated in 1846 for one reason and one reason only—to obtain freedom for the slave and his family.

Writers about the *Dred Scott* case long have suggested a variety of motives behind the suit. Many contemporaries, caught up in the emotional reactions to the decision, attributed the case either to proslavery or antislavery elements, each seeking a test case to substantiate its own particular point of view. Wild and unsubstantiated accusations were leveled against persons ranging from "anonymous" or "unknown" to Missouri Senator Thomas Hart Benton.[1] But as researchers sought the true story of the case, it became evident that it was not politically contrived at all—in its origins, that is—but that other factors brought it into being.

One unique theory was posed in 1907 by a lawyer, Frederick Trevor Hill, who argued that the primary reason was financial. Ostensibly a freedom case, the real purpose was to pave the way for a second suit against the Emerson estate for back wages once the court found that Scott had been held illegally as a slave.[2] Although some accepted the Hill theory, in 1929 Professor Frank Hodder pointed out that the Emerson estate was so small in the first place, and by 1846 it had been settled anyway, that the "back-wages" theory was unacceptable. Indeed, in his monograph on the *Dred Scott* case in 1951, Vincent Hopkins cites Hill's work in his bibliography, but omits it from his text as even a plausible cause for the origin of the case.[3]

It is now quite clear that the case originated only to obtain freedom for the Scotts and nothing more. One clue is the statute under which it was brought, a procedure by which a suitor might secure freedom. It contained no provision for indemnities; there were other statutes for that purpose.[4] The charge against Mrs. Emerson was *pro forma* trespass for assault and false imprisonment, and the damages a nominal ten dollars, as provided in the freedom statute.[5] If money had been the goal, the charge could have been different and the amount sought much greater, under a different statute.

Of even greater significance, though, were the points of law and arguments raised before the court. It seems entirely reasonable that one usually can find in arguments of counsel what a case is all about. Since the points of law and arguments of counsel are matters of record with a court, one simply looks into the court's records and all these questions should be answered. Unfortunately in the *Dred Scott* case it has not been that simple. The reason is that historians have never been able to locate all the records in the case. Reportedly "lost," the "missing" papers contained the key information: the points of law and arguments raised by counsel. Those papers were finally found by this author.[6] The contents of those long-missing documents leave no doubt that the only issue involved in the "original" *Dred Scott* case was freedom for the slave and his family. At no time were the politics of slavery, the morality of slavery, the views of any political or civic leader, financial considerations, or any other issues raised. The case purely and simply involved a Negro slave who sued for one thing and one thing only—to obtain his freedom.

Although there is no longer any doubt about why the suit was brought, uncertainty still exists about other aspects of its origins. Why was it filed when it was filed, and not earlier or later? What precipitated it? There are no clues in court records, but three later accounts are valid enough to consider. One was made a half century later by Arba N. Crane to historian John W. Burgess. Crane was a lawyer who worked for Roswell M. Field, the attorney who handled the case after it moved into the federal courts. Although not even in St. Louis when the case originated in 1846, Crane became active in its later stages as an assistant to Field and got to know Dred Scott fairly well. When Burgess wrote *The Middle Period, 1817-1858* in 1904, Crane recalled for him that the slave had told him (Crane) that Mrs. Emerson had "hired him out to different persons, and that he became dissatisfied with this treatment, and resolved to sue for his freedom."[7] Slightly different are accounts that appeared in newspapers

in 1857, shortly after the slave became a famous figure. One of these
was an unsigned letter in the St. Louis *Daily Missouri Republican,*
whose author claimed to have knowledge "derived from records, and
from persons conversant with the case." This anonymous writer stated
that Mrs. Emerson "propose[d] to sell them in 1846, and this occasioned
the institution of the suit for freedom."[8] A different account was given
in a sketch of Dred Scott that appeared the same day in *The Saint Louis
Daily Evening News.* This was the article that stated Scott had been with
Captain Bainbridge at Corpus Christi at the outbreak of the Mexican
War, and that "on his return from Mexico, he applied to his mistress,
Mrs. Emerson, then living near St. Louis, for the purchase of himself
and family, offering to pay part of the money down, and given [*sic*]
an eminent citizen of St. Louis, an officer in the army, as security for
the payment of the remainder. His mistress refused his proposition, and
Dred being informed that he was entitled to his freedom by the operation
of the laws regulating the Northwest Territory, forthwith brought suit
for it."[9] Each of these accounts is from a source claiming to know, and
yet each is different. One states very generally that the slave was dissatisfied with being hired out, one claims that Mrs. Emerson contemplated
selling him, and one indicates that Scott wanted to buy his freedom but
was refused. It is impossible to determine which is more accurate; corroborating evidence simply is not available. In all likelihood the truth lies
somewhere in those three accounts, and for that (or those) reason(s) Dred
Scott was impelled to sue for his freedom.

But several more questions remain to be answered. How did an illiterate
slave who could not even sign his name know that he had a legal basis for
freedom? The answer again remains unknown; one can only surmise that
a person or persons interested in his welfare informed him of that fact.
But once he knew that he had the right to sue, how could he obtain counsel
and finance such a suit? The answer in part, at least, is that certain persons
bonded themselves as security for costs that might accrue in the course of
the litigation. One might suspect at once that determined partisans may
have recognized this as an opportunity to secure a strategic judicial affirmation or denial of the power of the national government over slavery
in the territories. But that was not the reason they supported Dred Scott
in bringing his case into being; as has already been pointed out, there is
now conclusive proof that no issue was made of the validity or even the
morality of the laws of slavery under which Dred Scott claimed his freedom. The suit originated because Dred Scott genuinely wanted freedom

and because he secured the advice and assistance of friends whose only interest in the case, at the outset at least, was to aid him in obtaining that freedom.[10]

Finally, then, the question arises as to the identity of those "friends." Court records reveal a singular circumstance—the kinship of those who at various times posted Dred Scott's bond. Specifically, they were Henry Taylor Blow, Taylor Blow, Joseph Charless, Charles Edmund LaBeaume, and Louis T. LaBeaume.[11] The Blow brothers and Dred Scott all had been "raised" together, and obviously a long acquaintance existed between them. Charless and the LaBeaumes were brothers-in-law to the Blows and were also business partners at various times. All of them were closely related to each other, and all of them, at one time or another, contributed to Dred Scott's suit; indeed, Taylor Blow obtained final possession of the slave in 1857 and granted him his freedom, only a few weeks after the Supreme Court of the United States had denied it.[12] These factors point to Taylor Blow individually, or in concert with one or more of the others, as the "friend" or "friends" who assisted and advised Dred Scott and thus were the motivating force behind the suit for freedom.

But they were not his *first* "friends." There was someone else who posted bond *before* any of those men did, and it is probable that this man was responsible for the actual initiation of the suit and that the "friends" stepped in later. This entails yet another intriguing phase of the *Dred Scott* case, namely, the lawyers who were involved. As a matter of fact, one of the most frustrating aspects of the early stages of this case is the role played by various attorneys for Dred Scott. This is not so with Mrs. Emerson's attorneys, nor is it a problem when the litigation moved into the federal courts; the evidence is quite clear how those attorneys entered the case and what their motives were. But the roles played by Scott's lawyers in the state case are not nearly as manifest.

This is especially true of the first attorney associated with the case, Francis B. Murdoch, who, on April 6, 1846, filed the initial documents charging Mrs. Emerson with trespass and false imprisonment, and who, on that same day, signed a bond accepting responsibility for costs that might accrue in the case.[13]

But who was Francis B. Murdoch and how did he come to be associated with Dred Scott? Other than his name appearing on the documents of April 6, 1846, as "Plaintiff's Attorney," there is no further mention of Murdoch in any court records of the case or in any other documents or materials related to the litigation. He is indeed a "mystery man" in the *Dred Scott* case, and what little is known about him makes for some intriguing possibilities.[14] Francis Butter Murdoch was born in Cumberland, Maryland, on March 21, 1805. At the age of nineteen, he went to Bedford, Pennsylvania, to study law and soon was admitted to the bar of Pennsylvania. He settled briefly in Michigan, but after the death of his wife, he moved to Alton, Illinois, where he practiced law and was elected prosecuting attorney. On November 7, 1837, Elijah P. Lovejoy, Alton abolitionist minister and pamphleteer, was killed, and riotous mob action resulted in the death of several people, the destruction of property, and the unleashing of considerable vituperative and emotional proslavery and antislavery sentiments. As Alton's city attorney, Murdoch prosecuted both antislavery and proslavery zealots charged with capital offenses tied to slavery. Accounts of the trials indicate that he was fair and impartial in his official capacity, enforcing the law equally on both sides, but his political sympathies were on the side of those opposed to slavery. One aftermath of the Lovejoy episode was that many of the antislavery community moved away. Among them was Murdoch, newly remarried, who in 1841 went into law practice in St. Louis. Murdoch handled a variety of clients and cases, but no inordinate number for slaves or blacks to label him a "slave lawyer." Furthermore, nothing in the cases he handled tie him with anyone associated with Dred Scott, until the sudden appearance of his name on the documents of April 6, 1846.

Meanwhile, perhaps having nothing to do with Murdoch, and yet because of the singular circumstances possibly extremely significant, Harriet Scott had become a member of the Second African Baptist Church of St. Louis (later known as the Central Baptist Church). The pastor of the church was Reverend John R. Anderson. Born a slave and having purchased his freedom, Anderson became a typesetter for Lovejoy's abolitionist press in Alton and was there when the rioting occurred. Like Murdoch, Anderson also moved to St. Louis.[15] But here the facts end and the coincidences begin. The Scotts' pastor and lawyer both had antislavery sympathies, both came from the same small town, and both had been involved in the Lovejoy episode. There is no direct evidence that Murdoch and Anderson even knew each other, but the circumstances strongly suggest they did and that it was through Anderson that Murdoch came into the lives of Dred and Harriet Scott. The hard evidence shows only that Francis B. Murdoch filed the first papers in the *Dred Scott* case.[16] Then, shortly thereafter, in 1847, for reasons unknown, he emigrated to California, leaving behind both St. Louis and the *Dred Scott* case.

Additionally frustrating is that there is no apparent connection between Murdoch and the Blow family; yet once Murdoch left, there is no doubt that the Blows became involved. In fact, it is probable that only at this point did they do so, for when Murdoch left St. Louis, Dred Scott presumably was left without both counsel and assistance, and so he turned for help to "them boys" with whom he had been "raised." The hard evidence is not available that this is exactly why or how, but there is no question that from this point on the Blows and their relatives were integrally involved. That involvement was in two forms, financial and legal. The former is indisputably evidenced by numerous security bonds signed by members of the Blow family assuming responsibility for litigation costs. The evidence is not that easily available that the Blows also secured legal counsel, but an investigation into those attorneys leads to only one possible conclusion.

The first of these lawyers was Charles Daniel Drake. Drake's greatest fame was to come as a result of later achievements in Missouri during the Reconstruction period, but he was not an insignificant lawyer in St. Louis in 1846 and 1847, his name already associated with several prominent civic projects and legal activities. The obvious question is how and why such a prominent person happened to be the attorney for an insignificant slave. It should be recalled, however, that Drake had married one of the Blow girls, and even after his wife had died in 1842 Drake still remained close to the family, his sister-in-law Elizabeth Blow caring for his two children. Furthermore, in spite of his standing in the legal profession, Drake was experiencing financial difficulties and contemplated moving to Cincinnati, which meant that he might take his children away from the family with whom they were growing up. Under these circumstances it is not unseemly that the Blows helped him by sending any legal business they could. Since the Blows were aiding and advising Dred Scott in his litigations, it seems more than coincidental that their brother-in-law Drake became Scott's attorney.[17]

If Drake was an important figure among St. Louis lawyers, the man who succeeded him as Dred Scott's attorney was even more prominent. In June 1847 Drake did indeed move to Cincinnati, and the man who took over was Samuel Mansfield Bay. Bay was attorney-general of Missouri from 1839 to 1845 and then practiced private law in Jefferson City. In May 1847 he moved to St. Louis, where, among other lucrative achievements, he was attorney for the Bank of Missouri. Thus he was certainly no insignificant figure in the St. Louis legal scene, and again the question arises how a person of such stature became counsel for so obscure an individual as the slave Dred Scott. Once more there is no documentary proof, only interesting circumstances. Joseph Charless, brother-in-law of the Blows and one who signed as security for Dred Scott, had expanded into the banking business. One of the banks of which he was an officer was the Bank of Missouri, the same bank for which Samuel M. Bay was attorney. Certainly this proves nothing; but again, the circumstances are suggestive.[18]

If there are at least extenuating circumstances that relate to Murdoch, Drake, and Bay, there is even less to explain the two attorneys who were to be with the case longer than any of the others and who were to see it through to its conclusion in the state courts. This was the partnership of Alexander P. Field and David N. Hall. Very little is known of Hall except that he was a "scholar, a sound lawyer, and a worthy man."[19] Field had a stormy career before coming to St. Louis. A native Kentuckian, he moved to Illinois, where he was for eleven years secretary of state, only to be replaced in 1840, after a bitterly disputed intraparty struggle, by a rising young politician named Stephen A. Douglas. He then served briefly as secretary of Wisconsin Territory and in 1845 moved to St. Louis to resume private law practice. Field originally had been proslavery in his sympathies, but about 1828 he reversed his position radically. Although this can explain partially why he championed a slave's cause, it does nothing to explain directly how the firm of Field and Hall entered Dred Scott's case. Furthermore, St. Louis court records give no indication that Field and Hall handled any unusual number of cases for slaves or blacks, or that they did any legal work for the Blows or their relatives. Thus the only valid historical observation that can be made about Field and Hall is the simple fact that they became Dred Scott's attorneys.[20]

Explaining Mrs. Emerson's attorneys, however, poses far fewer problems. Her counsel was secured by her brother John F. A. Sanford. Sanford was a wealthy businessman; his widowed sister was being sued by her slaves. Besides, he had been designated executor in Dr. Emerson's will. That Sanford should help his sister is absolutely irreproachable,

and to attribute to him ulterior political motives—as was charged later—
is totally unjustified. In the St. Louis probate file of Sanford's estate is
recorded a three-hundred-dollar fee paid to Benoni S. Garland, for "10
years service attending to Dred Scott's case suing for freedom for self
and family, employing counsels, attending to hires and collecting same
at the request of Mr. Sanford from Nov., 1846 to Jan., 1857."[21] Garland
had already been handling Sanford family legal matters for several years,
and in 1846 he merely took on another.[22]

To handle Mrs. Emerson's slave case, Garland employed attorney
George W. Goode. A native of Virginia and a "pronounced proslavery
man," Goode became a leader of St. Louis' "states' rights Whigs." He
was also considered a good lawyer. These, it would seem, were credentials
enough for Garland to employ him.[23] Goode handled Mrs. Emerson's case
until 1849 when poor health forced him to retire. Garland then employed
the firm of Hugh A. Garland (not related) and Lyman D. Norris to take
over the case. Little is known about Norris, who was to make an unusually
significant contribution to the case later; he appears for the first time in
the St. Louis city directory in 1848. Garland, on the other hand, had an
impressive background in letters, law, and politics. Born and raised in
Virginia, he was educated at Hampden-Sydney College, where he became
professor of Greek. He practiced law in Virginia, was a member of the
Virginia legislature, and was also clerk of the United States House of
Representatives. In 1840 he retired from politics to devote his time to
literary studies (he later wrote a biography of John Randolph), but in
1845, as a result of poor investments and too liberal endorsing of friends'
notes, he lost his property and moved to St. Louis, where he resumed his
practice of law. Just why Garland and Norris were hired when Goode
retired from the case is not known, although they, too, certainly possessed
adequate credentials. At any rate, they took over in 1849 and continued
to handle Mrs. Emerson's case for the remainder of the time it was in the
state courts.[24]

Chapter 5

First State
Circuit Court Trial

DRED SCOTT AND HIS benefactor (or benefactors) anticipated little difficulty in securing his freedom, for unmistakable precedent existed in Missouri that slaves obtained freedom by virtue of residence in free territory. As early as 1824, in *Winny* v. *Phebe Whitesides*,[1] the Missouri Supreme Court had held that if a person was held in slavery in Illinois where slavery was forbidden, and then brought to Missouri and held there as a slave, too, that person was entitled to freedom by virtue of residence in free Illinois. The owner's right to the slave had been removed by the residence in a free state, and it did not automatically revive when the parties came to Missouri. Three years later, in *John Merry* v. *Tiffin and Menard*,[2] the court declared that a slave was emancipated by residence in any territory where slavery was prohibited by the Ordinance of 1787, and that Missouri courts would recognize such a person as free in Missouri. The validity and binding force of the Ordinance of 1787 was reasserted in *Francois La Grange* v. *Pierre Chouteau, Jun.*[3] and in *Theoteste alias Catiche* v. *Pierre Chouteau.*[4] In 1829, in *Philip Tramel* v. *Adam*,[5] the Court reaffirmed the principle declared earlier that residence in Illinois entitled a slave to freedom even though he afterwards came to Missouri. This was the basis for similar decisions in *Vincent* v. *James Duncan*,[6] in *Ralph* v. *Coleman Duncan*,[7] and in *Julia* v. *Samuel McKinney*.[8] In *Nat* v. *Stephen Ruddle*[9] the court rejected Nat's claim for freedom because the slave had gone to Illinois without his master's consent; but at the same time it declared that if such residence in Illinois did have the master's consent, there would be no question that the slave had acquired his freedom. In *Daniel Wilson* v. *Edmund Melvin*[10] the Court reaffirmed this principle in granting the slave Wilson his freedom.

Perhaps the most significant precedent, though, was *Rachael* v. *Walker*,[11] decided shortly before the *Daniel Wilson* case. Rachael, the slave of an army officer, had accompanied her master from St. Louis to Fort Snelling, had remained there for a number of years, and then had returned to St. Louis. She later sued for freedom because of her sojourn at Fort Snelling. The Missouri Supreme Court upheld Rachael's claim for freedom, and in doing so it declared that "an officer of the U.S. Army, who takes his slave to a military post, within the territory wherein slavery is prohibited, and retains her several years in attendance on himself and family, forfeits his property in such slave by virtue of the ordinance of 1787." The similarity to Dred Scott's case was strikingly unmistakable.

Between *Daniel Wilson* v. *Edmund Melvin* in 1837 and the time when Dred Scott filed his suit in 1846, no further decisions were handed down by the Missouri Supreme Court involving these principles. Thus, when Dred Scott initiated his action, the clearly settled doctrine in Missouri was that if a slave had resided, with the consent of his master, in any state or territory in which slavery was prohibited, that slave was entitled to freedom by virtue of such residence in that free state or territory; and even if he returned voluntarily to Missouri, this did not revive the former condition of slavery.

That some slaves would use these principles to seek freedom was undoubtedly anticipated, for among the statutes of Missouri, revised and published in 1845, was an act that set forth the procedure to follow. Any slave who thought he had a valid claim to freedom could petition a circuit court of Missouri, or its judge, for permission to sue the alleged master. If the judge believed the grounds set forth in the petition were valid, he was to grant the slave permission to sue. However, he was to set four conditions to such permission: first, that the slave must present "security, satisfactorily, to the clerk for all costs that may be adjudged against him or her"; second, that he "have reasonable liberty to attend his counsel and the court"; third, "that he be not subject to any severity on account of his application for freedom"; and fourth, "that he be not removed out of the jurisdiction of the court." The law further provided that the suit should be "an action of trespass for false imprisonment," and that the complaint instituting the suit should be "in the common form of a declaration for false imprisonment," containing "an averment, that the plaintiff, before and at the time of committing the grievances was, and still is, a free person, and that the defendent held, and still holds him in slavery." Prove this, and the slave would be declared free.[12]

On April 6, 1846, therefore, Dred and Harriet Scott filed separate petitions in the Circuit Court of St. Louis County, each outlining how they had been taken where slavery was illegal, and both now seeking permission to sue Irene Emerson for freedom. Neither Dred Scott nor his wife could write his or her name, and so they signed the petitions with their marks.[13] On the same day John M. Krum, Judge of the Circuit Court of St. Louis County, approved both petitions and granted permission to sue, at the same time ordering the four conditions required by law.[14] Accordingly *pro forma* charges of trespass for false imprisonment were filed, that Mrs. Emerson had "made an assault" upon them, and that she had "imprisoned" them "without any reasonable or probable cause whatsoever." Each charge also contained a statement that Mrs. Emerson was still holding the slave in servitude without a legal right to do so.[15]

Thus there were instituted in the Circuit Court of St. Louis County two separate but similar suits against Mrs. Emerson, one by Dred Scott and the other by his wife Harriet. *Dred Scott* v. *Irene Emerson* was docketed as No. 1 for the November term, 1846; *Harriet Scott* v. *Irene Emerson* was No. 2.[16] With the exception of the initial petitions of April 6, 1846, almost all the proceedings in the ensuing litigations were exactly the same. Then, on February 12, 1850, an agreement was made that "inasmuch as the points and principles of law to be decided [in the two cases were] identical," only *Dred Scott* v. *Irene Emerson* would be advanced, and any determination in that case would apply to Harriet's suit as well.[17] For purposes of clarification, therefore, the narrative hereafter will refer only to Dred Scott's case, unless otherwise indicated.

On the same day that the two litigations were initiated, April 6, 1846, two separate writs of summons were issued to Mrs. Emerson, ordering her to appear on the third Monday of November 1846 to answer to the charges. Endorsed upon one writ was Francis B. Murdoch's bond as security for costs that might accrue against Harriet. For some unknown reason no similar endorsement appeared on the writ for Dred's case.[18] The two writs were served on Mrs. Emerson on April 7. The next day, Mrs. Emerson's attorney, George W. Goode, indicated that he would seek dismissal of the suit "on the ground that the conditional orders by the Judge in this case directed have not been complied with." This was aimed obviously at the absence of satisfactory security to cover costs that might accrue against Dred. However, some satisfactory security was presented, although no actual document still exists, for Goode never submitted his motion to dismiss. Indeed, the next action in the case did not occur until six months later when on November 19, 1846, in compliance with the summons of April 6, Goode replied to the charges with a plea of "not guilty." He contended, of course, that Dred Scott was legally Mrs. Emerson's slave.[19]

The issue being drawn, the next step as provided by law was that Scott had to prove he was entitled to freedom. By this time Charles D. Drake had replaced Murdoch as Scott's attorney, and he proceeded to gather the needed evidence. On May 10, 1847, he took a deposition from Mrs. Catherine A. Anderson. Mrs. Anderson was the ex-wife of Lt. James L. Thompson who had been stationed at Fort Snelling with Dr. Emerson. She stated that she had hired Harriet for about two or three months, and that after Emerson had gone to Fort Jesup both slaves had remained at Fort Snelling, hired out to others. "During the whole time that I knew them at Fort Snelling," deposed Mrs. Anderson, "they were held in slavery by Doctor Emerson, or by persons to whom they were hired by him. They were universally known to be Dr. Emerson's slaves."[20]

On May 13 Drake secured further testimony, again in the form of a deposition, from Miles H. Clark, who had been stationed at both Forts Armstrong and Snelling when Emerson was at those posts. Clark was in St. Louis as a member of the volunteer "Missouri Guards" raised for service in New Mexico. The company was preparing to leave St. Louis, which is why Drake took the testimony by deposition beforehand rather than risk the chance of Clark's not being available when the case came to trial. Clark declared that he had known Scott at both Fort Armstrong and Fort Snelling, and that at both places he "was claimed by Doctor Emerson as a slave and used by him as such."[21]

Drake now had sufficient proof that Dr. Emerson had held Scott as a slave in both a free state and a free territory. But the suit was against Mrs. Emerson, not Dr. Emerson. It will be recalled that in March 1846 Mrs. Emerson had hired the Scotts to Samuel Russell of St. Louis. Drake therefore secured a written statement from Russell that he had hired Scott from Mrs. Emerson and that he had paid the money for the slave's hire to Mrs. Emerson and to her father Alexander Sanford.[22] Drake was now ready to go to court.

Dred Scott v. *Irene Emerson* was tried on Wednesday, June 30, 1847, in the Circuit Court of St. Louis County, Judge Alexander Hamilton presiding. The courtroom was in the St. Louis Courthouse, located on the city block bounded by Broadway, Chestnut, Fourth, and Market streets.[23] More than a year had elapsed from the time Scott had filed his original petition, but this was simply because the court had more cases than it could handle with sufficient dispatch. Although Drake had prepared the case, he left St. Louis in late May or early June 1847, and Samuel M. Bay handled the proceedings in court. Mrs. Emerson's attorney was still George W. Goode. Whether Mrs. Emerson or either of the slaves was in court is not clear; the official record of the trial states routinely: "This day come the parties, by their attorneys. . . ."[24]

After the jury was sworn in, Bay established that Dred Scott had been taken as a slave into free territory, that he had been brought back to Missouri, and that at the time the suit was instituted he was still being held there as a slave. Henry Taylor Blow testified that his father, Peter Blow, had formerly owned Dred Scott and had sold the slave to Emerson. The Anderson and Clark depositions were offered as evidence that Scott had lived as a slave at Forts Armstrong and Snelling. This established that Scott had been Emerson's slave in Missouri and had accompanied his master into free territory. Samuel Russell then testified that he had hired Scott from Mrs. Emerson and had paid for the hire to her and to her father, thus establishing that Mrs. Emerson still claimed Scott as her slave in Missouri. With these facts on record, Bay was satisfied that he had all the proof required by law. Other witnesses were present, but Bay saw no need for their additional testimony.[25]

Mrs. Emerson's attorney accepted without challenge the depositions of Mrs. Anderson and Clark and the oral testimony of Henry Taylor Blow. But he did cross-examine Russell, who admitted that he had not hired Scott himself, but that his wife either had done the actual hiring or had made the necessary arrangements for it. Russell conceded that all he really knew of the hiring was what he had learned from his wife, and that although he had paid money to Alexander Sanford, he "supposed that it was for Mrs. Emerson, but he did not know it" for sure. Goode was so satisfied with this cross-examination that he was now ready for the case to go to the jury.[26]

The issue raised in Goode's cross-examination was, of course, the admissibility of Samuel Russell's testimony, that it was hearsay and hence not valid evidence. After all, it was Mrs. Russell, not Russell, who had hired the slaves. Furthermore, Goode pointed out in his closing argument, Alexander Sanford's accepting money did not necessarily mean he was

Mrs. Emerson's agent. The defense, then, was the technicality that Dred Scott had not legally proved that it was specifically Mrs. Emerson who was holding him as a slave in Missouri.[27] It is of the utmost importance to note that Goode raised no doubts about the constitutionality of the Ordinance of 1787 or of the Missouri Compromise, nor was any issue made of Dred Scott's citizenship or of his right to sue. Equally significant is that the defense did not deny to Dred Scott his right to freedom by virtue of residence in free territory. This case clearly did not raise constitutional questions. It was a *bona fide* suit involving only one issue— freedom—and the technical validity of the evidence presented.[28]

The arguments concluded, Judge Hamilton instructed the jury that the defendant's procedural argument was correct—that Russell's testimony was not legal evidence to prove what the law required had to be proved, and that the assumption could not be made that Sanford's acceptance of money *ipso facto* constituted him an agent for Mrs. Emerson. Accordingly, the jury returned a verdict in favor of Mrs. Emerson, "that the said defendant is not guilty in manner and form as the plaintiff hath in his declaration complained against her." Thereupon Judge Hamilton ordered "that the said defendant go hence without day [*sic*] and recover of the said plaintiff her costs in this behalf expended."[29]

Dred Scott v. *Irene Emerson* elicited no particular interest or reaction in St. Louis or elsewhere, except to those people immediately concerned. It involved neither unusually prominent litigants nor extraordinary or controversial principles of law, and hence its occurrence passed almost unknown. Only one St. Louis newspaper even mentioned the case, and then only in a routine daily list of cases in the city's courts.[30] If any excitement occurred in St. Louis on June 30, 1847, it came not as a result of Dred Scott's suit, but rather because of the arrival on that day of Colonel Alexander W. Doniphan and a detachment of Missouri volunteers, returning from their triumphant Chihuahua campaign in the war against Mexico. But if St. Louis celebrated on that day, Dred Scott did not. He had lost his bid for freedom and was still Mrs. Emerson's slave.[31]

Chapter 6

First State
Supreme Court Appeal

IMMEDIATELY AFTER THE COURT denied Dred Scott his freedom, Samuel M. Bay moved for a new trial, contending that it was not the facts that were against Dred Scott, but rather the technicality of who had presented those facts; in other words, whether Samuel Russell's testimony was valid or hearsay evidence. That could be resolved very satisfactorily, suggested Bay, merely by calling Mrs. Russell herself. Judge Hamilton took the motion for a new trial under advisement, but the regular April term of the circuit court expired before he acted on it. It was not until the next term, on December 2, 1847, that he announced his decision, favorable to Dred Scott, when he ordered a new trial. He thus intimated two important points: first, that according to established doctrine in Missouri, Scott unquestionably was entitled to freedom; and second, that since the legal technicality could be rectified, it should not bar the slave from obtaining the freedom to which he was otherwise entitled.[1]

Meanwhile, on July 1, 1847, a completely different suit was initiated on behalf of Dred Scott. This was the occasion when Alexander P. Field and David N. Hall entered the case, and not only did they handle this new action, but they later took over Scott's original suit. Precisely when Bay dropped out of the picture is not clear. Court records indicate that all three worked together for awhile, but by March 1848, and certainly for the remainder of the state litigations, Field and Hall were Dred Scott's only lawyers.[2]

On July 1, 1847, then, Field and Hall instituted a new suit, in the same form as the earlier one (trespass and false imprisonment), but directed this time against three persons: Alexander Sanford, Irene Emerson, and Samuel Russell. It followed the same procedure as the original suit. First Scott filed a petition with Judge Hamilton requesting permission to sue his three alleged masters, detailing essentially the same account of his being in free territory with Dr. Emerson. He then charged that Sanford as administrator of Emerson's estate in Missouri, Mrs. Emerson as the person claiming Scott as a part of that estate, and Russell as the one actually employing him as a slave of that estate were all holding him illegally, because he had acquired his freedom by virtue of earlier residence in free territory. The next day, July 2, Judge Hamilton approved the petition and, conditioning his order with the provisions required by the law, granted the slave permission to sue. That same day Joseph Charless bonded himself to pay all costs that might accrue. The case was duly set for trial in the upcoming November term of 1847. Then, on July 31, the court noted that Scott was charging Mrs. Emerson with the same offense in two cases pending at the same time and ordered that one be dropped before the regular November term convened. The case finally dropped was the new one.[3]

The abortive case of *Dred Scott* v. *Alexander Sanford, Irene Emerson and Samuel Russell* is another of the enigmas of the overall history of the *Dred Scott* case. It appears suddenly and it disappears just as suddenly, with no supportive data to explain it, and thus one can only speculate. The obvious question is why it was instituted. One answer seems to stem from the earlier case—that since there was difficulty in pinpointing Mrs. Emerson as the owner, Scott's best bet was to bring all possible defendants into court and certainly one of them would be found guilty of the alleged offense. This suit was also the occasion for the entrance into Dred Scott's litigations of Field and Hall, and with them perhaps credence to the theory that financial reasons were behind the *Dred Scott* case. Field was reputed to be at his best when pursuing monetary damages for a client.[4] It may be significant that in Dred Scott's original suit against Mrs. Emerson the money claimed was a nominal ten dollars, whereas in this suit by Field and Hall the damages amounted to three hundred dollars, a considerable sum. But if this lends credence to the thesis that the goal of the slave's lawyers was money, it is confounded by the fact that when presented with the choice of the two suits, Field and Hall opted to continue the original case involving the much lesser amount. Once again, as in other instances in Dred Scott's struggle for freedom, the answers just are not there.

It will be recalled that on December 2, 1847, Judge Hamilton had awarded Dred Scott a new trial. This time Mrs. Emerson objected. Accordingly, on December 4, her attorney filed a bill of exceptions for an appeal to the Supreme Court of Missouri. The bill of exceptions was approved by Judge Hamilton, and a writ of error was duly served out to the lower court to send up a transcript of the earlier proceedings. But because of a bureaucratic delay in recording the disposition of *Dred Scott v. Alexander Sanford, Irene Emerson and Samuel Russell,* the resulting confusion held up the delivery of the transcript for three months. Finally, on March 6, 1848, the transcript was forwarded to Jefferson City, where the supreme court was shortly to meet.[5]

Before court convened, however, Mrs. Emerson relinquished direct control over her slave, but at the same time took measures to safeguard her ownership until the termination of the litigation. On March 17, 1848, as a result of a motion made by Mrs. Emerson's attorney, Judge Hamilton ordered the sheriff of St. Louis County to assume direct custody of Dred Scott and to hire him out "to the best advantage during the pendency of this suit." Anyone who hired Scott had to post a bond of six hundred dollars that he would not take him out of the jurisdiction of the court. All payments for the hire were to be made to the sheriff, who would account for these wages at the termination of the litigation to the party who won the suit. Thus, during the entire period that his case continued in the Circuit Court of St. Louis County, which was until March 18, 1857, Dred Scott remained in St. Louis, either in the custody of the sheriff or hired out by him.[6]

The Supreme Court of Missouri convened for its regular March term on March 20, 1848, at Jefferson City, Missouri. All three justices, William B. Napton, William Scott, and Priestley H. McBride, were present. Docketed as Case No. 14 of the March term, 1848, *Irene Emerson v. Dred Scott* was heard on April 3, 1848. Attorneys for both sides submitted arguments in written briefs; no oral statements were made.[7] The issue, it will be recalled, was not Dred Scott's freedom; it was the decision by the lower court granting Scott another trial. Goode contended that the lower court had erred in granting a new trial, because Dred Scott had failed to prove that it was Mrs. Emerson who held him as a slave in Missouri. As to the claim that Russell's questionable testimony could easily be rectified, Goode argued, that was actually an admission of that failure. Moreover, continued Goode, the new trial had been granted because Scott claimed to have lived in free territory, despite the fact that procedurally he had not proved what he was supposed to prove. In effect, Goode implied, Mrs. Emerson was being penalized because Scott's lawyer had failed to establish his case properly. It is significant that Goode did not deny to Scott his freedom by virtue of residence in free territory; he denied it only on the technicality that Scott had not properly proved it was Mrs. Emerson who was holding him as a slave in Missouri.[8]

Just as Goode had relied upon a technicality to secure the decision in the lower court against Dred Scott, so did Field and Hall now rely upon a technicality to uphold the granting of a new trial. They pointed out simply that the case was not properly before the Missouri Supreme Court, because it had been brought there on a writ of error. A writ of error, they insisted, can be issued only after a final judgment in the lower court. In this instance, they pointed out, the new trial had not yet taken place and no final judgment existed upon which a writ of error might be issued or an appeal be made. Not one word did they say about substantive issues or about slavery in the territories or its implications.[9]

The unanimous decision of the Missouri Supreme Court was announced on Friday, June 30, 1848, exactly one year after the first trial in the lower court. It was very brief and very terse: "There is no final judgment, upon which a writ of error can only lie." Accordingly, the writ of error was dismissed and the court refused to review the decision of the lower court. Dred Scott was assured of a new trial.[10]

These proceedings clearly indicate that the only issue before the Missouri Supreme Court was procedural, whether it had jurisdiction over the lower court's granting of a new trial. The court did not even consider the substantive facts. At no time did counsel of either side broach the issue of slavery in the territories, of the political implications of slavery, or of any allied subject, despite the fact that these questions were then very pronounced in the nationwide discussions unleashed by the Wilmot Proviso and the outcome of the war with Mexico. Thus, it is quite clear that at this stage of the litigation the *Dred Scott* case was still free of political interferences, and that it was still a genuine suit for freedom alone.

This explains why the second court action in Dred Scott's struggle for freedom passed by without causing any particular interest or public reaction. The only notice it received in the newspapers was in a routine listing of Missouri Supreme Court cases. Except for this very unobtrusive publicity—if it can even be called publicity—the only people aware of the litigation were still those very few directly involved in it.[11]

Chapter 7

Second State
Circuit Court Trial

ABOUT A YEAR AND a half passed before the new trial finally took place.
It was docketed first for February 27, 1849, and then again for May 2,
but both times postponed, once because of an overloaded docket and
once because some influential St. Louisans persuaded the court to take
up other litigations. It was docketed a third time for the latter part of
May. But on the night of May 17, 1849, a fire broke out on the St. Louis
waterfront, and before it was extinguished a large part of the city was
ravaged. Business all over came practically to a standstill, and few people
were willing to neglect urgent private affairs to attend court as jurors or
witnesses. To make matters worse, the dreaded cholera broke out, and
many who lived in the county feared, and actually refused, to come into
the city to attend court. Consequently Judge Hamilton advisedly suspended
court until after the critical times had passed. This, of course, once more
delayed Dred Scott's suit for freedom. The case was again set for hearing
in December 1849. Witnesses were summoned for at least three days
during that month, but still no trial. Finally, on Saturday, January 12,
1850, the case at long last was called.[1]

None of the lawyers who had participated in the first trial were involved in the retrial. Samuel M. Bay, who had argued for Dred Scott in
1847, fell victim to the great 1849 cholera epidemic, but he had been
replaced earlier anyway by Alexander P. Field and David N. Hall, who
already had handled the Emerson appeal to the Missouri Supreme Court
in 1848. Mrs. Emerson also was represented by new lawyers, Hugh A.
Garland and Lyman D. Norris, who replaced her former attorney George
W. Goode. As in 1847, the trial was held in the Circuit Court of St.
Louis County, in the Old Courthouse building, Judge Alexander Hamilton

presiding again. Whether the litigants themselves were in court is not clear; once again the official record states simply: "This day come the parties by their attorneys. . . ."[2]

Proceedings in the second trial followed very closely those in the first. Pursuant to the law under which Scott was suing, his lawyers established that he had been taken as a slave into free territory, that he had then been brought back to Missouri, and that at the time the suit was filed he was being held in Missouri illegally as a slave. They offered as evidence the same two depositions that had been presented at the first trial, those of Catherine A. Anderson and Miles H. Clark. Then, to prove that it was Mrs. Emerson who was holding Scott as a slave in Missouri (the controversial point in the 1847 trial), Field and Hall read into the record a deposition by Mrs. Adeline Russell, wife of Samuel Russell. Mrs. Russell deposed that she had hired the Scotts from Mrs. Emerson, who claimed them as her slaves. Asked how she knew that the slaves belonged to Mrs. Emerson, Mrs. Russell specified Mrs. Emerson as the one who actually hired them out to her. Samuel Russell then testified orally, as he had in 1847, that he and his wife had hired the slaves and that he had paid their wages.[3]

With this oral testimony and the three written depositions, Field and Hall rested their case. As in the first trial, additional witnesses for Dred Scott had been summoned, but once again they did not testify as evidently their testimony was not needed.[4] Mrs. Emerson's attorneys again offered no witnesses or other evidence whatsoever, not even a cross-examination.[5]

There was no longer any question about who had hired out Dred Scott as there had been in the first trial. Mrs. Emerson's attorneys could not, and did not, deny it. But they insisted in their summation that Mrs. Emerson had every right to hire him out because he was still her slave in spite of his travels with Dr. Emerson. The reason, they asserted, was that all the time Scott was at Fort Armstrong and Fort Snelling, he was under the military jurisdiction of the United States Army, and at no time while in free territory did he come under civil law. The same law applied to him, they insisted, that applied to Dr. Emerson—namely, military law. They made no effort to reconcile this with *Rachael* v. *Walker*, where the court had freed the slave Rachael in spite of the same military law argument.[6]

Summing up for the plaintiff, Field and Hall used the same reasoning

their predecessor Samuel M. Bay had used in the first trial: that Dr.
Emerson had taken his slave into territory where slavery was prohibited
by the Ordinance of 1787 as well as by the Missouri Compromise, and
that both effectuated the slave's freedom. They showed also that incontrovertible evidence now existed that Mrs. Emerson continued to hold
Scott in Missouri despite his legal right to freedom. They asked, therefore, that according to established law and precedent in Missouri, the
jury should return a verdict in favor of Dred Scott.[7]

It did not take the jury long to return that verdict, that "the defendant
is guilty of manner and form as in the plaintiff's declaration alleged."
Accordingly, Judge Hamilton ordered "that the plaintiff recover his freedom against said defendant and all persons claiming under her by title
derived since the commencement of this suit." Dred Scott was declared
to be a free man, and to have been free, as far as the law of Missouri was
concerned, ever since he had gone to Fort Armstrong in 1833. Not only
was Dred Scott free, but so, too, were his wife, Harriet, and their two
daughters, Eliza and Lizzie.[8]

Once again it is absolutely clear that the political issue of slavery in
the territories did not enter into the proceedings, despite the fact that
this question was then, in 1850, the subject of intense and bitter nationwide debate in the halls of Congress, in the press, and from the pulpit
and podium. At no time did any of the participants in the trial challenge
the validity of the slavery prohibitions in the Ordinance of 1787 or the
Missouri Compromise, nor did they even express any opinions about
them. Neither did anyone suggest doubting Dred Scott's citizenship or
his right to sue. All these were implicitly upheld by Scott's attorneys
and subsequently by the court. But more significant is the fact that
the defense, which might be expected to deny them, did not. Mrs.
Emerson's right to Dred Scott was defended on one ground only, that
civil law was subordinate to military law when applied to military personnel on active duty. By implication, the defense tacitly admitted
that if Scott had been outside the jurisdiction of the military establishment—that if Dr. Emerson had been a civilian and not in the army and
subject to its regulations—there would be no doubt that the civil law
made Dred Scott a free man. That, of course, was exactly the argument
of plaintiff's attorney—that it was precisely because of the operation of
the civil law (the Ordinance of 1787 and the Missouri Compromise)
that Dred Scott was free. Thus, the *Dred Scott* case remained in January

1850 as it had been when it started four years earlier in April 1846, still a genuine attempt on the part of a slave to secure his freedom and a genuine defense on the part of an owner to prevent the loss of what she considered to be her lawful property, with no political overtones whatsoever either explicitly or implicitly involved.

This undoubtedly explains why even a third court action involving the same parties went unnoticed and unheralded in the press. So unimportant and insignificant was this case that when its title was inadvertently omitted from routine newspaper listings of St. Louis court proceedings no one thought it worth the trouble even to print a correction.[9] Obviously the case aroused no interest outside of St. Louis either; indeed, since it was not even listed in the local papers, it undoubtedly was a nonentity elsewhere. So Dred Scott was free, but except for the few people directly involved, no one else either knew or cared—yet. But his freedom was not to last long.

Chapter 8

Second State Supreme Court Appeal

IMMEDIATELY AFTER THE DECISION granting Dred Scott his freedom, Hugh A. Garland and Lyman D. Norris instituted a series of moves that culminated in another appeal to the Missouri Supreme Court.[1] First they moved for a new trial, but that was overruled. Mrs. Emerson's only recourse, then, was to appeal directly to the state supreme court. On February 13 Garland and Norris filed a bill of exceptions; it was duly certified by Judge Hamilton, and the appeal procedure was set in motion. Subsequently, on a writ of error (now there was a final judgment in the lower court), a complete transcript was forwarded to the supreme court. The case was docketed as No. 84 for the March term scheduled to convene shortly in St. Louis.[2]

A number of important changes had occurred on the Missouri Supreme Court since Dred Scott's case had been before it in 1848. Two of the three justices had since been replaced; the court now consisted of William B. Napton, John F. Ryland, and James H. Birch, the latter two being new. The 1848 litigation had been held in Jefferson City; all the proceedings in this one occurred in St. Louis, where, since 1849, the supreme court had been authorized by the state legislature to hold semiannual terms.[3]

Another important change was the departure of Mrs. Emerson from St. Louis, leaving her slaves behind. Just what impelled her to leave is not clear, but it should be noted that she was only in her thirties and a widow with a small daughter. Sometime in 1849 or 1850 she moved to Springfield, Massachusetts, to live with her sister Mrs. James Barnes, whose husband was an engineer and, like the late Dr. Emerson, also an army officer. On November 21, 1850, Mrs. Emerson married Dr. Calvin Clifford Chaffee, a Springfield physician, and she lived there until her death in 1903.[4] Mrs. Emerson's departure from St. Louis had no effect on the case; it was not even noted in any of the proceedings. The same lawyers continued to defend her, and their arguments remained essentially the same, for a while, at least. Besides, Mrs. Emerson was not the one who looked after the legal affairs of her deceased first husband's estate anyway; it was done by her brother John F. A. Sanford, who went right on doing so even after his sister left St. Louis. Thus, there existed the unique situation in which Dred Scott, in the custody of the sheriff of St. Louis County, was suing Mrs. Emerson (now Mrs. Chaffee), who was living in Massachusetts. But the case continued in the Supreme Court of Missouri as though nothing had occurred.

The obvious question at this point is: why did Mrs. Emerson appeal to the Missouri Supreme Court in light of the long list of Missouri precedents that strengthened Scott's position? It is not insignificant that a shrewd and prosperous businessman (John F. A. Sanford) was handling Mrs. Emerson's legal problems, and he was not going to lose property and money when he thought there was a good chance to retain it. From the proceedings that ensued, it is clear that his attorneys were convinced there was a distinction between civil and military law over slave property, in spite of *Rachael* v. *Walker,* and that they could retain for Mrs. Emerson (or for their client Sanford) the financial investment the lower court had taken away.

This is unmistakably substantiated by Garland's brief for Mrs. Emerson. He stressed two important points. The first dealt with the consent of the master. According to *Nat* v. *Stephen Ruddle,*[5] a slave held in Missouri was entitled to freedom by virtue of residence in free territory only if that residence was with the master's consent. Garland argued that in Dred Scott's case Emerson had gone into free territory only because he was an army officer "subject to the order and direction of the Government, whose servant he was." He did not "voluntarily and of his own free will" go into free territory and therefore could not "voluntarily and of his own free will" have taken Dred Scott there with him. "Consent" was given neither explicitly nor implicitly; Emerson simply had no choice.

Garland's second point was a repetition of his argument in the lower court—that Forts Armstrong and Snelling were "under the military jurisdiction of the United States, which superseding the civil jurisdiction, abrogates to a certain extent the Missouri Compromise Act and Ordinance of 1787." Military law, not civil law, pertained in this case. Although

Garland referred to both the 1787 and the 1820 statutes, he did not intimate that their slavery prohibitions were even harmful or evil, let alone unconstitutional. He claimed only that they were civil law, and that in a jurisdictional conflict between civil law and military law the latter must prevail. It is patently clear that Garland's arguments neither involved nor were influenced by the political struggle then going on (in 1850) over the issue of slavery in the territories.[6]

David N. Hall filed the brief for Dred Scott. First he reiterated his lower court stance, that Scott was entitled to freedom because of his travels and Missouri law. Then he attacked the two points Garland had argued. Civil versus military law was a sham issue that had no bearing on the case. *Rachael* v. *Walker* (which Garland conveniently had ignored) already had settled that it made no difference whether a slave was on military or civilian property. As to the matter of consent, Hall conceded that an officer had to go where ordered, even though not "voluntarily and of his own free will." But when Emerson went to Fort Jesup and left Scott at Fort Snelling, in free territory, hired out as a slave to others, he did that voluntarily. Citing *Julia* v. *McKinney, Wilson* v. *Melvin, Nat* v. *Ruddle,* and *Ralph* v. *Duncan,* Hall insisted there was incontrovertible precedent that any slave thus hired out by his master in free territory was thereby entitled to his freedom, and that the decision of the lower court should rightfully stand.[7]

Ever since the Wilmot Proviso in 1846 had once more propelled slavery to the center of the national arena, that issue had unleashed passions and emotions that more and more were eroding the unity of the country. Only a few days before Garland and Hall filed their briefs, James Mason of Virginia read on the floor of the United States Senate John C. Calhoun's uncompromising declamation of sectionalism, which was followed shortly by Daniel Webster's equally stirring Seventh of March peroration. The nation was seething with disruptive debate, feelings were running high on both sides, and an explosion was feared momentarily. Yet the briefs filed on both sides indicate quite clearly that this was still a genuine freedom case, in no way influenced by the current emotionalism over slavery.

These briefs were filed on March 8, 1850, in time for the regular March term. But the schedule was unusually heavy due to the transfer of many cases from the Jefferson City docket, and the court was unable to take up the case during this term. By the time the court convened in

October 1850, for its next regular session in St. Louis, a decision had been reached. This decision, however, was based not upon the unbiased and genuine arguments and points of law that attorneys had presented in their briefs, but rather upon the judges' own prejudicial views toward the question that by now had become the main issue of a bitter and partisan struggle in Missouri—slavery in the territories. *Here, for the first time, politics was injected into the case, not by the parties, but by the judges of the Missouri Supreme Court in their intended decision.*

The background for this crucial transition in the *Dred Scott* case lay in the deep-rooted struggle to unseat Senator Thomas Hart Benton of Missouri.[8] Political conflict centering around "Old Bullion" was nothing new. The immediate issue arose from the highly partisan proslavery resolutions introduced by John C. Calhoun in the United States Senate on February 19, 1847, which asserted, in effect, that Congress had no power to prohibit slavery in the territories. Benton, a free-soil Democrat, vehemently opposed the resolutions, denounced them as erroneous "firebrand" abstractions, and campaigned against them both in Missouri and elsewhere. When Benton's enemies gained control of the Missouri state legislature, they sought to undermine his political power so they might unseat him in the senatorial election coming up in 1850. On March 6, 1849, they pushed through the so-called "Jackson Resolutions," which not only reaffirmed Calhoun's proslavery principles, but also instructed Missouri's senators to conform with them. Benton was in a precarious situation. If he abided by the Jackson Resolutions, he would have to support a precept that desecrated every freedom principle he had so strongly and so long supported. On the other hand, if he continued in what he believed to be right, he would be violating the instructions of the legislative body to which he soon had to look for reelection. Benton faced the situation squarely, and on May 26, 1849, in the famous "Appeal," he declared his position for the electorate of Missouri. Denouncing the Jackson Resolutions as a political plot against him and accusing its sponsors as nullifiers and disunionists, Benton appealed to the people of Missouri to stand by him to maintain the Union. The stage was set for a bitterly vitriolic senatorial campaign.

The attitudes of the Missouri Supreme Court justices toward Benton played an important part in the events that now transpired in the *Dred Scott* case. Ryland was pro-Benton, but the other two, Napton and Birch, were his bitter enemies. Indeed, Benton publicly accused Napton of being

the real instigator behind the Jackson Resolutions deliberately to undermine his (Benton's) political platform. Napton denied the specific charge,
but did not hide his political differences with Benton. The animosity
between Benton and Birch went deeper; they were intense personal
enemies as well.[9]

It was under such circumstances that Mrs. Emerson's appeal came
before the Missouri Supreme Court in March 1850. As already indicated,
the court adjourned its March term before reaching the case. However,
the judges were keenly aware of the slavery principles it involved. Napton
frequently had discussed them with William Scott, who had been on the
bench with him when Dred Scott's case had been before the supreme
court in 1848. Both Napton and Scott had decided then that as soon as
an opportunity presented itself, they would overturn all decisions that
recognized the validity and binding force of any slavery prohibitions
based on the Ordinance of 1787. Napton communicated this to Ryland
and Birch as his view toward the *Dred Scott* case. Ryland disagreed; he
felt that the prior decisions should stand undisturbed. Birch, however,
agreed to follow Napton's lead; in fact, he was willing to go even further
and declare unconstitutional all congressional legislation restricting
slavery in the territories, including the Missouri Compromise. Napton
feared that was going too far, because so sweeping a declaration was not
essential to this case; but he had no qualms about overthrowing precedents based only on the Ordinance of 1787.[10]

The accusation has been made that Napton and Birch saw in the
Dred Scott case not only their long-awaited chance to overthrow past
decisions based on the Ordinance of 1787, but also a glorious opportunity
to deliver a crushing blow to their hated political foe Thomas Hart
Benton. It was part of a grand conspiracy, charged Edward Bates, then
a prominent St. Louis Whig and later President Lincoln's attorney-
general, aimed at uniting anti-Benton Missouri Democrats with vacillating
Whigs. The anti-Benton Democrats would give their support to the Whig
candidate Henry S. Geyer; in return Geyer would support proslavery and
states' rights measures when he got into the United States Senate. To
give the coalition needed moral strength, the Missouri Supreme Court,
with Napton and Birch taking the lead, would reaffirm judicially the
political views of Benton's enemies, even though it meant overturning
previous decisions of Missouri's courts on the subject of slavery. Coming
from so estimable an institution as the state's supreme court, such a

declaration would be tantamount to a judicial sanction to crush Benton. If the plan worked, Benton would be defeated, the Whigs would be compensated with a senator, and the anti-Benton Democrats would be in control of Missouri. The *Dred Scott* case, by pure coincidence before the Missouri Supreme Court at the time, provided the ideal opportunity for the judicial phase of the conspiracy.[11]

Whether such an orchestrated plot actually existed cannot be proved, but that is what did happen in the ensuing senatorial campaign.[12] Furthermore, there is no doubt about the attitudes of the Missouri Supreme Court justices toward the slavery principles involved in the election as well as in the *Dred Scott* case: Napton and Birch, both resolute anti-Benton Democrats, favored a proslavery decision overturning the previous decisions upholding the validity of the Ordinance of 1787; Ryland, on the other hand, wanted to retain the old precedents as they existed, and he was prepared to write a dissenting opinion expressing this view. These were the opinions the three held when the Missouri Supreme Court met in St. Louis on October 25, 1850, for its regular October term.[13]

Shortly after the court convened, Ryland changed his mind and agreed to concur with Napton and Birch so a unanimous decision could be delivered. He did this for several reasons. In August 1850 a new Missouri state legislature had been elected, and the composition of that body indicated that Benton might not be reelected anyway; indeed, when the legislature met, it chose Geyer to replace Benton. With Benton already defeated, his enemies no longer needed that strong proslavery pronouncement from the supreme court. Another factor was that Napton finally was able to convince Birch that the decision need not go so far as to declare the Missouri Compromise unconstitutional. This meant that the Napton-Birch majority decision could be toned down considerably, making it more palatable to Ryland. The latter, not one of Missouri's most consistently distinguished jurists anyway, had in the meantime modified his thinking toward the anti-Benton viewpoint, although not nearly as proslavery as Napton's and Birch's. As a result Ryland agreed to concur with a majority opinion that, although not as strongly anti-Benton as originally planned, nevertheless still would overturn all Missouri precedents that upheld the binding force of the Ordinance of 1787. The documents in the *Dred Scott* case were thereupon turned over to Napton to write the now unanimous decision.[14]

But Napton never wrote that decision. He intended to include in it passages from Lord Stowell's classic opinion in the *Slave Grace* case. These materials, though, were not available in the Missouri state library, and Napton sent away for them, putting off writing the decision until they came. But in August 1851, before the materials arrived, in an election of judges for Missouri courts, Napton lost his seat on the Missouri Supreme Court. His failure to write the decision before the election meant, of course, that the case would pass over to the newly elected court. That court now consisted of Hamilton R. Gamble, John F. Ryland, and William Scott.[15] Only the "moderate" Ryland remained from the previous court. But he and Scott—a majority of the new court— already had committed themselves to overthrowing precedents based on the Ordinance of 1787.

The newly elected court met in St. Louis on October 20, 1851. At first it appeared that a heavy schedule might push the *Dred Scott* case to the next term, but at virtually the eleventh hour Field succeeded in getting it placed on the docket.[16] (His partner Hall had died on March 28, 1851, and Field continued alone as Dred Scott's counsel.) Following the doctrine that the judges who decide a case should be those who hear arguments, and inasmuch as the supreme court often decided cases on written rather than oral argument, Field resubmitted the same briefs that both sides had filed in 1850. For some reason he neglected to notify Mrs. Emerson's attorneys. Subsequently, now docketed as No. 137, on November 29, 1851, the case was finally taken under consideration, on written briefs alone. A decision was reached and Justice Scott was designated to prepare the court's opinion.[17]

At this point Mrs. Emerson's counsel somehow learned of the resubmission of the original briefs. Norris was preparing a new brief anyway, but had not yet completed it—and here his case had already been decided! At first he considered a special oral argument, but deciding this might not be proper, he obtained permission to file the new brief, even though belatedly.[18]

This brief is of particular importance because it marks a significant change in the legal arguments. Up to this point, neither side had challenged the validity of the slavery prohibitions in either the Ordinance of 1787 or the Missouri Compromise, although the idea had already occurred to the judges. But now Norris for the first time raised doubts about those two acts.[19] True, he did not go so far as to challenge their actual constitutionality; that was to come later, in the federal courts. But by questioning the applicability of these laws, and especially by his choice of words, Norris indicated that the burning political issues of the day were now influencing the arguments of the attorneys as they already had affected some of the judges of the Missouri Supreme Court. In fact, in the very opening paragraphs of his new brief, Norris described quite succinctly his "sober second thoughts" about this case:

> When the case was first presented to the consideration of your honors predecessors it was thought by the appellants counsel (upon a partial Examination) to present no new points for the decision of this Court. . . . "Sober second thoughts" superinduced by deeper study have led us to doubt the correctness of our first conclusion. . . . Our own convictions [are] that the whole tenor of [past] decisions upon the subject of Freedom are based upon false legal principles & untenable to the last degree.

Here, then, as a result of "sober second thoughts," the defense for the first time challenged congressional prohibition of slavery in the territories. What partisan judges had failed to achieve earlier was now accomplished by an equally partisan defense counsel, for Norris's proslavery doctrines, if not his law, were to be incorporated in the Missouri court's final decision. *From this point on, the* Dred Scott *case clearly changed from a genuine freedom suit to the controversial political issue for which it became infamous in American history.*

Norris's brief was a sweeping denunciation of the authority of both the Ordinance of 1787 and the Missouri Compromise. But he fell short of denying their constitutionality; he argued only that laws based upon them were unenforceable within the state of Missouri. Stated another way, he did not deny the authority of Congress to free a slave in the territories; what he did challenge was the concept of "once free, always free." He buttressed his attack on the Ordinance of 1787 with quotations from the recent decision of the United States Supreme Court, only a few months earlier, in *Strader* v. *Graham,* which declared that the Ordinance had been supplanted by the Constitution and therefore any enforcement of its provisions or principles stemmed only from the Constitution of the United States or the constitutions and laws of the respective states. Because the Ordinance ceased to be in force, Norris maintained, it followed that no longer could it be "the source of Jurisdiction" of any law or decision in Missouri. Yet it was, in the precedents cited by Dred Scott's counsel. But those decisions, now asserted Norris, were based upon "false legal principles" and should be overthrown.

Norris's assault on the Missouri Compromise was much less a legal discourse than a partisan political harangue. Instead of citing legal precedent as at least he had done in his derogation of the Ordinance of 1787, he outlined the history of Missouri's struggle for statehood, punctuating it regularly with sectional and proslavery diatribes. His most caustic barbs were directed at the hypocrisy of northern courts for not treating free blacks equally with whites: "Before this Court should recognize any of the rights of freedom claimed under [the Missouri Compromise], those rights should first be enforced & perfected by the tribunals of that country north of the line 36°30'." Besides, he added, the Missouri Compromise was federal law and therefore should be enforced by federal rather than state courts. If the federal courts did their job correctly, they would be guided by *Strader* v. *Graham* that a slave was subject to the laws of the state in which he was residing, no matter where he had been before.

Norris reiterated the "military-law" argument that had been in the earlier Garland brief, but he developed it singularly, referring to "property recognized as such by the Constitution of the United States." That, of course, was the extreme proslavery view. But it also was a step toward the interpretation made by Chief Justice Taney later, that an umbrella of substantive due process protected slavery as property under the Fifth Amendment.

The capstone of Norris's brief, though, was its closing, a racist harangue that not only revealed the prejudices of its author, but also indicated how the *Dred Scott* case had become a vehicle for the expression of such views:

> Neither sound policy nor enlightened philanthropy should encourage in a Slaveholding State, the multiplication of a race whose condition could be neither that of freemen or slaves & whose existence & increase in this anomalous character, without promoting their individual comforts & happiness[,] tends only to dissatisfy and corrupt those of their own race & color remaining in a State of Servitude.

What had started as a routine freedom case had now stirred up two explosive issues that already were plaguing the nation and that were to become even more important later: the political status of slavery and the attitudes of white America toward blacks. If the earlier abortive cabal by the Missouri Supreme Court was the real thing, it apparently involved directly, at least, only the first of these issues—slavery as a political institution. What Norris injected into the case was in the long run much more disruptive to American history—the undisguised and ignoble argument that blacks were inferior to whites. Chief Justice Taney would later stir up the proverbial hornet's nest with this same theme, in his racist declamations about rights of Negroes that whites were or were not bound to respect. But it was Lyman D. Norris, in this brief, who introduced those dogmas of racial bigotry that henceforth would play such an important role in the *Dred Scott* case.

With Norris's new brief added to the record, the supreme court adjourned on December 24, 1851. It moved to Jefferson City to hold a term there and then, on March 15, 1852, convened in St. Louis for its regular March term. There, on March 22, 1852, it announced the decision in *Dred Scott v. Irene Emerson*.[20]

Justice William Scott delivered the Opinion of the Court, with Justice Ryland concurring.[21] Cases of this type were not new to Missouri courts, said Scott, and slaves frequently had been accorded freedom on the basis of residence in territory where slavery was prohibited. These decisions seemingly were based, however, on grounds "that it is the duty of the Courts of this State to carry into effect the Constitution and laws of other States and territories, regardless of the rights, the policy, or the institutions of the people of this State."

Scott then asserted that the courts of Missouri were under no obligation to recognize the laws of any other state if they conflicted with the laws of Missouri. This comity among state courts was necessary and good, Scott continued, but:

> Every state has the right of determining how far in a spirit
> of comity it will respect the laws of other States. Those
> laws have no intrinsic right to be enforced beyond the
> limits of the State for which they were enacted. The respect
> allowed them will depend altogether on their conformity

to the policy of our institutions. No state is bound to carry
into effect enactments conceived in a spirit hostile to that
which pervades her own laws.[22]

Although comity existed—and he repeatedly applauded it—Scott insisted
that it had only a "tacit" existence, which ended if any laws became
"repugnant" to the policy or "prejudicial" to the interests of any one
state. "It is a humiliating spectacle," he decried, "to see the courts of
a State confiscating the property of her own citizens by the command
of a foreign law."

Scott then discussed "foreign law" vis-à-vis the slavery prohibitions
of the Missouri Compromise and the constitution and statutes of Illinois
and their force in Missouri's courts. He did not deny the constitutionality
or validity of the slavery prohibition of the Missouri Compromise; indeed, he declared, that prohibition was "absolute"—but only in the
particular location where it applied, which by the wording of the law
itself was limited to that portion of the Louisiana Purchase territory
north of $36°\,30'$ but not including the state of Missouri. Thus, if a slave
crossed the western border of Missouri, he could unquestionably obtain his freedom under the Missouri Compromise prohibition, but such
action would have to be in a court in the free territory, not in a Missouri
court. The same applied to a slave who crossed into Illinois; he could also
obtain his freedom, but he would have to do so in Illinois. But, remon-
strated Scott, employing states' rights proslavery rhetoric widely heard
on the political stump:

> Those governments are capable of enforcing their own laws,
> and if they are not, are we concerned that such laws should
> be enforced and that too at the cost of our own citizens?
> . . . On almost three sides, the State of Missouri is surrounded
> with free soil. If one of our slaves touch that soil with his
> master's assent, he becomes entitled to his freedom. Con-
> sidering the numberless instances in which those living along
> an extensive frontier would have occasion to occupy their
> slaves beyond our boundary, how hard would it be, if our
> Courts should liberate all the slaves who would thus be
> employed. How unreasonable to ask it.[23]

Significantly, Scott did not deny that a slave could attain freedom by going into free territory; indeed, he clearly recognized that principle, as had Norris. But what happened when the slave returned to Missouri? Did he remain free? No, insisted Scott, in the face of the many precedents to the contrary. "Once free" did not necessarily mean "always free." The precept applicable now was that pronounced by the Kentucky Court of Appeals in *Graham* v. *Strader,* in which that court had held "that the owner of a slave who resides in Kentucky, who permits his slave to go to Ohio in charge of an agent for a temporary purpose, does not forfeit his right of property in such slave." The reason was that upon his return to Kentucky that slave came under the jurisdiction of Kentucky law, which sanctioned slavery, and even though he had been a free man in Ohio, he reverted to slavery when he voluntarily returned to Kentucky. Thus, when Dred Scott voluntarily returned to Missouri, he too reverted to slavery under Missouri law, regardless of what he might have been in Illinois or in Wisconsin Territory.[24]

Thus the majority opinion was based upon an interpretation of the law of comity rather than upon an interpretation of the law of slavery. Also, Scott deliberately relied upon the Kentucky decision in *Graham* v. *Strader* rather than the United States Supreme Court decision in *Strader* v. *Graham.* A careful reading of the latter reveals that its decision did not deal with the merits of slavery legislation. Instead, the case was returned to the Kentucky high court for lack of jurisdiction, which meant that the state court's decision prevailed. That decision declared Kentucky's right not to extend comity toward certain laws that emancipated slaves. Norris had misconstrued *Strader* v. *Graham;* he had read into it the substantive principle that a state categorically can decide whether a slave "once free" is "always free." Others would make the same mistake. But Justice Scott did not. His racist law may have been reprehensible; but his legal process was sound.[25]

Scott concluded with passages that reveal the prejudicial and sectional biases that influenced his decision. To begin with, Scott proclaimed from the bench a justification of slavery as the will of God. He contrasted the condition of the slave in the United States with that of the black man in Africa, and declared: "We are almost persuaded, that the introduction of slavery amongst us, was, in the providence of God, who makes the evil passions of men subservient to his own glory, a means of placing that unhappy race within the pale of civilized nations." But perhaps the most significant passage is the one in which Scott bluntly admitted that, despite all precedents in the Missouri Supreme Court, the decision in this case rested upon completely different reasoning:

> Times now are not as they were, when the former decisions on this subject were made. Since then not only individuals but States have been possessed with a dark and fell spirit in relation to slavery, whose gratification is sought in the pursuit of measures whose inevitable consequence must be the overthrow and destruction of our government. Under such circumstances, it does not behoove the State of Missouri, to show the least countenance to any measure which might gratify this spirit. She is willing to assume her full responsibility for the existence of slavery within her limits, nor does she seek to share or divide it with others. Although we may for our own sake regret that the avarice and hardheartedness of the progenitors of those who are now so sensitive on the subject, ever introduced the institution among us, yet we will not go to them to learn law, morality or religion on the subject.[26]

This "times now are not as they were" declamation clearly reveals the radical transformation in the erstwhile genuine freedom case. In all likelihood Norris's brief did not change the two-to-one verdict of the court, for even before he submitted it Scott and Ryland had indicated their intention to overthrow the "once free, always free" precedents. But undoubtedly Norris contributed to the extremism of the majority opinion, for clearly his racial and sectional prejudices are found there.

That this elicited serious concern is borne out in the dissenting opinion of Justice Hamilton R. Gamble.[27] Indeed, at the very outset Gamble identified the unique circumstances that impelled him even to write a dissent: "The questions involved in the case, and the present condition of feeling in the country, seem to require that I should state the grounds of the dissent."

Gamble dealt first with comity. Every slave state had statutory provisions for emancipation that had always been recognized as valid in all other slave states, even though the mechanisms for emancipation differed from state to state. Gamble saw no reason why this comity should suddenly cease. True, comity was not mandatory; but anything else was immoral, illogical, and senseless, leading only to disorder and anarchy. The Constitution did not give the national government power to regulate slavery; that was left entirely to the states. But being free to adopt or reject slavery as it saw fit, each state had to recognize and accept that its neighbors might view slavery differently. Those differences had always been honored in the courts.

So, too, in Missouri. Knowing that Illinois prohibited slavery, a citizen of Missouri should not take his slave there in the first place; if he did, he had no just complaint when Illinois law emancipated that slave. Indeed, the very taking of the slave into Illinois was itself a tacit act of emancipation. The principle had existed for a long time that a slave was considered free if his master even indirectly recognized him as such, and taking him where slavery was forbidden was at the very least a tacit recognition of that freedom. Gamble then cited the long list of precedents that substantiated comity by Missouri courts toward freedom attained in free states and territories. "These decisions," he summarized, "which come down to the year 1837 . . . have so fully settled the question that since that time there has been no case bringing it before the Court . . . until the present."

Gamble did not rely upon Missouri cases alone. He cited decisions of other slave states—Louisiana, Virginia, Mississippi and Kentucky—that upheld the emancipation force of the Ordinance of 1787. Bolstering his argument for comity, he pointed out that in all these decisions the principle was either expressly declared or tacitly admitted that "where a right to freedom has been acquired under the law of another State or country, it may be enforced by action in the Courts of a slaveholding State."

In concluding, Gamble appealed for judicial calmness and impartiality in the face of the turbulent slave issue. He deprecated the situation in which those "who have no concern for the institution of slavery" interfered with the domestic affairs of others under the guise of morality and philanthropy. It was only natural that slaveowners, "when denounced in terms that would be appropriate if they had actually kidnapped the slaves from the coast of Africa, or had inherited the fortunes accumulated by such iniquitous traffic, should feel exasperated by such wanton and unfounded attack." This made it especially imperative that "the judicial mind, calm and self balanced," should adhere to sound principles established when there were no undue emotions to warp interpretations of fundamental legal questions:

> Times may have changed, public feeling may have changed, but principles have not and do not change, and in my judgment there can be no safe basis for judicial decisions, but in those principles which are immutable.[28]

So by a two-to-one decision the Missouri Supreme Court overturned all precedents and asserted that "the voluntary removal of a slave, by his master, to a State, Territory, or Country, in which slavery is prohibited, with a view to a residence there, does not entitle the slave to sue for his freedom, in the courts of this State."[29] Accordingly on March 22, 1852, the court declared that the judgment of the lower court "be reversed, annulled, and for nought held and esteemed," and that the case "be remanded to the said Circuit Court for further proceedings" so a new judgment might be delivered "according to the opinion of this court herein delivered."[30] Dred Scott's freedom had been short-lived.

The decision of the Missouri Supreme Court was recognized as important by some newspapers; others did not consider it so. The St. Louis *Daily Missouri Republican* described the majority opinion as "strong and conclusive," and even though it overturned all former decisions on the subject of slavery in the territories it was nevertheless "in consonance with reason and good sense" and "predicated on the soundest principles of law." At the same time the paper declared that "this decision has almost become necessary by the new order of things and the current of recent events," indicating that it approved for more than legal reasons.[31] Other Missouri newspapers either gave a brief resume of the decision but without editorial comment, or made no mention of it at all.[32] Outside Missouri, the *Dred Scott* case was noted in the Washington, D.C., *Daily National Intelligencer,* which printed a very small news item merely reporting the bare details of the decision, but with no editorial comments.[33] Thus the decision of the Missouri Supreme Court aroused no particularly impressive approval or indignation in Missouri, and the brief article in the *Daily National Intelligencer* indicates that the case was considered important enough to be mentioned, at least, outside of Missouri. But it should be kept in mind that the slavery controversy that had swept the country during the period of the Wilmot Proviso and the Compromise of 1850 had now lapsed into a temporary lull. Professor Allan Nevins very aptly described this quiescent period as one during which the "tiger" was asleep, and he likened the Missouri Supreme Court's decision to that animal merely "stirring" in its slumber.[34]

The decision of the Missouri Supreme Court was officially transmitted to the Circuit Court of St. Louis County on April 10, 1852. Meanwhile, on March 23, the day after the decision had been announced, measures already were instituted for the sheriff of St. Louis County to turn over to Mrs. Emerson all proceeds of the Scotts's hire since 1848. But on June 29, 1852, Judge Hamilton surprisingly overruled what would appear to be a routine formality. The court's journal says only: "Said motion be overruled." Nothing more appears on the records for almost one and one-half years, until January 25, 1854, but it explains the earlier action: "Continued by consent, awaiting decision of Supreme Court of the United States." For on November 2, 1853, a new case had been instituted in the United States federal courts, with every expectation that it would go all the way to the very top. In the meantime the sheriff held on to the money earned by the Scotts. Also in the meantime the Scotts remained slaves.[35]

PART III
THE FEDERAL COURTS: *DRED SCOTT V. JOHN F. A. SANFORD*

Chapter 9

From State Case
to Federal Case

EXACTLY WHEN AND HOW the transfer to a federal action was conceived is not absolutely clear because the evidence is spotty. One contributing incident undoubtedly was Mrs. Emerson's move to Massachusetts. As already indicated, her departure had no effect at that time on the litigation, and her prosperous brother John F. A. Sanford continued to handle his sister's case. What is so confusing about this is that although Sanford had been named in Dr. Emerson's will, he had not legally qualified as and therefore had never actually been appointed executor by the Iowa Probate Court, nor had he been designated administrator of the ancillary estate in Missouri.[1] Missouri probate law was quite clear that "no executor by virtue of being named in the will has any power, *until letters are granted,* to intermeddle with the estate," and that "the power of an executor . . . to act as such is derived, not so much from the will of the testator, *as from the appointment of the court* and a compliance with the law."[2] Yet contemporary evidence indicates that after Mrs. Emerson left St. Louis, Sanford continued to act for her in good faith, not only as her brother, but also because he believed he had the legal right by virtue of having been named in the Emerson will. Why no one questioned it is another of those inexplicable mysteries of the *Dred Scott* case. But no one did question it.[3]

Sanford contributed in yet another way to setting the stage for the new case. Like his sister, he, too, changed residence. A prosperous merchant, he moved to New York to take charge of his firm's operations there. For personal and business reasons, though, he often returned to St. Louis for extended periods. He was therefore available to help his sister when Dred Scott brought suit against her in 1846 and to continue legal assistance even after she moved from St. Louis.[4]

Perhaps the most important new development was the involvement of a new attorney for Dred Scott, Roswell M. Field (no relation to Alexander P. Field), a native of Vermont who had moved west in 1839 and had become St. Louis' "leading land lawyer."[5] Working in Field's office was a young lawyer, Arba N. Crane. At least two sources name Crane as the instigator in bringing the suit into the federal courts. Both these sources cited conversations with Crane himself as the basis for their information, although both did so more than fifty years after the event. One was the historian John W. Burgess, who included the substance of his conversation with Crane in his book *The Middle Period, 1817-1858,* published in 1904. The other was a St. Louis attorney, John F. Lee, who recalled a conversation with Crane in a letter that he (Lee) wrote to the librarian of the Missouri Historical Society in 1907. According to these accounts, one evening (but exactly when was not indicated) Crane happened to be in Field's office while Scott, employed as a janitor, was cleaning up. The two entered into a casual conversation, and the young lawyer learned of Scott's legal adventures in the Missouri courts. Convinced that the slave was entitled to his freedom, Crane apprised Field of what he had learned, and then, with his employer's permission, "went to work on the case."[6] That Crane did very much for Scott cannot be denied, but there is reason to question whether his efforts began as early as he intimated.[7] Crane did not even come to St. Louis until after he had graduated from Harvard Law School in 1856; by then the *Dred Scott* case was already well along toward its concluding stages before the Supreme Court.[8] It would appear, then, that Field became involved in some other way.

That "other way"—and there is no reason to dispute it because it comes from Field himself—was through Charles Edmund LaBeaume. A brother-in-law of the Blows, LaBeaume had been one of Dred Scott's benefactors from the beginning of the litigation in 1846. On April 9, 1851, he hired Scott from the sheriff of St. Louis County, and Scott remained in his employ through the remainder of the litigation. A lawyer, LaBeaume shared office space first with Samuel M. Bay and then with Alexander P. Field and David N. Hall. There is no evidence that LaBeaume did any of the legal work in the case for any of them. But it is reasonable to assume that being in the same law offices as Scott's attorneys, LaBeaume would have more than a cursory knowledge of what was transpiring and what was involved.[9] According to Field himself, sometime shortly after the Supreme Court of Missouri rendered its decision on March 22, 1852 (and undoubtedly before June 29, 1852, when, as noted above, an arrangement already had been made to bring suit into the federal courts), LaBeaume informed Field of the case and sought his advice. In talking to Field, though, LaBeaume indicated that Scott and his family had since been sold to Sanford. Under these circumstances Field advised a diversity suit in the Circuit Court of the United States by Scott as a citizen of Missouri against Sanford as a citizen of New York.[10]

But LaBeaume had misinformed Field about the ownership of Dred Scott, because the slave had never been sold to Sanford. It is undoubtedly true that when the federal case was instituted, an agreed statement of facts averred that shortly before the commencement of the suit Scott and his family had been "sold & conveyed" to Sanford. But this statement was inaccurate and erroneous.

The evidence is unmistakable. In the first place, the agreed statement asserted that it was Dr. Emerson who had "sold & conveyed" Scott to Sanford; yet Emerson had died some ten years earlier. Even more conclusive are the circumstances surrounding Scott's eventual emancipation. On May 26, 1857, two and one-half months after the Supreme Court declared him still a slave, Scott was granted his freedom by Taylor Blow, to whom the slave in the meantime had been sold—not by Sanford, but by Dr. and Mrs. Chaffee.[11] Sanford had died in New York only three weeks earlier, on May 5, 1857; but probate records of his estate in both New York and St. Louis indicate that Scott never was a part of that estate. Undoubtedly many slaves were sold without a record being made of the sale; but for the executor or the administrator of an estate to make such a transaction without recording it in proper probate records is highly unlikely. Anyone selling anything from Sanford's estate certainly would have left some record of it. But there is none. (Note the intriguing similarity to the situation twenty-five years earlier involving the Peter Blow estate.) Of course, Sanford himself might have sold the slave; that is, he might have sold Scott to the Chaffees, for resale to Taylor Blow, sometime after the Supreme Court's decision but before he died. But this could not have happened either. During that entire period Sanford was in an asylum and unable to transact any personal business—it had to be done for him—and under these circumstances, records of any power of attorney transactions undoubtedly would have been kept; but none exist.[12]

Tending to muddy the waters is a notation by Samuel L. M. Barlow, one of the executors of Sanford's estate, that he (Barlow) owned Scott as a part of that estate. Surely Barlow knew that executors are not "owners"; yet he so described himself. Furthermore, Scott was not even part of that estate. If he had been, only Barlow could have conveyed him to the Chaffees who subsequently transferred him to Taylor Blow for emancipation. But if Barlow had done this, he must have accounted for it in the probate records of Sanford's estate. The absence of any such record indicates that Barlow neither owned nor conveyed Scott, because he was never a part of that estate to be owned or conveyed.[13]

If he did not belong to Barlow and if he did not belong to Sanford, to whom, then, did Dred Scott belong? There is no evidence—at any time during the entire litigation, from its inception in 1846 to its conclusion in 1857—that Scott was the property of anyone except Mrs. Emerson and then Dr. Chaffee after she married him in 1850. Moreover, when Chaffee, an avowed abolitionist, married Irene Emerson, he had no knowledge that she even owned any slaves; he did not learn of them until shortly before the Supreme Court decision in 1857. Under Massachusetts law, however, he became their owner as part of his wife's property. Thus Dred Scott belonged only to Mrs. Emerson (Chaffee) and to her abolitionist husband; but because Sanford was simply assumed to have some legal connection with his deceased brother-in-law's estate, and because both Sanford and his sister moved away from St. Louis, it was Sanford against whom a new suit was filed in the federal court on the grounds of diversity of citizenship.[14]

Two questions immediately present themselves on this Sanford "ownership." If Sanford did not own Dred Scott, why did LaBeaume inform Field otherwise? Certainly LaBeaume must have realized that Sanford did not "own" Scott in the usual sense of that word. But all the available evidence indicates that LaBeaume along with others assumed that Sanford was executor of the Emerson estate, and that as executor he had a relationship toward the slave that was not too unlike that of an actual owner. If LaBeaume sought a new case in the federal courts, he could avoid legal hairsplitting over the relative status of owner vis-à-vis executor simply by asserting that Sanford outright "owned" the slave rather than indicating that Sanford was the executor. But this is still not sufficient proof that LaBeaume's aim was a *test* case to challenge any of the legislation relating to slavery. Undoubtedly LaBeaume sought a *new* case in the federal courts, for he was well aware of what had already transpired in the state courts. But why did he want a new case? Was he, a long-time acquaintance and benefactor of Dred Scott, altruistically seeking another means to obtain freedom for the slave—and nothing more—and going into the federal courts only as a last legal resort because the litigation in the state courts had failed? Or did LaBeaume seek a case primarily to test certain slavery principles, and only tangentially to seek freedom for Dred Scott? Either could result from identifying Sanford as Scott's owner.[15]

Unfortunately very little is known about LaBeaume or his motives. Like Francis B. Murdoch earlier, Charles Edmund LaBeaume is another "mystery man" in the *Dred Scott* case. A native of St. Louis, LaBeaume was conservative in some political and social matters, but the opposite in others. He was, for instance, an early member and active in the American party in St. Louis; yet he celebrated the overthrow of the French monarchy in 1848 and actively supported liberal elements in central Europe. He was unmistakably opposed to slavery. From these few facts alone it obviously is impossible to conclude why LaBeaume might have desired a new *Dred Scott* case. In truth, all that can be said with any historical accuracy is that LaBeaume played a significant role at this critical stage of the *Dred Scott* litigation in two ways: first, he called it to Field's attention; and second, he did it in a way that prompted a suit in the federal courts. *What* LaBeaume did is clear; *why* he did it is not as apparent.[16]

Another obvious question related to the "ownership" of Dred Scott is: if Sanford did not own Scott, why did he admit to ownership when he could have terminated the litigation at its outset merely by showing that he did not own the slave as alleged? His failure to do so almost *prima facie* suggests collusion. The correspondent of the *Morning Courier and New-York Enquirer* later accused Sanford of just that, conceding, however that he "consented to place himself in the attitude of a defendant [only] after enduring an amount of importunity, badgering, and worrying, from persons having no other than a political interest in the case." Since Sanford was an "active worker" for the New York Democracy, one might expect that if he consented to such a scheme it was to benefit his own political party, and that those with "political influence" were proslavery Democrats.[17] The accusation was made widely, but there was never any proof who did the "importuning" or the "badgering." There

were only bits of admittedly suggestive circumstances that collectively
satisfied some that the case came into the federal courts as the result of
collusion.[18]

In spite of these suspicious circumstances, there is no clear evidence why
LaBeaume brought Scott's case to Field's attention or why Sanford did
not disclaim ownership. Indeed, it is entirely conceivable that LaBeaume's
original intent was solely humanitarian in Scott's behalf, and that Sanford's
reaction was a genuine defense of his sister's property under the assumption
that he was the executor of the estate, and that these reasons alone prompted the *initial* actions of LaBeaume, Field, and Sanford.

But once LaBeaume called the case to Field's attention, there is no
doubt that other considerations then came into play, for developments
at this point were much too palpable to be merely circumstantial. For
example, the statement of facts alleging the sale of Scott to Sanford was
drawn up by both attorneys, Hugh A. Garland and Roswell M. Field.
Garland had been handling the case for several years and certainly knew
that Sanford had not purchased Scott. As a matter of fact, there was no
need even to involve Sanford; after all, Mrs. Emerson (Mrs. Chaffee)
was now a resident of Massachusetts, and a new suit against her just
as readily could provide the diversity to place the case in the federal
courts. Yet Garland agreed to a stipulation that was both untrue and
unnecessary. Garland openly expressed strong proslavery and prosouthern
sympathies.[19] On the other hand, Field was an outspoken abolitionist.
He accepted the case and worked on it without pay—which itself proves
nothing, but considering his abolitionist sympathies it raises legitimate
suspicions.[20] Furthermore, once the case was in the federal courts,
LaBeaume published and distributed a volatile antislavery diatribe and
appeal for funds in Scott's behalf and in behalf of the freedom principles
involved in his suit.[21] Conversely, Taylor Blow, who also helped finance
Scott's suit, and who ostensibly was seeking the freedom of a slave with
whom he had been raised, was not an abolitionist; in fact, he was even a
Confederate sympathizer during the Civil War.[22] These circumstances explain why numerous allegations were made against proslavery and antislavery partisans, that each, either separately or even in collusion with the
other, intrigued to bring in a test case on the power of Congress over
slavery.

Of all the alleged motives of the alleged conspirators, only one is actually

documented. Without question Field wanted the Supreme Court to settle
the vexing question whether residence in a free state or territory permanently freed a slave; he clearly articulated that desire to Montgomery Blair when
he requested the latter to argue the case before the Supreme Court.[23] There
was no question at all of the constitutionality of any prohibition of slavery,
whether in the Ordinance of 1787 or in the Missouri Compromise. That
came later, before the Supreme Court, and it came from Sanford's attorneys. In this first stage of the federal litigation, the issue was the decision
of the Missouri Supreme Court that Missouri law could remand to servitude
one who had been emancipated previously by residence in free territory. It
was this decision, after all, and not the constitutionality of the Ordinance
of 1787 or of the Missouri Compromise, that Field had to contend with.
No one questioned that slaves were *emancipated* by residence in free territory; at issue was whether that freedom was *lost* by returning to a slave
state.

It is precisely this point, framed in the context of the roles of LaBeaume,
Field, and Sanford, that explains why a new case not only was created,
but also why it had to be created. Whether LaBeaume was interested in
Scott's freedom became immaterial. If that was his concern, the least
circuitous, the cheapest, and the fastest way to reverse the Missouri
decision was to appeal directly to the Supreme Court of the United States.
But if that were done, it would be foredoomed to failure. For only two
years earlier, in *Strader* v. *Graham,* the nation's highest tribunal had already indicated that it would honor as the final word on a state's slavery
law whatever that state's own supreme court decreed.

But Field knew that *Strader* v. *Graham* had been decided on uniquely
procedural rather than substantive grounds.[24] *Strader* v. *Graham,* 10
Howard 82 (1850), had come to the United States Supreme Court from
the Court of Appeals of Kentucky, that state's highest court. It was
originally a damage suit for the value of three slaves hired by a Kentucky
slaveowner (Christopher Graham) to an Ohio resident (Jacob Strader),
from whose steamboat the slaves had fled into Ohio and then to Canada.
The Kentucky courts had awarded Graham three thousand dollars in
damages for the loss of his slaves, basing judgment on Kentucky law.
Strader then appealed directly to the United States Supreme Court for
redress of damages, on the grounds that the slaves had become free in
Ohio by operation of the Ordinance of 1787. Chief Justice Roger Brooke

Taney's unanimous Opinion of the Court, augmented by separate concurring opinions by Associate Justices John McLean and John Catron, declared that Strader's claim of freedom for the slaves under the Ordinance of 1787 could not be sustained—not because the law was invalid, but because it was simply not applicable. When the constitutions of the United States and of the state of Ohio had been drawn up, said the Court, they had superseded the Ordinance of 1787. Strader's claims therefore should have been based on them; instead, he injudiciously chose to argue the applicability of the Ordinance of 1787, a law obsolete and inoperative *in this particular instance.* Since, as Taney stated, nothing in the United States Constitution "can in any degree control the law of Kentucky upon this subject," and, as McLean concurred, "all questions of freedom [under the Ordinance of 1787] must arise under the constitution [of Ohio], and not under the ordinance [of 1787]," the Court had no choice but to return the case for lack of jurisdiction. This meant sustaining the Kentucky court's decision. It also precluded any examination of Strader's arguments on their merits. In a tone of almost ominous foreboding, McLean wrote: "This, in my judgment, decides the question of jurisdiction, which is the only question before us. And anything that is said in the opinion of the court, in relation to the ordinance, beyond this, is not in the case, and is, consequently, extrajudicial."[25]

Strader v. *Graham,* therefore, skirted the volatile substantive slavery issues by denying jurisdiction. Field astutely recognized this, and he feared that *Dred Scott* v. *Irene Emerson,* if appealed directly from the Missouri Supreme Court, would suffer the same fate. The only way for Dred Scott to have a chance for freedom was to force an examination of emancipation achieved by a congressional prohibition of slavery in the territories. Although in Scott's case this included both the Ordinance of 1787 and the Missouri Compromise, the latter was really not the issue. The basic legislation and the basic principles were in the earlier Ordinance of 1787; an analysis of that act and those principles would necessarily cover all ensuing congressional prohibitions of slavery in the territories. But the only way to force an examination of the Ordinance of 1787 was to bring a case to the Supreme Court via a route that would ensure that *Strader* v. *Graham* could not be a precedent. That meant a case in the federal court system, to be appealed from a lower federal court rather than from a state supreme court.[26]

Dred Scott v. *John F. A. Sanford* came into existence, therefore, because Charles Edmund LaBeaume called to Roswell M. Field's attention the circumstances surrounding the slave Dred Scott. LaBeaume may have hoped altruistically to aid Scott achieve the freedom the Missouri courts had denied him. He also may have had political motives, seeking a judicial solution to the vexing issue of slavery in the territories. But there is no doubt about Field's motives. The first was to determine whether a slave state could revive the status of slavery once an erstwhile slave had been emancipated by residence in a free state or territory. The second was to ensure that the Supreme Court did not evade that substantive issue by falling back on *Strader* v. *Graham.* Both could be achieved by a new case in the lower federal court. Once Dred Scott came to Field's attention, he and LaBeaume as well as Garland (presumably whatever he did as Sanford's attorney was with the latter's consent and approval) all said and did things that clearly indicate Dred Scott's freedom or the preservation of Mrs. Emerson's or Sanford's property rights no longer was the sole or even the primary motive in prosecuting or defending the suit. When that transition occurred, the case inexorably became the *cause célèbre* that made it so important in American history.

Chapter 10

U. S. Circuit Court

SO IT WAS, THEN, that after he was approached by Charles Edmund LaBeaume, Roswell M. Field brought suit in Dred Scott's behalf against John F. A. Sanford. On November 2, 1853, Field filed in the Circuit Court of the United States for the District of Missouri a *vi et armis* action in trespass accusing Sanford, "a citizen of the State of New York," *pro forma* of illegally assaulting, holding, and imprisoning Dred Scott, "a citizen of the State of Missouri," Harriet Scott, and their daughters Eliza and Lizzie.[1] Since the case involved diversity of citizenship, the court of original jurisdiction was a circuit rather than a district court.[2] On the same day, November 2, 1853, Charles Edmund LaBeaume and Taylor Blow bonded themselves to cover "all the costs and fees which may accrue by reason of the prosecution of the said suit." The case was set for the April term, 1854, and docketed as No. 692.[3]

The circuit court convened in St. Louis on April 3, 1854, Judge Robert W. Wells presiding. On April 7 Sanford and his attorney Hugh A. Garland replied to charges and filed a plea in abatement denying the jurisdiction of the court. (A *plea in abatement* is a petition to a court requesting the quashing or overthrow of a previous action; in this case, a plea that the court not even accept Scott's declaration charging Sanford with trespass.) Sanford asserted that Scott was not a citizen of Missouri as alleged and therefore, since the case did not involve legitimate citizens of different states, the court did not have jurisdiction and could not even accept Scott's declaration. Sanford then went on to explain why Scott was not a citizen of Missouri: ". . . Because he is a negro of African descent—his ancestors were of pure African blood and were brought into this country and sold as negro slaves." Thus was interjected into the *Dred Scott* case for the first time the right of a black person to be a citizen of the United States.[4]

One week later, on April 14, Field entered a demurrer to the plea in abatement. (A *demurrer* is a challenge to a particular plea, that it does not show sufficient cause why the litigants should not proceed with the case.) Field argued that the plea in abatement "& the matters therein contained are not sufficient in law to preclude the Court of its jurisdiction of this cause"—that although Scott was a Negro of African descent, that fact did not bar him either from citizenship or from the right to sue. Thereupon Field requested that the court set aside the plea in abatement and require Sanford to defend himself upon the merits—the facts of the case and the law as it applied to those facts. Garland "joined" in the demurrer; that is, he took issue with Field's arguments. Legal procedure now required that before either side could continue, this matter must be adjudicated first.[5]

The legal issues involved in the plea in abatement and the demurrer were argued on April 24. Garland cited a number of decisions that Negroes were not citizens within the meaning of Article IV, Section 2 of the Constitution ("citizens of each state shall be entitled to all privileges and immunities of citizens in the several states") and since they were not citizens in that respect, Garland argued, neither were they citizens within the meaning of Article III, Section 2, which established the jurisdiction of the federal courts over cases between citizens of different states. Field, on the other hand, asserted that "citizenship to give jurisdiction means nothing more than residence." He pointed to the requirements for voting in different states of the Union and showed that although Negroes were prohibited from voting in some, they could vote in others. Because the right to vote was one indication of citizenship, Field insisted, it was clear that at least *some* Negroes of African descent were citizens. Thus, he concluded, just being a Negro of African descent did not of itself bar one from citizenship.[6]

Judge Wells's decision came the following day, April 25: the plea in abatement was "insufficient" and Field's demurrer was sustained. Wells recognized that granting to a free Negro the right to sue was a policy with which the slave states disagreed. But he pointed out also that if a free Negro could not sue because he was not a citizen, neither could he *be* sued, and thus obtained a very substantial privilege and immunity that free white citizens did not possess. Furthermore, he continued, a

Negro could sue in the United States courts if he was an alien subject
to a foreign country; why should not a native-born American Negro have
the same right? Accordingly, Wells concluded, "every person born in
the United States and capable of holding property was a citizen having
the right to sue in the United States courts." If Scott was free, he had
the right to sue. The fundamental issue was not whether Scott was a
Negro, but whether he was free. Whether he was free, pointed out Wells,
depended on those laws that applied to his residence in free territory.[7]

Inasmuch as this decision by Judge Wells later became the subject of
great dispute, it is essential that it be clearly understood. Wells drew a
very fine line in distinguishing between rights of a free Negro and a slave
Negro. Where Wells was treading on extremely delicate ground was that
his decision sustaining the demurrer could be justified only after the court
had heard the case and granted Scott his freedom based upon the substantive facts. But if that substantive decision remanded Scott to slavery,
then Wells's sustaining of the demurrer could be open to much criticism,
for it would have allowed a slave, otherwise not eligible, to have sued in a
United States circuit court. Although Field was himself an abolitionist, as
a lawyer he recognized here grave consequences. If Wells's principle was
allowed to stand, virtually any *fugitive* slave (Dred Scott, of course, was
not a fugitive slave) could subvert the laws of return; for once a slave
escaped into free territory, even if recaptured there, he could use this
precedent, bring suit for his freedom, and a partisan abolitionist jury
could make a shambles of the fugitive slave laws.[8] When the decision
was finally determined in this case, the Supreme Court declared that
Dred Scott was still a slave; and thus Wells's decision sustaining the demurrer not only was without foundation, but it also presented the very
dilemma Field recognized as a way of subverting the already controversial
fugitive slave laws. For these reasons, then, the decision sustaining the
demurrer was very critical and it is understandable why later it became
the center of heated legal arguments.

As soon as Wells sustained the demurrer, Field and Garland agreed
upon two points of procedure. The first was that the defendant would
file a new plea to the charges made in Scott's original declaration of
November 2. This was necessary because Sanford's first reply, the plea
in abatement, had been overruled, and if the case was to proceed the
defendant had to take a new stand.[9] The second agreement was that,
to facilitate the inevitable trial, "an agreed case should be made up by

them," and this agreed statement of facts would be presented to the court for its action.[10]

The filing of the plea in abatement on grounds of citizenship suggests that up to that point, at least, neither Sanford nor Garland was yet party to any action seeking to force a case on the merits of the Ordinance of 1787. The plea appears to have been a genuine defense to prevent any discussion at all on the issue of a slave's residence in free territory. Had either Sanford or Garland wanted a test case, why would they have attempted to get it thrown out of court for a reason completely different? Of course, there is the possibility that both sides wanted to test the question of Negro citizenship, too, but there is absolutely no hint of this anywhere in the evidence. On the contrary, the citizenship argument has every semblance of a genuine attempt by the defendant to avoid being sued. It was only after the plea in abatement was overruled that the two sides agreed to a procedure for arguing the case on its merits. If Garland and/or Sanford became a party, along with Field, to a test case, it was at this juncture that it occurred, because the next court action, on May 4, 1854, was the introduction of the agreed statement of facts—some of which were less than accurate—establishing the substantive grounds for the suit. This statement, similar to earlier declarations in the state case, briefly traced Scott's travels with Dr. Emerson to Forts Armstrong and Snelling and back to Missouri. It averred also that Emerson then sold Scott to Sanford who was holding him in slavery in Missouri even though he should be free. (See Appendix B.)

The trial of *Dred Scott v. John F. A. Sanford* occurred on Monday, May 15, 1854, in the Circuit Court of the United States for the District of Missouri, Judge Wells still presiding.[11] Contrary to widespread local St. Louis tradition, the trial was not conducted in the historic Old Courthouse. It was held instead in an inauspicious upstairs room in a private building, the Papin Building, at what was then 38 Main Street. Normally the federal courts held their sessions free of charge in the courthouse. But that building was owned by the state and state courts had priority on the use of the courtrooms, and if there was no room the United States marshall simply had to rent another location. In April 1854 the United States Circuit Court faced this housing situation, and so the private room at 38 Main Street was rented.[12]

The trial itself was very unpretentious and modest. Attorneys were Field for the plaintiff and Garland for the defendant. Whether Scott and

Sanford themselves were in court is not clear; the official record states: "This day come again the parties by their attorneys . . . ." The only evidence presented was the agreed statement of facts that Field read to the jury; no further testimony was given by either side. Field then requested the court to instruct the jury that upon the facts in the case the law was with Dred Scott. He contended, obviously, that Scott was free by the operation of the Ordinance of 1787, the constitution of Illinois, and the Missouri Compromise. But Wells refused to give such instructions. Instead, although he personally sympathized with Scott's cause, he instructed the jury that the law covering the facts of the case did not operate to grant the slave his freedom.[13]

Inasmuch as the appeal taken to the Supreme Court stemmed directly from these instructions, they bear careful scrutiny. Wells explained to the jury that the removal of a slave by his master into Illinois did not free the slave but simply suspended the condition of slavery temporarily, and that upon their return to Missouri, the master's right to the slave, dormant while they were in Illinois, was revived. Furthermore, Wells explained, the provisions in the Illinois constitution and statutes that emancipated slaves were actually penal in nature against slaveholders and therefore the courts of other states were not bound to enforce them.[14] These were the reasons given by the majority of the Missouri Supreme Court in *Dred Scott* v. *Irene Emerson* in 1852, and, as Wells stated, "The U. S. Courts follow the State courts in regard to the interpretation of their own law. I was bound to take the interpretation of the laws of Missouri in this case, from the Supreme Court of the State."[15]

On the basis of these instructions, a verdict was returned in favor of the defendant Sanford, that he was not guilty of Scott's accusation of assault, trespass, and false imprisonment, and that Scott, his wife, and their two daughters were "negro slaves the lawful property of the defendant. . . ." Field immediately moved to set aside the verdict and grant a new trial "because the court misdirected the jury in the matter of law on said trial." Wells overruled the motion and ordered "that the defendant John F. A. Sanford go hence without day [sic] and recover against said plaintiff Dred Scott the costs by him expended in the defence of this suit."[16] Field thereupon instituted an appeal to the Supreme Court of the United States. He presented a bill of exceptions detailing the earlier proceedings with a statement of his objection. Wells duly approved the bill of exceptions, and the appeal procedure was begun.[17]

The most significant new issue in this phase of the litigation was the citizenship of blacks. It was a totally unexpected issue and certainly not one of Field's motives for filing the suit, but was injected into the case only tangentially by Garland. Eventually it would become a major issue—made so not by the parties to the case, but by the Supreme Court itself. Neither side would say much about citizenship in arguments before the Supreme Court because neither side considered it that important to the case; their major concern was the permanence of freedom attained under the Ordinance of 1787. But the Supreme Court's first consideration, albeit routine, had to be jurisdiction—and the citizenship issue, considered at first a subsidiary matter, became paramount. Indeed, one of the main reasons the Supreme Court would order a second argument was so counsel could clarify points of law about citizenship, which they had slighted in their first presentation.

Of equal significance is that the lower court proceedings paved the way for the assault on the Missouri Compromise, although apparently no one anticipated it. True, Field expressed concern that the ruling on the plea in abatement might open a Pandora's box vis-à-vis citizenship and fugitive slave laws. But certainly he should have seen that that ruling also opened the door for an analysis of the constitutionality of *any* legislation prohibiting slavery in territories, including the Missouri Compromise. After all, if the critical question was not Scott's color— as Garland argued—but whether Scott was free or slave—as Field argued— and if that in turn depended upon the law that applied to his living in free territory, then by Field's own argument Scott's status as free or slave before he returned to Missouri had been legitimately opened to inquiry. There is no doubt that Field expected that inquiry to look into the Ordinance of 1787, confidently anticipating that it would vindicate the principle of permanent emancipation. There is no evidence that any of the litigants included the Missouri Compromise in that examination. Yet it is hard to believe that they could have been so naive as not to foresee its eventual inclusion, even though when Field had become associated with the case in the spring of 1852 the "sleeping tiger" of sectionalism was still exhibiting the tremulous lethargy it had sunk into immediately after the Compromise of 1850. Then on January 4, 1854, Stephen A. Douglas reported the Kansas-Nebraska bill onto the floor of the United States Senate. Snarling violently, that tiger awakened, its fangs bared and its razor-sharp claws poised. How could one expect the protagonists of slavery not to jump at the opportunity suddenly available in the *Dred Scott* case to spread anti-Missouri Compromise doctrine before the Supreme Court and to use that body to legitimize and legalize their political views toward slavery in the territories? Roswell M. Field's vehicle to reinforce the freedom provisions of the Ordinance of 1787 was to backfire and become the instrument for the invalidation of the Missouri Compromise.

In spite of the great excitement it boded for the immediate future, these court proceedings still elicited little attention. Even with two prominent local lawyers, Field and Garland, arguing it, and despite the fact that such important principles were involved, very little mention of the proceedings was made in the St. Louis newspapers. Other cases were discussed at some length, as was the absence of adequate quarters for the court. With only one exception, St. Louis newspapers made absolutely no mention of the *Dred Scott* case; it was not even included in routine newspaper listings of cases decided.[18] Only the antislavery *St. Louis Daily Morning Herald* printed a brief summary and, then, evidently cognizant of the behind-the-scenes arrangements, concluded: "Dred is, of course, poor and without any powerful friends. But no doubt he will find at the bar of the Supreme Court some able and generous advocate, who will do all he can to establish his right to go free."[19] The then United States district attorney in St. Louis and later lieutenant governor of Missouri aptly described the case as so unimportant then that it did not even "create a local stir."[20] But if the Dred Scott case did not create a local stir, it was progressing inexorably toward creating quite a national stir.

Chapter 11

U. S. Supreme Court: First Arguments

ON MAY 30, 1854, only two weeks after the decision in St. Louis, President Franklin Pierce signed into law the Kansas-Nebraska Act, which repealed the slavery prohibition of the Missouri Compromise and replaced it with the vague principle of popular sovereignty. The "sleeping tiger" of sectionalism was now awake and seething with fury. The press, the pulpit, and the public forum, both North and South, raged with denunciation and defiance. The vehement exchange was not limited to the Missouri Compromise issue; slavery in all its aspects and ramifications now came in for a thorough and extremely partisan examination. It was in this highly charged atmosphere that the *Dred Scott* case was appealed to the Supreme Court of the United States. On December 30, 1854, it was filed officially, placed on the docket as Case No. 137 for the December term, 1854. More than thirteen months elapsed, however, before the case was finally argued. Although the principles involved were of the utmost current interest and importance, there was no discernible intentional delay or postponement at any time; the docket was just extremely crowded, and the Court simply did not reach the case until February 1856.[1]

In the meantime more important personnel changes occurred. On October 14, 1854, Hugh A. Garland died.[2] By this time the Kansas-Nebraska bill had become law, and those acquainted with the case recognized its potential impact on current politics. Under these circumstances, "a southern gentleman"—but otherwise unidentified—approached Reverdy Johnson, one of the country's most eminent lawyers, and "mentioned" to him the questions associated with the *Dred Scott* case. "Always entertaining the opinion afterwards announced by the Supreme Court, and seeing . . . how deeply the country was interested in their decision," Johnson

volunteered to argue the case for the defendant John F. A. Sanford.
Senator Henry S. Geyer of Missouri also volunteered his services in behalf
of Sanford.[3]

Both Johnson and Geyer were outstanding men in their profession. A
resident of Maryland and formerly a senator (1845-49) and attorney-
general of the United States (1849-50), Johnson was regarded by many
as perhaps the leading constitutional lawyer in the country, compared
often with greats such as William Wirt and Daniel Webster. He was acclaimed equally by the English bar.[4] Geyer was one of the most eminent
attorneys of the West. Also a native of Maryland, he moved to St. Louis
in 1815 after distinguished service in the War of 1812. He was active in
Missouri politics, serving in various leadership capacities in the state legislature, and earned the reputation as the "greatest lawyer at the Missouri
bar." In 1850 he attained nationwide fame by defeating Thomas Hart
Benton for the Senate.[5] Thus the attorneys who took over Sanford's
case were among the most highly esteemed in the country, and both
volunteered their services so they could discuss before the Supreme
Court issues they considered to be of the utmost importance.

In the meantime Dred Scott also acquired new counsel, Montgomery
Blair. The son of Francis Preston Blair, a close friend of Andrew
Jackson's, Montgomery Blair grew up in St. Louis where he became one
of the leading opponents of slavery in Missouri. His legal experience included a position in the law office of Thomas Hart Benton as well as
the judgeship of the St. Louis Court of Common Pleas. In 1852 Blair
moved to Silver Spring, Maryland. Held in very high regard by his colleagues, in 1853 Blair was recommended for the office of attorney-
general of the United States. Although he did not receive the position,
he was appointed, in 1855, as solicitor of the newly created federal
Court of Claims. Dred Scott's new attorney, then, was as eminent a
figure as were the new attorneys for Sanford.[6]

As early as May 25, 1854, Roswell M. Field asked Blair to take the
case when it came before the Supreme Court. But Blair had gone to
California to complete the settlement of the estate of his deceased
brother James, who had accumulated a fortune there during the gold
rush days, and he did not return to St. Louis until late in October.
Field, in the meantime, sought the assistance of other "prominent"
antislavery attorneys—exactly who, however, is not known—but without
success.[7]

At the same time, Charles Edmund LaBeaume also attempted to secure financial as well as legal assistance. He published a twelve-page pamphlet detailing the record of the case in the lower federal court. The preface contained a stirring appeal, signed with his mark by Dred Scott:

> My fellow-countrymen, can any of you help me in my day of trial? Will nobody speak for me at Washington, even without hope of other reward than the blessings of a poor black man and his family? I can only pray that some good heart will be moved by pity to do that for me which I can not do for myself; and that if the right is on my side, it may be so declared by the high court to which I have appealed.[8]

The pamphlet was widely distributed throughout the abolitionist community, but surprisingly neither appreciable funds nor legal assistance was forthcoming. Considering their enthusiastic support in other causes, the nonparticipation of abolitionists in this instance is inexplicable.[9]

On December 24, 1854, Field once more wrote to Blair, again asking him to take the case. He informed him, though, that neither the slave nor "his friends" had the means of paying for Blair's services; but since the case involved such important principles, perhaps he would take it without charge. Blair was undecided at first. He conferred at Silver Spring with his father, who urged him to accept it. He then consulted with Gamaliel Bailey, the crusading editor of the antislavery *National Era*. Blair was willing to serve without his fee if some way could be found to pay for other expenses. Bailey confidently volunteered to assume that responsibility; and with this assurance, Blair agreed to take the case. On December 30, 1854, the same day that the case was filed and docketed, Blair informed Field of his decision.[10] Meanwhile the Court ground through its docket, but by the end of the term in May 1855, it had not yet reached the *Dred Scott* case. It was redocketed for the next term as Case No. 61.[11]

During this interval the only other important development was the preparation of legal arguments. Blair was in St. Louis in late March 1855, as a pallbearer in the funeral of Mrs. Thomas Hart Benton; he may have used this occasion to discuss the case with Field and others.[12] Blair and Field also communicated by mail. Field indicated his concern over Judge Wells's denying the plea in abatement, pointing out how it could open

the way for evading fugitive slave legislation. He warned Blair that Sanford's attorneys undoubtedly would recognize this, too, and therefore
might create a diversion by unduly exaggerating the citizenship issue
raised in the plea in abatement. Even though it would be "very desireable
. . . to obtain the opinion of the Court upon it," Field expected that the
Court would reject the citizenship question as not germane and would
consider only whether Dred Scott was restored to slavery when he returned
to Missouri. That, after all, was specifically why the writ of error had been
granted.[13] Undoubtedly Field's comments influenced Blair, for the latter
did offer a defense for Negro citizenship, even though he felt it an extraneous issue. It proved to be anything but that.

Field was unremitting, though, for a decision on the effect of residence
in free territory, and he repeatedly emphasized to Blair why the Supreme
Court must not evade a decision on the merits as it had in *Strader* v.
Graham. "That case," Field insisted, "decides only that the question is
not such as gives a foundation for writ of errour [*sic*] to a *state court*
under the 25th section of the judiciary act"; it could not be a precedent
for an action that arose in the *federal* court system.[14] *Scott* v. *Sanford*
therefore must be decided upon the merits. In that way, said Field, no
matter how the decision resulted, "at all events a much disputed question
would be settled by the highest court in the nation."[15]

On December 3, 1855, the Supreme Court convened for its December
term. As the judges progressed slowly through the crowded docket, it
became apparent early in February 1856 that they would soon reach
Scott v. *Sanford*. On February 7, therefore, Blair filed his brief in support of his client's claim to freedom.[16]

Dealing first with the merits,[17] Blair indicated that the lower court
based its decision on the same two premises as the Supreme Court of
Missouri in *Dred Scott* v. *Irene Emerson*: first, that the master's right
to a slave revived when they returned to Missouri; and second, that the
emancipation provision in the Illinois constitution was penal and therefore
unenforceable by comity in courts of other states.

Blair dealt first with the notion that the master's ownership revived
upon return to a slave state. It was a principle that stemmed from Lord
Stowell's oft-cited 1827 decision in the famous *Case of the Slave Grace*,
a landmark in the history of slavery in the British Empire. Departing from
the earlier *Somerset* principle, Lord Stowell held that freedom had to be
based upon a specific local statute; in the absence of such a statute, a slave

could not be emancipated.[18] Blair did not quarrel that the principle
existed, although he disagreed with it in substance, but he argued that in
this instance there was a local statute, and it had *freed* Dred Scott—it
was the constitution of Illinois, which expressly prohibited slavery in
that state. The very principle the lower court had relied upon to enslave
Scott in Missouri, argued Blair, in fact had emancipated him in Illinois.

But was that freedom permanent and valid in Missouri? Yes, asserted
Blair, until the Missouri Supreme Court had chosen to consider the Illinois freedom provisions as penal. But the Missouri court had reached
that conclusion only by injecting current political views into its majority
decision, because "the times are not now as they were when the former
decisions on this subject were made." Blair quoted extensively from
Gamble's dissent, citing the many Missouri precedents as explicitly prov-
ing the question "conclusively settled by repeated adjudications." Blair
cited similar precedents in Virginia, Mississippi, and Kentucky, all slave
states, and all supporting the doctrine of permanent emancipation.[19]
He referred also to decisions of the Supreme Court of the United States,
which repeatedly recognized the Justinian and common law principles
that "liberty, once admitted, cannot be recalled," and "once free,
always free."[20]

Then, not because he considered it a major issue, but because he anticipated his opponents would raise it as a procedural diversion, Blair turned
to the jurisdictional question raised by the plea in abatement: whether
"a negro of African descent" could be a citizen of the United States.
Readily conceding that blacks did not possess all rights of citizenship,
Blair concentrated on showing that blacks had at least some. He made
no attempt to differentiate between state and national citizenship; his
citations indicate an assumption that a citizen of a state was a citizen
of the United States. His primary thrust was to show that unless blacks
were explicitly excluded from a particular constitutional right, they
had that right along with other citizens. This was particularly important vis-à-vis the right to sue in a federal court. Perhaps most persuasive
was Blair's documentation of numerous suits that had been brought in
the federal courts both by and against free blacks, and their status as
citizens having the right to sue or be sued had never been denied. He
drove the point home adroitly by identifying counsel in one of those
cases as none other than the incumbent chief justice himself, Roger
B. Taney.[21] The upshot of Blair's entire argument, of course, was that

Dred Scott clearly had the right to sue and that Sanford could not circumvent the merits by claiming that the Supreme Court lacked jurisdiction because Scott was not a citizen. The only way the case could be
decided was to examine substantively the permanence of emancipation laws.

On February 8 Geyer filed his brief. Unfortunately, no copy is in
existence and so its contents are unknown.[22] (Geyer's later oral arguments probably contained the same materials, but there is no detailed
record of that either.) That same day a little noticed action by the Court
foreshadowed the importance of coming events. Reverdy Johnson asked
the Court to allow each counsel to have an unprecedented three hours
for oral argument instead of the usual two. The request was granted.[23]
Three days later, on February 11, the case came up for argument.

Despite the relevance of these arguments to contemporary issues,
it is surprising that no advance publicity was given to them. Newspapers
throughout the country printed stories about other important slave
cases—the *Sherman Booth* case in Wisconsin, the *Jonathan Lemmon*
case in New York, and the *Passmore Williamson* case in Philadelphia—
but little or no mention was made of the *Dred Scott* case.[24] Even the
Washington correspondent of the home town St. Louis *Daily Missouri
Republican,* periodically reporting on "important" cases before the
Supreme Court, not once referred to this one.[25] In Congress, where
both houses were involved in heated debate over slavery in the territories,
no one mentioned the crucial case that was nearing argument.[26]
Very correctly, then, did a Washington newspaper say: "The public of
Washington do not seem to be aware that one of the most important
cases ever brought up for adjudication by the Supreme Court is now
being tried before that august tribunal."[27]

On Monday, February 11, 1856, Case No. 61, *Dred Scott* v. *John
F. A. Sanford,* was argued before the Supreme Court of the United
States. On the bench were the following: Roger Brooke Taney of Mary-
land, chief justice; Associate Justices John McLean of Ohio, James
Moore Wayne of Georgia, John Catron of Tennessee, Peter Vivian
Daniel of Virginia, Samuel Nelson of New York, Robert Cooper Grier
of Pennsylvania, Benjamin Robbins Curtis of Massachusetts, and John
Archibald Campbell of Alabama.[28] Blair opened the argument on Monday,
February 11, occupying the full three hours allotted on that day. The
next day, February 12, Geyer presented his argument for the defendant,

followed on the next day, February 13, by Johnson. When Johnson finished, Blair resumed his argument, completing it on the following day, February 14.[29]

Unfortunately, no detailed record exists of exactly what those three eminent attorneys said. The Court did not record oral arguments; that was left up to counsel, to preserve a record or not as they individually wished.[30] A number of newspaper correspondents heard the arguments, but they reported only the highlights. Thus, aside from the bare notice that Blair spoke "very ably" for Dred Scott, about the most one finds about his argument was that it was "a calm, learned and conclusive speech."[31] Presumably, though, Blair repeated and elaborated upon the two points he had established in his brief; that is, that a slave once emancipated in a free state remained free even after he returned to a slave state; and that a free Negro had the right to sue as a citizen in the federal courts.

Not much more was written about the arguments of Geyer and Johnson, but enough was reported to reveal that they were of monumental significance. *For the first time the* Dred Scott *case was referred to as involving the constitutionality of the Missouri Compromise.*[32] The point that Geyer and Johnson made, obviously, was that Dred Scott had never been free in the first place because Congress did not have that authority. (None of the press reports detailed reasons.) This was a dramatic and traumatic new tack in the case. Except for the flimsy military personnel argument, there had never been any denial heretofore that Scott was entitled to freedom (albeit temporarily) by virtue of residence in free territory. The substantive issue all along had been the action of Missouri taking away that freedom, not where or how Scott had attained it. That was why Blair had not even bothered with the issue of emancipation in the territories; establishing Scott as free anywhere—in this instance Illinois —was sufficient. There was no reason to complicate the picture by suggesting a possible differentiation between freedom acquired in a free state and freedom acquired in a free territory, if indeed there was any difference. Besides, the Missouri Compromise had been repealed; why resurrect it and risk extraneous issues that might lead to another evasion as in *Strader* v. *Graham*? But all that was now abruptly subverted by Geyer and Johnson. The issue was no longer whether Dred Scott could lose his freedom; the issue now was whether he had ever been free in the first place, by either the Ordinance of 1787 or the Missouri Compromise. Blair's failure to anticipate that the Missouri Compromise might be open to review had come home to roost.

But what about the constitution and laws of Illinois? Here Geyer and Johnson did what Blair did not do: they distinguished between freedom by residence in a territory and freedom by residence in a state. They denied the former because Congress did not have the authority to prohibit slavery in the territories; but they conceded the latter because states did have that residual constitutional power. Thus Scott could have been free in Illinois. But that did not matter; he had returned to Missouri of his own free will. The voluntarism of his return, they asserted, falling back on the argument used in the state case, was the key fact. That remanded him to slavery.[33]

If the scanty newspaper accounts are correct—and they were consistently similar in their reporting—both Geyer and Johnson either shunned the citizenship issue completely or said very little about it. Why they did so is not clear; one would suppose that competent lawyers would not overlook such an important point in the transcript.

On the other hand, perhaps they surmised, as some of the justices did, that it was not even before the Court. It seems reasonable, though, both being long-time opponents of legislation restricting slavery in the territories and both being in the forefront of the political battles to repeal the Missouri Compromise, that both would concentrate on the territory issue. At the same time, Blair did not even touch this matter, undoubtedly because he saw it as not pertinent to the case. When the Court met later to consult, it faced two major issues: jurisdiction and citizenship as raised in the plea in abatement and the merits of slave legislation as raised in the evidence presented. Sanford's counsel said little or nothing about the former. As to the latter, one side dealt primarily with an issue not even suggested in the lower court (the Missouri Compromise), and the other side concentrated on completely different merits: the impact of slave laws on a person emancipated in a free state. If counsel were so divergent on the issues, what was the Court to decide? Is it any wonder that a reargument was in the offing?

Despite the importance of the oral arguments, surprisingly little attention was paid them in the press. The major Washington papers printed routine daily lists of cases, but added only a few general sentences describing the arguments of the three attorneys.[34] On February 13 the *New York Daily Tribune*, *The New York Herald*, and the Baltimore *Sun* were the first newspapers outside of Washington to publicize the case. The Boston *Post* carried the first news in New England on February 16. On February 18 the case was reported for the first time in the South, in a very brief dispatch in *The Savannah Daily Republican*. Within a few days it was similarly reported in the Augusta *Daily Constitution* and *The Charleston Mercury*. On February 20 the case received its first notice in the Philadelphia press, in the *North American and United States Gazette*. That same day the St. Louis *Daily Missouri Republican* brought the news to the West.[35] All these reports were very short, mentioning only that a litigation was before the Supreme Court involving the constitutionality of the Missouri Compromise, the citizenship of blacks, and the rights of slaveholders to take their slaves into free states. There were neither details nor editorial comment. Once these brief notices had been printed, the only additional mention of the case came in sporadic dispatches of Washington correspondents who followed developments in the Court's consultations. *Dred Scott* was totally overshadowed by the sectional struggles over Kansas and slavery, by the international crises in the Crimea and India, and especially by the approaching presidential election of 1856. The antislavery Washington, D.C., *National Era* ruefully observed: "Little attention seems to have been given to a case which was last week argued before the Supreme Court, in which are involved highly interesting legal and constitutional principles."[36] Little attention indeed; but the storm was soon to break.

Chapter 12

The Court Consults

SPECULATION STARTED EVEN BEFORE consultations began.[1] One newspaper suggested that the Court would deal with two important substantive issues: congressional power over slavery in the territories and the right of slaveholders to take their slaves into free states.[2] Then a rumor developed that the Court would focus instead on the voluntarism of Scott's return and thereby avoid controversial issues. The *New York Daily Tribune*'s James E. Harvey, who wrote under the pseudonym "Index," reported that the Court was leaning five to four toward this narrow approach, but he admitted that his information was founded only on "speculation . . . which almost amounts to conviction." He anticipated several "strong" dissenting opinions, but did not indicate by whom.[3] Still another rumor was that the whole case was fictitious and that the Court therefore would not even decide on it.[4] A correspondent of the St. Louis *Daily Missouri Republican* denied that the constitutionality of the Missouri Compromise was involved, even though Sanford's counsel had argued it; the main question instead was the right of blacks to be citizens of the United States.[5] Obviously interested observers were both confused and misinformed.

Their quandary manifests how the problem before the Court was more than a legal one. For years politicians had warily evaded the divisive question of the power of Congress to regulate slavery in the territories. Although there was agreement in principle that Congress had that power, there was widespread disagreement on the extent of that power. Because it was so volatile an issue, many congressmen had tried to push it into the courts. Thus the Compromise of 1850 and the Kansas-Nebraska Act both virtually invited judicial resolution by specifically stipulating that disputes over slavery and personal freedom could be appealed to the Supreme Court of the United States. Many expected a litigation to come out of the territories emanating directly from one of those statutes. Instead, it was the *Dred Scott* case, raising questions far beyond the narrower territorial issue. The problem now before the Court, as Professor David M. Potter succinctly put it, was whether nine justices, regarded as largely outside the orbit of politics, "would decide to rush in where Congress had feared to tread."[6]

On February 22 the Court consulted on the *Dred Scott* case for the first time. The discussion was brief and no conclusions were reached, but several opinions reportedly expressed at that meeting led the outspoken anti-slavery correspondents of the *New York Daily Tribune* and the Philadelphia *North American and United States Gazette* to report that the Court might overrule the lower court and grant Scott his freedom. Just how these correspondents received their information is unknown, but Justice Catron later pointed out that the publication of these views indicated a "gross breach of confidence, as the information could only come from a Judge who was present."[7]

A few days later a second consultation was held and the issues discussed in more detail. The first question raised was the jurisdiction of the Court to decide the case in the first instance, a procedural matter that was basic before any deliberations could take place. Immediately it became apparent that there were sharp differences of opinion. Specifically, the question was whether they should review the lower court's action on the plea in abatement. Four of the nine justices—John McLean, Robert Grier (northerners), John Catron, and John Campbell (southerners)—thought the plea in abatement was not even a matter for consideration and that the Court already had jurisdiction. Their view was that once the lower court had denied the plea in abatement and sustained the demurrer, Sanford had then defended himself on the merits of the case; and when the appeal was made to the Supreme Court, it was made against the decision of the lower court on those merits, not against its decision on the plea in abatement. The issue before the Court was those merits alone, not the question of jurisdiction. Four other justices—Roger B. Taney, James Wayne, Peter Daniel (southerners), and Benjamin Curtis (northerner) held that the plea in abatement and the related issue of jurisdiction, as a part of the total record transmitted to the Supreme Court, were subject to consideration and should be taken up first. Samuel Nelson of New York, who held the balance, was undecided. Thus the first discussion on jurisdiction ended in a deadlock, two northerners and two southerners on one side, one northerner and three southerners on the other side, and one northerner undecided.[8]

Although these consultations were traditionally confidential, some of the abolitionist press were able to report that the Court might evade the "direct issues" by declining jurisdiction. In this way, it was alleged, the Court would "prevent the expression of dissenting opinions on the constitutionality of the Missouri Compromise." Nevertheless, the *New York Daily Tribune* reported, "an effort will be made to get a positive decree of some sort, and in that event there is some hope of aid from the Southern members of the Supreme Bench." Neither the "aid" nor the "Southern members" were identified, nor was the source of information. There was, though, the ominous hint that some forces were attempting to squelch a strong antislavery dissent.[9]

On February 28 the Supreme Court adjourned for one month to deal with matters on circuit. No more than the usual scant publicity was given to the Court's adjournment, and only a very few newspapers added that the Court had not yet reached a decision in the "case involving the constitutionality of the Missouri Compromise."[10] During March 1856, while the judges were on their circuits, there was of course no chance for further consultation. Temporarily, at least, *Dred Scott* was out of the public eye. Even in Congress, where the issue of Kansas statehood triggered acrimonious debate on the power of Congress to legislate over slavery in the territories, no direct mention was made of the litigation that involved that same vexing problem, although many legislators must have been aware of it.[11]

On Tuesday, April 1, the Supreme Court reconvened in Washington, and on Saturday evening, April 5, the justices consulted for the third time on the *Dred Scott* case. Once more Taney opened with the question of the plea in abatement and jurisdiction, and again no decision could be reached. As after the earlier consultations, only some of the abolitionist press reported on these tentative proceedings, and the rest of the press apparently awaited more definitive developments. The *New York Daily Tribune* correspondent, himself not an unbiased observer, repeated earlier assertions that the slanted political views of the individual justices were influencing their regard for the "true" interpretation of the law. Southern members of the Court wanted to evade the "real issue" by deciding the case on the technical question of jurisdiction. If they succeeded they would keep the Missouri Compromise issue out of the decision and there-by prevent the minority northern justices from rendering powerful dissenting opinions. "For it must be known," he added in a tone of undisguised political partiality, "that the sectional sentiment which united the South in Congress is also felt and manifested in the highest judicial tribunal."[12]

The integrity of these slashing journalistic attacks is highly suspect, however, for the division of the Court on reviewing the plea in abatement was not sectional. Their alignment had not changed one bit since the earlier consultation. It was still Taney, Wayne, Daniel (southerners), and Curtis (a northerner) in favor of reviewing the plea in abatement as part of the total record; and McLean, Grier (northerners), Catron, and Campbell (southerners) holding that the writ of error was to the merits only; and Nelson (a northerner) remained undecided.[13] It is not inconceivable, though, that outsiders were confused by what the Court's division was all about. It was not on actual jurisdiction; it was on whether they should even discuss jurisdiction. Thus, while both Taney and Curtis agreed that the plea in abatement was subject to consideration, they differed on the outcome of that consideration—Taney holding that the plea in abatement should be sustained and therefore the Court did not have jurisdiction, Curtis contending that the plea in abatement had been properly overruled because the Court did have jurisdiction. Yet the abolitionist press saw fit unjustifiably to accuse the Court of dividing along sectional lines.

Although the blatant reporting of false information cannot be explained and certainly not condoned,[14] there was a self-serving reason why at least some of the abolitionist press wanted the Court to deal with the merits of the case. They were convinced that the "minority" was "ready to vindicate the constitutionality of the Missouri Compromise" and that the new Republican party could make political capital of such judicial declarations in the coming presidential election. Specifically, they were convinced that McLean, long an outspoken opponent of slavery and an avowed candidate for the Republican presidential nomination, would issue a strong dissent justifying congressional control over slavery in the territories, and they expected that Curtis and Grier probably would do the same.[15] McLean's views were already widely known, having been disseminated for many years through private correspondence and in the press. Horace Greeley, forceful editor of the *New York Daily Tribune,*

personally opposed McLean's candidacy, but he was nevertheless anxious
for a decision that could bring out McLean's antislavery arguments. At
the same time, James E. Harvey, Greeley's Washington correspondent
"Index," was a strong McLean man. This could explain why the *Tribune,*
at least, was one of the few newspapers—all Republican, not coincidentally
—that followed the consultations and pressed for a decision on the merits
rather than a denial of jurisdiction. Certainly they must have realized that
a partisan minority view could evoke a strong proslavery majority statement; still they believed their own interests would best be served by a
McLean dissent.[16]

On April 7, 9, and 12 the Court consulted again, but the only reliable
information about these meetings is both sparse and conflicting. According to Cambell and Nelson, in recollections made one and one-half
decades later, the deadlock on the plea in abatement remained unbroken,
and therefore the decision was finally made to reargue the case in hopes
of clarifying the law and making a final judgment possible.[17] Yet on a
different occasion Campbell indicated that the deadlock was broken and
that a five-to-four majority was reached on jurisdiction, but that it was
shortly thereafter changed back to a decision to reargue.[18] A reconstruction of the scanty evidence indicates that the consultations on April 7
were heated and intense; some justices even expressed concern that the
Court was being manipulated, perhaps unscrupulously, into involving
controversial and delicate points of law that the facts of the case possibly
did not demand.[19] Then came a break in the deadlock; there was some
indication by Nelson—although not in a formal vote—that he was leaning
toward the Taney-Curtis-Wayne-Daniel view of delving into the citizenship issue. Thus on April 8 Curtis was able to write to his uncle (in confidence, he hoped) that "the court will not decide the question of the
Missouri Compromise line,—a majority of the judges being of opinion
that it is not necessary to do so."[20]

But the April 9 and 12 consultations saw a return to deadlock. First
a vote was taken and Nelson did indeed swing the balance as Curtis
had anticipated. But as the discussions continued, Nelson had second
thoughts, apparently kindled by what his colleagues were saying. Perhaps
he was not completely convinced that the matter of citizenship should
be discussed after all. Perhaps he was concerned that it might have un-
welcome ramifications in his home state of New York where free blacks
were already victims of racial discrimination. Perhaps Nelson feared that a

controversial decision might embroil the Court in national politics and, as Campbell later hinted, Nelson wanted to avoid such a "collision with a popular election."[21] Indeed, the most widely accepted reason historians have given for Nelson's action has been that it was to prevent McLean from issuing a politically motivated dissent. Little or no consideration has been given to Nelson's concern about the judicial credibility of the Court, fearing it might be undermined if the Court became involved in partisan politics. But whatever his motives, shortly after the five-to-four vote was taken, Nelson changed his mind and moved for a reargument of the entire case at the following term. The motion was carried.[22]

While these consultations were going on, the press contributed to the confusion by reporting both fact and rumor, and especially by speculating on what the eventual decision might be. On April 8 and again on April 10, the day after each of the first two consultations, reporters for the *New York Daily Tribune* and the Philadelphia *North American and United States Gazette* informed their readers that the Court had already decided to accept jurisdiction, and they announced that McLean and Curtis, and probably Grier, would sustain the Missouri Compromise in strong dissenting opinions. Where they obtained this erroneous information is unknown, and certainly their observations about dissents supporting the Missouri Compromise do not jibe with Curtis's statement to his uncle that the Court would not decide that question. Nevertheless the *Tribune* correspondent jubilantly declared: "There is such a thing as a minority left on the bench, notwithstanding the Court has been denounced as a 'Citadel of Slavery'; and unless all the impressions are erroneous, Judge McLean will fortify their positions with an opinion that cannot fail to confound those who are prepared to repudiate the judgment of Southern Courts and the practice of Southern States." He predicted that Curtis would also contribute "a powerful exposition of the case," and that Grier would concur with both. "The decree will be delivered next week," he concluded, "and the opinion will make a sensation."[23]

But the decision was not delivered in the following week. In fact, nothing more was heard of the *Dred Scott* case for more than a month. Then, on May 12, the Court unexpectedly and tersely announced that it had ordered the case to be reargued by counsel at the next term.[24]

A number of reasons have been given why the Court took this action. Senator William Pitt Fessenden, Republican of Maine, in a speech delivered in the United States Senate on February 8, 1858, accused the Court of

deliberately postponing judgment until after the 1856 presidential election for political reasons. As did Abraham Lincoln and many others after
him, Fessenden accused proslavery Democrats of fitting the *Dred Scott*
case into a gigantic conspiracy to establish slavery all over the United
States. The first step was the repeal of the Missouri Compromise, to be
followed by a favorable decision from the Supreme Court justifying
that repeal. This, in turn, would pave the way for the legalization of
slavery in the entire country. But there was a danger that the timing of
the court decision—right before a presidential election—might be im-
propitious, and so the "conspirators" decided to postpone the decision
until after the election. Neither Fessenden nor any others who made
these allegations could buttress their charges with valid evidence, and
so they must be considered only as expressions of partisan distaste for
the decision as finally rendered.[25]

The most widely accepted reason for the decision to reargue is that
it was to prevent McLean from delivering a dissent that might either
propel him into the Republican presidential nomination or at the very
least make available authoritative judicial doctrine for the Republican
campaign. This was first expressed by James E. Harvey, the "Index"
of the *Tribune*, in his dispatch from Washington on May 13, 1856, when
he reported that the "majority" had devised the idea of a reargument
as a means of "restraining those who are known to be ready to vindicate
the constitutionality of the Missouri Compromise from expressing their
convictions."[26] Thirteen years later, in a speech delivered in the House
of Representatives on February 13, 1869, Congressman James M. Ashley
of Toledo, Ohio, charged that the Court deliberately muzzled McLean
to prevent him from using a dissenting opinion as a stepping-stone to
the Republican presidential nomination.[27] McLean's biographer believes
there was no jaundiced intent to impede McLean's personal ambitions.
The delicate problem was how to restrain McLean enough to prevent
the Court from becoming embroiled in partisan politics, but still not
prevent him personally from becoming a viable candidate for the Republican nomination. The only way, apparently, was a watered-down dissent
or no dissent at all. This view has been widely accepted by historians
and was at least implied by one of McLean's own colleagues on the bench,
Justice Campbell.[28]

There is, however, better reason to believe the action of the Court was
not entirely motivated by the political circumstances of the time, but was

instead a genuine desire for a more thorough review of the issues. There can be no disputing that McLean was an outspoken opponent of slavery and that he had long before been and still was, in 1856, a contender for the presidency. There is no doubt that McLean's political views already were widely known and that both he and his backers were making many efforts to publicize them even more. Nor is there any doubt that many who differed with McLean also were willing to go to great lengths to stifle those views.[29] Yet, with regard to McLean's position in the *Dred Scott* case, some significant points must be noted. First is the vote on Nelson's motion to reargue. It was approved *unanimously*.[30] If McLean was truly "champing at the bit," as claimed, to deliver his opinion on the Missouri Compromise before the 1856 presidential election, he unquestionably would have raised some sort of objection to this motion. But he voted for reargument, along with Curtis, who was also supposed to have favored a strong declaration in favor of the Missouri Compromise, and along with all the rest of the Court, northerners as well as southerners, those favoring as well as those opposing the constitutionality of congressional control over slavery in the territories. Thus it appears that the real reason behind the decision for reargument was not to avert a sectional political dissent by McLean at all; on the contrary, it was a genuine effort, *with McLean's own consent and approval,* to clarify the delicate question of jurisdiction as raised in the plea in abatement.

As a matter of fact, far from pressuring for a dissent at that time, McLean was himself not indisposed to postponing the decision. In the first place, little that McLean might say in his dissent could be new, for his views were already widely publicized. Besides, those views may not have been as strong as reputed; leading abolitionists thought McLean's judicial record on slavery was actually overrated.[31] If so, a McLean dissent would not have the impact some thought it might have. Second, it could actually work to McLean's benefit not to deliver a dissent, for then his supporters could portray him as the martyred hero who had been muzzled and bridled by conspiring slaveholders; and as things materialized, that was precisely the strategy his backers followed after the reargument was ordered.[32] Third, McLean had reason to postpone the decision to allow another case to be heard, from which he might strengthen his own arguments in the *Dred Scott* case. On May 2, 1856, Joseph Blunt, one of the lawyers for the state of New York in the *Jonathan Lemmon* slave case, wrote to McLean and requested a postponement of the decision in the *Scott* case "to allow the state of New York to be heard on the same question." The main issue in the *Lemmon* case was the status of slaves residing temporarily in a free state. Blunt had learned through the newspapers that a decision covering this principle was imminent in the *Scott* case. Convinced that the *Lemmon* case would eventually be appealed to the Supreme Court, Blunt asked McLean if it was possible to delay the *Scott* case until the *Lemmon* case also could be argued. "Would it be asking too much," wrote Blunt from New York, "taking into consideration the great importance of the principle and the momentous consequences involved, to ask a postponement of the decision or in case that be deemed improper to order a rehearing when the counsel representing this state might present their views on that question."[33] If a decision in the *Dred Scott* case could be postponed, not only would additional antislavery arguments be forthcoming in the *Lemmon* case, but the authorities and principles cited there could provide additional weight to McLean's own opinion when it came in the *Scott* case.[34]

Undoubtedly all these contributed to the decision to reargue. But historians have focused so much on McLean that they have overlooked the obvious and main reason: that it was a genuine effort on the part of the *entire* Court to clarify the jurisdiction and citizenship issue. After all, when the case came into the lower federal court, the issue was slavery in the territories, not citizenship of blacks. In spite of the plea in abatement, that did not change when the case was appealed to the Supreme Court. Why else then did Montgomery Blair argue citizenship only obliquely and Henry S. Geyer and Reverdy Johnson so little if even at all? But once the Court began its consultations, it became apparent that the controversial slavery question still could be evaded, in spite of Roswell M. Field's and Montgomery Blair's insistence to the contrary, by falling back on *Strader* v. *Graham*. Conceding that *Strader* did not apply procedurally, the Court still could have used the principle inferred from that case—and one it had used for so long anyway—that the federal courts accept a state supreme court's interpretation of state law. But what could not be evaded was the question of jurisdiction. No matter what the Court's decision, it could not dodge the fact that the plea in abatement *was there* as part of the record. If the Court decided only on the merits, it was implicitly overturning the plea in abatement. If it refused to decide on the merits, it was implicitly sustaining the plea in abatement. Whatever the Court said or did, it had to say or do in the face of that plea. It was precisely the dilemma

Field had noted earlier. Moreover, it was compounded because argument by counsel was totally inadequate. Even McLean, in spite of an apparent attempt to muzzle him, voted to hear reargument on this perplexing issue.

If there was any doubt, Taney made it abundantly clear. On Monday, May 12, when he announced the Court's decision for reargument, he instructed counsel to deal "especially" with:

> 1. Whether or not the facts admitted by the demurrer to the plea to the jurisdiction and adjudgment given that the defendant answer over, and the submission of the defendant to judgment by pleading over to the merits, the appellate court can take notice of these facts thus admitted upon the record in determining the question of jurisdiction of the court below to hear, and finally dispose of the case—and
>
> 2. Whether or not, assuming that the appellate court is bound to take notice of the facts thus appearing upon the record, the plaintiff is a citizen of the State of Missouri within the meaning of the 11 par. of the judiciary act of 1789.[35]

The reaction—what little there was of it—to this development was mixed. The *New York Daily Tribune,* showing little regard for the truth, denounced the Court's move as "a most ingenious, but not particularly creditable expedient" for evading a final judgment. "The black gowns have come to be artful dodgers," its correspondent contemptuously wrote. "The minority were prepared to meet the issue broadly and distinctly; but the controlling members were not quite ready . . . to open the opportunity for a demolition of the fraudulent pretences that have been set up in Congress on this question."[36] The Philadelphia *North American and United States Gazette* was of similar opinion, calling the postponement of a final judgment "little more than a convenient evasion." "But the fact can not be disguised," it charged, "that the . . . independence which once existed no longer exists, and the same sectional feeling which excites men in other branches of the public service has tainted this tribunal of last resort."[37]

The reaction of other Republican newspapers, however, was different. The *Morning Courier and New York Enquirer* and the *Boston Daily Advertiser* both praised the Court for its action. "This order," they declared, "proves that the great tribunal to which the country has been taught for nearly three-quarters of a century to look up to for the dispensation of justice upon the principles of law, is not prepared to rush into the political arena and ruffle its ermine in the strife of politicians and the squabbles of demagogues."[38]

Despite this undeniable interest in the *Dred Scott* case shown by a few newspapers, most expressed no reaction at all to the decision to reargue. Such prominent journals as the Washington, D.C., *Daily National Intelligencer* and *The New York Herald*, for instance, merely listed the *Dred Scott* case by title only in their routine daily summaries of action taken by the Supreme Court. The Baltimore *Sun* briefly mentioned the Court's action in a very small article, but aside from noting a rumor that the case might be fictitious, it merely cited the order for reargument without further comment. The strongly antislavery Washington, D.C., *National Era* printed a very small article noting the adjournment of the Supreme Court, but it made no mention of the *Dred Scott* case—and its own editor, Gamaliel Bailey, had assumed financial responsibility for the case while it was in the Supreme Court![39] The fact is that most of the country's newspapers made no mention at all of what had transpired in the case. Very few people knew about it or discussed it, despite its great importance. It was not until seven months later, in December 1856, when it was argued for the second time before the Supreme Court, that the *Dred Scott* case finally received the widespread publicity and notoriety that made it so famous.[40]

Chapter 13

U. S. Supreme Court: Second Arguments

SEVEN MONTHS ELAPSED BEFORE the *Dred Scott* case was argued for the second time. During that brief period the sectional breach between North and South became even wider. On May 21, 1856, a band of proslavery "border ruffians" virtually destroyed the city of Lawrence, center of the free-state population of Kansas Territory. The next day Representative Preston S. Brooks of South Carolina brutally assaulted Senator Charles Sumner at his seat in the United States Senate shortly after the Massachusetts abolitionist delivered a virulent attack on slavery. Two days later came John Brown's blood bath at Pottawotomie Creek. Like the peals of the proverbial "firebell in the night," the news of these violent events spread alarmingly throughout the country, exacerbating the hostility and rancor already existing between North and South, and driving more and more people from a willingness to coexist in compromise to receptivity to Rhettian and Garrisonian disunion.

It was in this charged atmosphere that the presidential election of 1856 took place. The campaign was bitterly contested, one of the most vociferously discussed issues being slavery in the territories. The Republican party, appearing for the first time in a presidential campaign, nominated the colorful and charismatic John C. Fremont, with William L. Dayton as his running mate. Avowedly antislavery, the Republican platform declared in unmistakable terms that "the Constitution confers upon Congress sovereign power over the Territories of the United States," and that Congress therefore had "both the right and the duty" to prohibit slavery in the territories. The Democrats, whose standard-bearers were James Buchanan and John C. Breckinridge, maintained on the other hand that the doctrine of "popular sovereignty" was the only sound and safe solution of the slavery question in the territories. Two other parties entered the field, the remnant of the once great Whig party and the new American or Know-Nothing party.

The campaign developed primarily into a battle between the Democratic and the Republican parties. The core of the Republican message was a moral one, conveyed in both intellectual and partisan ways. Republicans argued that the founders of the country had expected the eventual extinction of slavery, that the Missouri Compromise had been a manifestation of that desire, and that the best hopes for the nation were bound up with the restriction of slavery as much as possible until viable means could be found for its gradual abolition. But with blood flowing in Kansas and corresponding hostility reflected in the debates in Congress and on the political stump, intense resentment was expressed on all sides, and sectional feelings ran very high.

The *Dred Scott* case was of no consequence in this election. Despite the outpourings of a few McLean supporters when the Court announced its decision to reargue, there was no recurrence of this line of attack. Of course, since no final judgment had been rendered, there could be no reference to any decision. But on several occasions at least the pendency of the case was mentioned, and in some instances even gross misinformation was evident. Congress was in session throughout the summer of 1856 and much of its deliberations dealt with House Bill 411 for the admission of Kansas as a free state. Both sides repeatedly referred to favorable Supreme Court decisions, and occasionally a member of Congress mentioned the current suit. On June 20, for instance, Congressman Henry Bennett, New York Republican, discussing the possible power of one branch of the federal government to compel a state to recognize slavery, declared:

> This question has been recently before the judges of the Supreme Court of the United States, and, as I am informed, virtually decided, although the case was dismissed. And mark that decision! It is that slaves can be held as property in a free State! It is said, too, that this decision is made by the pro-slavery judges from slave States! And that every judge who heard the case from a free State held a contrary opinion.[1]

He wanted for accuracy. Equally misinformed was Congressman Mason W. Tappan, Republican from New Hampshire, who stated on July 29: "It is understood that a majority of the judges of the Supreme Court of the United States are ready with an opinion, confirming the slavery side of this question."[2] Meanwhile, Congressman Alexander H. Stephens of Georgia was more cautious in his reply to a question posed by his colleague from Ohio, Lewis D. Campbell. As the debate drifted to the constitutionality of slavery in the territories, Campbell pointedly asked Stephens why, if he was so certain the Missouri Compromise was unconstitutional, had he not taken it into the courts long ago, where it would have been readily declared unconstitutional and so much sectional agitation could have been avoided. Stephens made a rather veiled reply about a case "of that sort" being currently before the Supreme Court. Campbell did not push for an elaboration of the remark, nor did Stephens volunteer more, and their discussion drifted away from the pending case back to the issue of the Missouri Compromise.[3]

In addition to these references in Congress, mention was made also from the political stump. Addressing a large Democratic rally in Philadelphia on October 25, Reverdy Johnson referred briefly to the case in which he was counsel. Attacking the Republican party for advocating congressional prohibition of slavery in the territories, Johnson declared:

> It must serve as a consolation to us to know that the question is now pending for adjudication before the Supreme Court of the United States. It was argued at the last term, but the Court thought proper to direct a reargument at the next term; and I trust in Providence, (as I believe,) that when that argument shall have been had and the judgment of that high tribunal shall have been announced, it will be found that there is no such power in the Constitution.[4]

Aside from these brief references, there seems to have been little or no other public mention of the pending case.[5]

The presidential election of November 4, 1856, resulted in a narrow Democratic victory. Nevertheless, the cessation of the inflammatory campaign rhetoric, accompanied by a general restoration of peace in Kansas, gave a delusive hope that Buchanan's administration might enter into office on a note of renewed harmony and unity. "For a few happy weeks, in fact, Americans ceased to think of slavery, feuding settlers, and disunionist plots," writes Allan Nevins of the period, and attention was turned instead to other less divisive affairs.[6]

But the deep-rooted sectional conflict was quickly reopened when Congress assembled in December. It was expected that in his last annual State of the Union message on December 2, President Franklin Pierce would avoid controversial issues and seek to close his term in an atmosphere of harmony. Instead, reviewing the significance of the late election, he digressed into a partisan denunciation of the Republican party. This alone was enough to incite Republican congressmen, but Pierce added more fuel to the flames of sectional discord. Summarizing congressional controversies over slavery in the territories, he declared, as he referred to the recent Kansas-Nebraska Act:

> In the progress of constitutional inquiry and reflection, it had now at length come to be seen clearly that Congress does not possess constitutional power to impose restrictions of this character upon any present or future State of the Union. In a long series of decisions, on the fullest argument, and after the most deliberate consideration, the Supreme Court of the United States had finally determined this point in every form under which the question could arise.[7]

Pierce's message rekindled the sectional controversy. Hardly had he finished speaking when Senators John P. Hale of New Hampshire and Lyman Trumbull of Illinois demanded to be shown the decision in which, as Pierce had stated, "the Supreme Court of the United States had finally determined this point."[8] The sessions of Congress in the days that followed witnessed similar outpourings of indignation by other Republicans and replies in the same vein by proslavery Democrats. As Nevins has aptly stated, "All the billingsgate of the campaign were brought into use again."[9] It was in such a politically charged environment that attorneys argued the *Dred Scott* case before the Supreme Court for the second time.[10]

On December 2 Henry S. Geyer filed the printed brief for the defendant-in-error John F. A. Sanford.[11] Earlier he had either ignored or dealt superficially with citizenship; now, in response to the Court's order, Geyer devoted a considerable portion of his brief to it. The core of his argument was

that Scott's status as free or slave was immaterial; the critical factor was
his color. To be a citizen eligible to sue in the federal courts, Geyer argued,
one first must be a citizen of the state in which he lived, and Missouri did
not grant such rights to blacks. True, a black person could be free in Missouri, but that freedom still did not make him a citizen. Nor did it make
any difference that Scott was born within the United States. Many native-
born people were not citizens, such as children of foreign diplomats and
Indians. So, too, with blacks, asserted Geyer, who were "natural born
subjects, not citizens." Although noncitizens might become naturalized,
blacks could not, even free blacks. Geyer touched vaguely on a concept
of dual citizenship, state and federal, but he denied blacks the right to
either. He ignored citizenship rights granted blacks in some free states,
although he stressed opposite examples of rights denied. The sheer racism
of his argument in many ways matched the bigotry expressed earlier in
the Missouri Supreme Court.

Before rearguing the unconstitutionality of the Missouri Compromise,
Geyer made two other observations. One was that the Illinois constitution
and the Missouri Compromise, although both prohibited slavery, did not
actually emancipate anyone. Like enabling laws, they required additional
implementing legislation. It was their effect rather than their substance
that foredoomed to a slaveowner any possibility of legally enforcing
the status of slavery. It was an argument not unlike what Stephen A.
Douglas would expound two years later at Freeport in his debate with
senatorial candidate Abraham Lincoln.

Geyer also went into a lengthy distinction between a slave's temporary
or permanent residence in free territory. Concluding that Scott's was
only temporary, Geyer cited *Groves* v. *Slaughter* and *Rankin* v. *Lydia*
that "slaves attending their owners sojourning in or travelling through a
State where slavery does not exist by law, are not thereby emancipated."[12]
Strader v. *Graham* then doubly protected the owner's rights by accepting the law of the state to which both returned. Curiously, permanent
versus temporary residence had not been a controversial issue heretofore in this case; one might wonder why Geyer injected it here. One
reason may be that Geyer anticipated the *Lemmon* case, which involved
slaves in transit, and he hoped to defuse that potentially volatile issue
before it even reached the Court.

At the same time, though, there was a ring of contradiction in Geyer's
arguments. He devoted more than half his brief to reasons why the Mis-

souri Compromise was unconstitutional and why Dred Scott therefore had never been free in the first place. Still, in his "implementing" and "temporary residence" arguments, Geyer implied that emancipation could occur legally, assuming appropriate implementing legislation in the first instance and permanent residence in the second. But the authority behind both was congressional legislation abolishing slavery in the territories, an authority Geyer now insisted was unconstitutional and invalid in the first place. Geyer never reconciled these contradictions, nor were they reconciled by the Court.

On December 15, the same day on which the oral argument commenced, Montgomery Blair filed a supplementary "Additional Brief" for the plaintiff-in-error Dred Scott.[13] Having already dealt with citizenship and jurisdiction in his first brief, he merely referred to the authorities and law cited there to justify Scott's right to sue. Nevertheless, he still pointed out that procedurally citizenship should not be an issue, having been eliminated when Sanford pleaded to the merits after the demurrer had been upheld; citizenship could be an issue only had Sanford appealed the action taken on the plea in abatement. Blair then added a very brief statement refuting Geyer's argument concerning permanent and temporary residence. He pointed out that nothing in the record indicated that Emerson or Scott had either a permanent or a temporary residence in Missouri or elsewhere, and therefore it could not be an issue in this case.[14]

Blair devoted most of his supplementary brief to the constitutionality of the Missouri Compromise, a matter he had not dealt with earlier because it had not then been at issue in the case. First he reviewed historically the development of the general power of Congress over the territories, beginning as early as 1780, when the Second Continental Congress asked individual states to cede their western lands to the Congress. Citing the language of documents involving eighteen separate land cessions, Blair showed that by 1787 the framers of the Constitution unquestionably intended for Congress to have absolute power over the territories, limited only of course by protections included in the Constitution itself. Then he narrowed his focus to the power of Congress over slavery in the territories. Once more he documented his argument with historical evidence, citing thirteen acts of Congress that legislated over slavery, either protecting it or abolishing it, in various territories. To these Blair added excerpts from four authoritative jurists (Joseph Story, James Kent, William Rawle, and Thomas Sargeant) and references to fourteen decisions, decided in northern, southern, and United States courts, all of which recognized the constitutional right of Congress to legislate over slavery in the territories. It was a most imposing array, establishing an indisputable basis for his major thesis that the constitutionality of the Missouri Compromise could not be an issue in this case. There was no question that Congress had the authority. If Congress chose to legalize slavery, that was its prerogative; if Congress chose to abolish slavery, that, too, was its prerogative. Slavery in the territories, Blair maintained, was exclusively a legislative matter; it was not for the courts to decide, it was not "within the scope of judicial inquiry." Exercise judicial restraint, he exhorted.

But Sanford's counsel had challenged the legality of the Missouri Compromise. On what grounds? Certainly not because it exceeded any authority of Congress under the Constitution. Their objection, Blair indicated, was that the 1820 statute conflicted with a *state* law as interpreted by a *state* supreme court, that "a species of property recognized in the laws of the states cannot be held in the Territories." If state authority superseded federal authority, it would "subject Congress to the State legislatures," and this to Blair was both unthinkable and not even arguable. Although he did not mention Calhoun by name, Blair totally rejected the South Carolinian's states' rights philosophy. Thus Blair would not even deign to argue the constitutionality of the Missouri Compromise on the right of Congress to legislate over slavery in the territories. That principle was too well established even to be debated.

By not taking up that argument, Blair may have been diminishing the scope of judicial review—perhaps even abdicating its role completely— and suggesting an authority for Congress that could upset the delicate separation of powers balance among the three branches of the federal government. Indeed, within a decade the Reconstruction era would convince many that what Blair had suggested had come to fruition.

Yet Blair should not be so quickly faulted. After all, even though the concept of judicial review was firmly established, the overthrow of an act of Congress by the Supreme Court had occurred only once before, fifty-three years earlier, in 1803, in *Marbury* v. *Madison,* and that decision by the great John Marshall had been met with anything but universal rejoicing.[15] More than a century after the *Dred Scott* case, and especially since the post-World War II civil libertarian era, lawyers are quick to suggest unconstitutionality when congressional legislation is merely displeasing, let alone oppressive. But in the 1850s such was not yet the case. The notion of unconstitutionality as a legal strategy was as uncommon and as potentially volatile as a "higher law" strategy. By insisting that constitutionality was not involved, Blair was trying to avoid issues he believed transcended the case, and that, in the explosive environment of 1856, might trigger a national catastrophe—which, of course, is exactly what did eventually happen.

At the same time, by calling for judicial restraint and not arguing the Missouri Compromise, Blair remained consistent with every view he had expressed heretofore in this case. From the moment he became associated with it, the issue in *Dred Scott* v. *John F. A. Sanford* was what the Supreme Court had evaded in *Strader* v. *Graham:* whether a slave, once emancipated by congressional or free state action, could be remanded to slavery by returning to a slave state. The power to emancipate never was the issue. Blair refused to be sidetracked, even though Sanford's counsel were determined to do so.

Furthermore, by not arguing the Missouri Compromise on its merits, Blair actually was making a strong case for its constitutionality. His reason, as he stated so clearly and documented so authoritatively, was that the principle that Congress could legislate over slavery in the territories, whether "up" or "down," was so firmly established that it was beyond challenge. Questioning it was unthinkable and unacceptable. The constitutionality of the Missouri Compromise was totally extraneous to the case.

The printed briefs having been submitted, all parties waited for the Court to work through its docket so oral arguments might be presented. Despite the importance of the case, it elicited surprisingly very little press comment. Of the major newspapers of the country, only one, the Washington, D.C., *Daily Union,* gave any advance notice, in a very small article announcing that the case would be argued on December 15 if all the justices were present. Only two sentences in length, this notice nevertheless was prophetic: "Seldom, if ever, has there been a case before this high tribunal of greater importance, or one in which such a general and deep interest is felt." Although that "general and deep interest" was not reflected in widespread newspaper publicity, apparently advance notice was no longer necessary. The *Daily Union* had been correct; when the Supreme Court convened for the rearguments in the *Dred Scott* case, its chambers in the basement room of the Senate wing were packed with a "superior audience" of "many distinguished jurists and members of Congress."[16]

On Monday, December 15, 1856, *Dred Scott* v. *John F. A. Sanford*
came up for reargument before the Supreme Court of the United States.
All nine justices were present. The oral argument lasted four days, three
hours each day. It was opened by Montgomery Blair for the plaintiff-in-
error Dred Scott, and he occupied the full three hours allotted to the
case for that day.[17]

Blair prefaced his remarks with an announcement that he had tried
unsuccessfully to secure assistance in arguing the important constitutional
principles involved, but that he would continue alone if necessary. Either
that day or the next, George Ticknor Curtis, a prominent Boston attorney and brother of Justice Benjamin Robbins Curtis, joined with
Blair to argue the question of the power of Congress over slavery in the
territories.[18] For reasons that cannot be documented, but that seem
self-evident, Blair drastically changed his tactics, at virtually the last
moment, toward discussing the Missouri Compromise. From a posture
in his written brief—submitted that very same day—that the constitutionality of congressional legislation abolishing slavery in the territories was
not an issue, Blair's oral arguments were devoted almost entirely to a
substantive justification of that power in Congress. Blair spent most of
his three hours on that topic; and on the concluding day, even though
Curtis had joined him by then, Blair devoted almost two more hours to
that same issue. Undoubtedly considerable pressures convinced Blair
that the original reasons for instituting the suit had now been supplanted
by the more volatile Missouri Compromise question, and that he had to
meet the issue face on.

Blair's oral arguments reiterated and elaborated the points he had
made in his two briefs.[19] He dealt first with the issues of jurisdiction
and citizenship, as requested in the order for reargument. Reviewing
the chronology of the case, he pointed out that Sanford's attorneys
had not objected to the lower court's decision on citizenship, else
they would have appealed that; instead they proceeded with the merits.
For procedural reasons alone, then, the citizenship question was not an
issue in the appeal and consequently was not properly subject to review
by the Court.

Aside from the procedural reason, Blair added substantive reasons
why the Court had jurisdiction, because Dred Scott was a citizen and a
proper plaintiff. Again he elaborated on what was already in his briefs,
stressing the term *white male citizens* in many constitutions and laws,
thereby indicating that there was another class of citizens, the "non-

white male citizens," and that only express legislation could deny them
of privileges they otherwise possessed. He then added a most telling
point that had not been made before, that an act of the Missouri
legislature, passed in 1845, explicitly recognized the citizenship of free
Negroes by expressly enabling those *recognized as citizens by other states*
to come into Missouri.

Blair then turned to the merits. He pointed out first that regardless of
the constitutionality of a slavery prohibition for a territory, there could
be absolutely no denial of the validity of such a prohibition by a state,
in this case Illinois. Dred Scott's going to Illinois alone made him free.
Blair decried the refusal of the Missouri Supreme Court to extend comity
and recognize that freedom, charging that "it was not law, but passion
and politics which invaded Judge William Scott's mind" in the controversial decision in *Dred Scott* v. *Irene Emerson.*

After briefly rejecting the issue of temporary residence, as he had already done in his brief, Blair turned to the constitutionality of the Missouri Compromise, devoting the rest of his time (more than two hours)
to an issue he had up to then insisted was totally extraneous to the case.[20]
Elaborating on the chronology in his brief, he gave an extensive historical
sketch of congressional laws over slavery in the territories, both protecting
it and prohibiting it, concluding that there was never any doubt of their
constitutionality. Any serious differences were over *how* the power should
be exercised, not over *whether* it could be exercised. The framers of the
Constitution believed that way, that principle had always been recognized
since, and there was no sound reason for the Court to declare otherwise.[21]

The next day, Tuesday, December 16, after the Court handed down
decisions in three other cases, Geyer argued for the defendant-in-error
Sanford. As did Blair the day before, Geyer occupied the full three hours
allotted. He prefaced his remarks by observing that "some portion of the
press" was giving the impression that this was not a genuine suit, but
rather a feigned issue created to get from the Supreme Court a decision
on the important slavery questions involved. He denied the allegation and
declared publicly that the case was genuine, brought up in the regular
manner and for the same purpose as any other case—to decide upon the
facts of that one particular suit.[22]

Geyer pointed out that the Court had to review the plea in abatement;
otherwise, how else could it know whether it had jurisdiction?[23] He then
discussed the citizenship issue, reviewing what he had included in his
brief, and concluding that a Negro, whether slave or free, could not be

a citizen of the United States and therefore could not sue in the federal courts.

Geyer then turned to the merits, arguing first that Dred Scott was not entitled to freedom by virtue of his residence in Illinois. He stressed the point he had made in his brief that the constitution and law of Illinois merely prevented the state legislature from establishing slavery in that state, but had no effect on someone brought into the state who was already a slave, especially if that slave was merely passing through or residing only temporarily within the state boundaries. As to Scott's residence at Fort Snelling, Geyer maintained that it also did not change his status as a slave. Slavery had existed in the Louisiana Purchase territory long before the passage of the Missouri Compromise act, and Congress had no constitutional power to abolish it. Geyer readily agreed that Congress had the power to institute municipal governments for the territories, but that power existed only to initiate the process toward eventual statehood, and not because Congress could control persons and property in the territory. Power over local institutions lay only with the inhabitants of the territory themselves. Examining at length the power of Congress to legislate over those inhabitants, he took the very narrow neo-Jeffersonian interpretation of the Constitution that there was no express grant of such power; the only basis for it was implied from the power of Congress over commerce. Championing the principles of Douglas's popular sovereignty, he argued that the Missouri Compromise was a base violation of the sovereignty of the people because it took away from them powers over local institutions they alone rightfully possessed. Besides, he declared, this "so-called compromise" had been acquiesced in under duress, for only to save the Union had the South been willing to sacrifice principle and agree to such a measure. Dred Scott could not claim freedom by virtue of residence in Missouri Compromise territory, for the act of Congress prohibiting slavery there was unconstitutional and hence null and void.

The next day, Wednesday, December 17, Reverdy Johnson spoke for the full three hours. Before he commenced it was announced that George Ticknor Curtis had joined Blair and would assist him in arguing the case for Dred Scott.[24]

Johnson opened with a discussion intended to show that the Constitution of the United States did not consider Negroes to be citizens, but his reasoning was more important in its conclusions on the nature of property.[25] He pointed out that the Constitution not only maintained the principle that man can have property in man, but it also pledged the force of the Union to protect that property right. His reference to Fifth Amendment property rights was to be noted by Taney later in one of the more far-reaching sections of the decision.[26]

Johnson devoted the greatest portion of his argument to the unconstitutionality of the Missouri Compromise.[27] As Geyer had the day before, he posited a narrow interpretation of governmental powers, arguing at great length that nothing in the Constitution gave Congress the express power to prohibit slavery, but that that power had been usurped without a valid constitutional basis. As for the clause in the Constitution giving Congress power to make rules and regulations for the territories, Congress could do nothing that was detrimental either to the United States or to any one state. By prohibiting slavery in the territories, Congress was legislating against the interests of the slave states; yet if it permitted slavery in the territories, Congress would harm the interests of the free states. From the constitutional point of view, Johnson could see only one viable solution to this dilemma: he could not go so far as to say that the Constitution protected slavery in the territories (he seemed to be contradicting his own earlier stance on Fifth Amendment property rights) but he was convinced that there was nothing in the Constitution either that gave Congress the power to prohibit slavery in the territories. Hence, he declared, the act of March 6, 1820, prohibiting slavery in the Louisiana Purchase territory north of 36°30' was unconstitutional and therefore null and void. How and why, then, did Congress pass this unconstitutional measure in the first place? As Geyer had the day before, Johnson acclaimed the South for placing patriotism to the Union above self-interest, even though it meant compromising on an unconstitutional measure.

Oral arguments in the *Dred Scott* case were concluded on Thursday, December 18. All four attorneys spoke on that day—Blair for two hours, Curtis for one, and Johnson and Geyer making only brief remarks. Johnson opened the day's proceedings by presenting a few precedents to support his position that Negroes were not citizens.[28] Blair then held the floor for two hours, arguing once more in support of the jurisdiction of the Court and of the right of Negroes to citizenship.[29] He repeated and emphasized the same principles he had declared a few days earlier and added several more authorities to support his views. Then he turned to a lengthy analysis of the constitutionality of the Missouri Compromise, even though Curtis was prepared to discuss that subject at length. Blair's approach, though, was more philosophic than legal, focusing on the classic controversy over narrow *versus* broad interpretation of the Constitution: could Congress exercise only that power which was specifically authorized, or could Congress exercise a power as long as it was not specifically prohibited? The latter had always been the constitutional position on congressional authority over slavery in the territories, Blair pointed out, until recent sectional political expediency propelled the narrow interpretation into prominence. National integrity demanded that the Court not be the instrument of that sectional political expediency, but that it reach a decision instead based upon the well-established political philosophy that had guided constitutional thinking from the beginning of our national being.

Geyer followed with a few short remarks to the effect that when the Missouri Compromise was agreed to in 1820, there were indeed doubts of its constitutionality. James Madison has expressed such an opinion, and President Monroe had actually written a rough draft of a veto message on the grounds that if the measure was not unconstitutional, at least it was repugnant to the "general sentiment of the States."

In the hour that remained, George T. Curtis closed the argument with what was universally described as a "scholarly"presentation confined to the constitutionality of the Missouri Compromise.[30] Curtis limited his comments to Article IV, Section 3, of the Constitution, which contains two paragraphs: the first giving Congress the power to admit new states into the Union, and the second giving Congress the power to "dispose of and make all needful Rules and Regulations respecting the Territory or other Property belonging to the United States." Going into a thorough history of the period immediately preceding and contemporaneous with the framing of these two provisions, as well as into the debates in the Constitutional Convention, Curtis concluded that the clear intent of the framers of the Constitution was that Congress should have absolute authority over a territory while it remained in that status, subject only to any limitations prescribed in the Constitution. Not until after the territory became a state did the state alone have the right to decide upon its local institutions. Nothing in the Constitution limited Congress from legislating over slavery in the territories, either for it or against it. Consequently, the Missouri Compromise act of March 6, 1820, which prohibited slavery in the Louisiana Purchase territory north of $36°30'$, was constitutional. Dred Scott was therefore entitled to freedom by virtue of his residence at Fort Snelling.

So the arguments were completed. Now it was up to the Court.

Chapter   14

The Court Consults Again

IN CONTRAST WITH THE sparse publicity before, news of the oral arguments now was disseminated in the press throughout the country. Many newspapers carried in full the telegraphic dispatches of the Associated Press reporter who recorded the arguments. Many printed special reports from Washington correspondents. Many reprinted articles from other newspapers. Yet, surprisingly, only a few papers reacted editorially, apparently waiting for the final decision; when it did come, very few then refrained from commenting![1]

Some papers, though, did react to the arguments. Most agreed that the efforts of all four attorneys were exemplary and very able. The correspondent of the antislavery *Morning Courier and New-York Enquirer* predictably described Henry Geyer's argument as "a stump speech . . . not very far removed from those passionate and detestable diatribes which filled the columns of *The Richmond Enquirer*, and the *New Orleans Delta*, during the Presidential contest."[2] On the other hand he praised Reverdy Johnson for his "usual excellent" work and George T. Curtis for what many considered one of the finest arguments ever presented before the Supreme Court. Curtis was commended even by several southern senators, albeit they disagreed with the doctrines he propounded. Some papers criticized Montgomery Blair after his first argument of December 15 for having failed to secure an associate counsel and then, after Curtis joined him, for taking up two hours of the allotted time on December 18 and leaving only one hour to Curtis.[3]

Even before the arguments were completed, speculation about the outcome began. Horace Greeley's *New York Daily Tribune* commented repeatedly that the Court was controlled by southerners who would render a biased and politically inspired decision favorable to slaveholders. Especially acrimonious were the dispatches of the *Tribune*'s Washington correspondent James M. Pike, who was certain that the justices would divide along sectional lines. He denounced their "Jim-Crow attitudes," and even advocated the dissolution of the Union rather than allow supporters of slavery to control the government.[4]

Other antislavery papers also attacked the Court, although not in such callous tones. A correspondent of the *Morning Courier and New-York Enquirer* wrote that it would be a "voluntary abandonment" of their rights if free people submitted any questions concerning those rights to such a partial Court. "They are learned, wise, and good men," he wrote, "but they are only men. To expect them to sit, hear, and resolve, unswayed by the passions of those who placed them where they are, and by the interests of that institution which now controls every other department of the Government, would be to suppose them more than men."[5] A correspondent of the Philadelphia *North American and United States Gazette* declared prophetically that if the Supreme Court held the Missouri Compromise unconstitutional, "an impetus would be given to a new strife, which moderate men might in vain seek to control."[6] Similar fears were expressed in other Republican papers, with special emphasis on the ominous consequences should the division of the Court be along sectional lines.[7]

Among the fiercest denunciations were those by the *Morning Courier and New York-Enquirer* and *The New York Herald*. A correspondent of the former accused certain unnamed Democratic politicians of fomenting the case at its very outset "to procure from it a decision adverse to the Republican party and to the Free States." He charged that sometime after the case had been concluded in the Missouri courts, some "Washington politicians" had contrived with John F. A. Sanford to bring the case into the federal courts for the express purpose of obtaining a decision declaring the Missouri Compromise unconstitutional and spreading slavery to the territories. "Had the decision been rendered after the first argument and before the 1856 election," this correspondent wrote, "it would have been issued by millions of copies to prove the constitutionality of the Democratic party, and the Supreme Court would be permanently arrayed as a piece of partisan machinery on the side of the Democratic party."[8] He did not explain, however, why the decision had not been rendered earlier, nor did he give any proof of his allegations. Nevertheless, many newspapers reprinted the story, spreading the false accusation that the *Dred Scott* case was fabricated by proslavery Democrats to get a favorable decision from the Supreme Court. Even though the correspondent retracted his accusation against Sanford, the charge remained against the Supreme Court, accusing it of being the tool of proslavery Democrats.[9]

Particularly acrimonious was *The New York Herald,* which leveled its attack more on the judges than on the expected decision. The Court could not decide the constitutionality of the Missouri Compromise, said the *Herald;* what could be more ludicrous than the notion that one trial concerning so insignificant an individual as the "nigger Dred Scott" could settle a question that affected the entire country? Then it turned to personalities, launching a series of venomous personal invectives that were no more than the basest of partisan harangues. The chief justice, it declared, was "a Jesuit in morals and politics . . . greatly impaired by old age and ill health; but although unfit for the duties of the station, he holds on to the office for the sake of the salary." John McLean was a grasping and often-rejected politician; John Catron was denounced as "free from any qualifications of a Supreme Court Judge as the horse he is said once to have groomed." Peter V. Daniel was "narrow minded, ignorant, and bigotted beyond the extremest measure of Virginia politicians," and Benjamin R. Curtis was "a wooden nutmeg." Similar "compliments" were paid to the other justices as well as to counsel. "These are the parties who have been playing the farce of 'Dred Scott,' and such are the men who are to pass judgment upon a measure sanctioned by statesmen, lawyers, and jurists, the least of whom was far superior to the whole talent and wisdom now on the Supreme Bench," declared the *Herald*, concluding that it was foolish to believe such a Court could possibly settle the validity of the Missouri Compromise.[10]

In view of what they said even before the decision was reached, it is no surprise that this same segment of the press reacted with such rancor after the Court finally did speak. Their emotional minds were already made up. As far as they were concerned, the Court's action was a foregone conclusion; it was going to decide the case along sectional lines, and the decision was going to be bad, no matter what reasoning was followed. All that remained was to await the actual wording of the decision, and then the full-scale assault upon the Court could be launched. Unbiased and objective journalism was experiencing one of its most trying times.

Nevertheless, not all the reaction to the arguments was adverse. As already mentioned, the general opinion of the efforts of the attorneys was that they were praiseworthy. *The New York Journal of Commerce* expressed relief that the vexing slavery questions might finally be settled, but it feared that if the Court should divide along sectional lines "their decision will have less weight than it may be entitled to."[11] Similar views were expressed in newspapers throughout the country, among them the Baltimore *Sun*, *The Charleston Daily Courier*, the Philadelphia *Daily News*, the *New York Dispatch*, the *Boston Post*, and the *St. Louis Daily Evening News*. The very location of these newspapers indicates that the reaction to the arguments was not sectional. On the contrary, with the exception of *The New York Herald,* which was a Democratic journal (but free-state Democratic) the opposition to the expected decision was led by Republican newspapers, whose openly avowed policy of prohibiting slavery in the territories was in danger of being declared unconstitutional by the Supreme Court. Most newspapers with other party affiliations, regardless of their geographic location, looked forward to the decision in the fervent hope it might finally settle the issues that had caused so much strife in the past.[12]

Public anticipation to the pending decision was not confined to the newspapers; it was the subject of discussion in Congress, too. In a heated dialogue between Representatives Lawrence Branch of North Carolina and Benjamin Stanton of Ohio about slavery in the territories, both anticipated a decision from the Supreme Court, but neither would anticipate what it might be. In the Senate on the same day, Senator James C. Jones of Tennessee referred specifically to the case "at this very time" before the Supreme Court, and he expressed the fervent desire not only that the Court would settle the vexing issue of slavery in the territories "in a few short days," but also that everyone would "bow submissively to the decision, be it what it may."[13]

In private circles, too, the *Dred Scott* case was the topic of considerable interest. Alexander H. Stephens wrote to his brother Linton that he hoped the Court would not evade a decision on the Missouri Compromise as it had done earlier. "I have been urging all the influences I could bring to bear upon the Supreme Court to get them to postpone no longer the case on the Missouri Restriction before them, but to decide it," he wrote. "If they decide, as I have reason to believe they will, that the restriction was unconstitutional . . . then the question—the political question—as I think, will be ended as to the power of the people in their Territorial Legislatures."[14] Two weeks later Stephens again wrote to his brother, saying that the coming decision would "have greater political effect and bearing than any others of the day. The decision will be a marked epoch in our history."[15] Stephens was not the only one who looked forward to such a great step. Robert J. Walker expressed to Stephen A. Douglas his hope, too, that the whole question of slavery in the territories at last would be settled by the Supreme Court. "Such a result," he expected, "would give renewed confidence, at home and abroad, in the stability of our institutions."[16] Whereas Stephens and Walker anticipated a decision declaring the Missouri Compromise unconstitutional, others hoped for an opposite result; significantly, though, most seemed willing to accept the decision and finally resolve this vexing issue.[17]

Public interest in the *Dred Scott* case intensified on January 1, 1857, when a Washington correspondent of *The New York Herald* reported that the Court had reached a decision, to be "formally announced in a few days by Chief Justice Taney." By a seven to two vote, McLean and Curtis in the minority, the Court would declare the Missouri Compromise unconstitutional. The next day, however, the *Herald* retracted its statement as a false rumor. Nevertheless both the unfounded rumor and its refutation found their way into the nation's press and kindled expectations for an early decision.[18]

Despite all this anticipation and speculation, nothing actually occurred until the judges met in consultation on Saturday, February 14. Perhaps they would have discussed it earlier, but on January 4 Justice Daniel's wife died in a tragic fire in the family home in Washington. Daniel suffered minor burns attempting to save his wife, and as a result of both his injuries and his personal grief, he was unable to attend Court until February 9.[19] Another reason for delay was the illness of Justice James M. Wayne.[20] But finally, on February 14, when all nine justices were available, they took up the *Dred Scott* case. It was discussed at a number of consultations, but exactly when is not known. Several, at least, occurred between February 14 and February 19, and one as late as March 5.[21]

The first question raised was jurisdiction. As it had earlier, the Court again divided on this issue, and in the same way. McLean, Catron, Grier, and Campbell held that the plea in abatement and Scott's citizenship were not before the Court and that the case should be decided upon its merits alone. Taney, Wayne, Daniel, and Curtis maintained that citizenship and jurisdiction had to be decided before going into the merits. Nelson again held the balance, and again he broke the tie. But in a reversal from his temporary stance earlier, Nelson now joined the McLean-Catron-Grier-Campbell group, providing a five-to-four majority—one that was *not* sectional, it should be noted—against discussing the plea in abatement and citizenship.[22]

This meant the Court would decide the case only upon the facts. A great deal of heated discussion ensued,[23] but finally a majority—although the evidence is not clear who constituted this majority—determined that the case could and should be decided without ruling on the constitutionality of the Missouri Compromise.[24] This would be done by upholding the decision of the lower court on two specific grounds. The first was the long-held principle that a federal court, called to pass upon a question involving state law, normally accepts that state supreme court's interpretation of the law. The second was the principle inferred from *Strader* v. *Graham* that the free or slave status of a Negro depended upon the law of the state where he was and not where he had been. In both instances, Scott's status depended upon the law of Missouri as interpreted by Missouri's Supreme Court in *Dred Scott* v. *Irene Emerson*. The Supreme Court would thereby avoid citizenship of Negroes and the constitutionality of the Missouri Compromise and instead decide the case on well-established, noncontroversial principles.[25]

To Justice Nelson was delegated the duty of preparing the Opinion of the Court. In assigning to him this responsibility, the Court instructed Nelson not to touch upon either the citizenship of Negroes or the constitutionality of the Missouri Compromise, to limit his statement very carefully to the particular circumstances of Dred Scott, and not to make any generalizations that might associate the decision with any partisan political doctrines.[26] It was understood that Nelson's statement would not be a unanimous Opinion of the Court, but that McLean and Curtis would dissent, with McLean writing a brief dissenting opinion for both. This dissent also would avoid citizenship of Negroes and the constitutionality of the Missouri Compromise and would argue only in generalizations that a slave became free and remained free by virtue of residence in a free territory.[27]

It was at this point that all the latent forces hitherto in the background now came to the fore. Considerable misunderstanding surrounds who precipitated the next action, although three justices have been accused—

McLean, Curtis, and Wayne.[28] Catron wrote on February 19 that "two dissentients" caused the majority to change its attitude and decide to discuss the questions of Negro citizenship and the Missouri Compromise.[29] According to Grier, in a letter he wrote on February 23, "it appeared that our brothers who dissented from the majority, especially Justice McLean, were determined to come out with a long and labored dissent, including their opinions and arguments on both troublesome points."[30] Campbell substantiated these charges when, in reminiscing over these events thirteen years later, he declared: "My impression is, that several opinions had already been begun among the members of the Court, in which a full discussion of the case was made, before Justice Wayne made this proposal."[31]

On the other hand, according to Curtis and persons conversant with him, it was Wayne, a proslavery Georgia Democrat, who was responsible for triggering the Court to reverse itself. "It was in vain," wrote George Ticknor Curtis, "that Justices McLean, Nelson, and Curtis, in the conferences of the court, explained in the strongest terms that such a result, instead of putting an end to the agitation in the North, would only increase it."[32] Wayne's biographer mentions two separate instances that support the contention that Wayne precipitated the action. He refers to Wayne telling Senator David L. Yulee of Florida, on the very day that this decision was made, that he (Wayne) had "gained a triumph for the Southern section of the country, by persuading the chief justice that the court could put an end to all further agitation on the subject of slavery in the territories."[33] Wayne's biographer also cites Congressman James M. Ashley of Ohio as quoting Wayne, who "so expressed himself to his friends, 'that if the Supreme Court could be brought to make a unanimous decision in the Dred Scott case . . . it would settle the question for all time to come.'"[34]

There is also a great deal of evidence that outsiders exerted pressure on the Court to invalidate congressional prohibition of slavery in the territories. Alexander H. Stephens, for instance, declared bluntly that he was "urging all influences [he] could bring to bear upon the Supreme Court" to decide on the Missouri Compromise, because he felt confident the Court would declare it unconstitutional.[35] J. Glancy Jones of Pennsylvania, a very close political and personal friend of President-elect Buchanan, deemed it of the utmost importance that the Supreme Court should decide "favorably" on the issue.[36] Buchanan himself was deeply concerned, and he corresponded with several of the justices in an effort to determine before his inauguration what the decision might be.[37] Montgomery Blair justifiably expressed to Martin Van Buren, as early as February 5, 1857, his fears that "outside pressure" was being placed on the Court to declare the Missouri Compromise unconstitutional.[38]

These conflicting accounts leave it unclear whether it was Wayne's new proposal that caused McLean and Curtis to write the dissents they did, or if it was McLean and Curtis who first determined to include the slavery issue in their dissent and thus precipitated Wayne into his action. But there is no question that influential partisan pressures were being exerted on the Court to declare the Missouri Compromise unconstitutional.

There is no question either that after Nelson had already begun to write his noncontroversial opinion, *Wayne proposed that the decision should include the two vital questions Nelson was omitting.*[39] Wayne also proposed that Taney write the Opinion of the Court. After a brief discussion a majority agreed. That a majority was so quick to adopt Wayne's proposal seems surprising offhand; but, according to Campbell, "the apprehension had been expressed by others of the Court, that the Court would not fulfill public expectations or discharge its duties by maintaining silence upon these questions." So once the idea had been broached, they agreed to it.[40] McLean and Curtis disagreed; Grier was undecided; and Nelson was ill and not even present at this critical consultation.[41] The remaining five, then—Taney, Wayne, Catron, Campbell, and Daniel—*the five justices who came from slave states*—formed the bare majority that now decided it could peacefully settle the slavery issue by declaring the Missouri Compromise unconstitutional. This was the turn of events that enabled Wayne to say he had gained not only a great triumph for the South, but also a very important point for the peace and quiet of the country.[42]

It is thus still not absolutely clear what precipitated this momentous change—the threat of the McLean and Curtis dissents or the Wayne desire to "gain a triumph" for the South. Although most historians have accepted the former, there is stronger reason to feel, as Allan Nevins suggests in his brief essay on responsibility for the *Dred Scott* decision, that much more than minimal responsibility belongs to Wayne.[43] It was he who proposed the change, and it was he who convinced Taney and Catron to go along. Without his prodding, the original, less provocative decision would have resulted.

Scholars have focused so much on McLean, Curtis, and Wayne that they have given little or no attention to others. Yet as early as February 6, more than a week before the first consultation, Catron wrote that even though Daniel was still distraught over the death of his wife, "that Judge will surely deliver his own opinion in the case, *at length.*"[44] "That Judge" was the most extreme proslavery protagonist on the Court. Nevins characterizes him as a "bigot" with a "fanatical temper" who referred to opponents of slavery as "monsters."[45] In fact, the sectional and anti-black diatribes in his opinion were far more racist than the widely publicized excerpts from Taney's opinion. If Daniel augured an opinion "*at length*," this could have spurred McLean and Curtis to reply. Could not Daniel, then, bear some responsibility for the Court's traumatic change of direction?

Nor can Chief Justice Taney be blameless. Of course he would take considerable abuse later for the contents of his opinion, but could he have forestalled that? Perhaps Taney did not take the initial step to change the Court's action, but he did not prevent it either. True, Supreme Court judges are—and should be—independent individuals; yet Taney, like John Marshall before him, had established an unmistakable leadership, and it seems reasonable that once the Court had decided on the safe Nelson route, Taney might have exerted appropriate leadership to keep the Court within the bounds of judicial restraint. Instead he needed very little prodding to go along with Wayne. His several biographers agree that the chief justice was intensely devoted to the South, that he saw the Court as perhaps the ultimate protector of southern agrarianism against northern "aggression," even if it meant adopting unpopular interpretations of history and law. Professor Don Fehrenbacher indicates that Taney's opinion in *Dred Scott* "was essentially visceral in origin—that law, logic, and history were distorted to serve a passionate purpose."[46] That "passionate purpose," according to Nevins, was "to bulwark his own people and their institutions," and "now was the moment, if ever, to strike a judicial blow for Southern rights in the Territories."[47] Taney even agreed to write a new Court opinion. Wayne, who proposed the change, could have written that opinion; in fact, he already had started one, but gladly deferred to the chief justice.[48] Indeed, Taney's acceding to the Wayne proposal may even have assured its acceptance.

What is incontrovertible, though—and this cannot be tossed aside lightly if one is looking to place responsibility—is that once Wayne made his proposal, the majority that approved it was purely southern and sectional—the five justices from slaveholding states. Theirs was the ultimate action that transformed what otherwise might have been undesirable but at least acceptable into what history records as the infamous *Dred Scott* decision.

These developments were known by very few persons. Among the few who did know was President-elect Buchanan. Ever since his election, Buchanan was plagued with the realization that the northern and southern wings of his party held conflicting interpretations of the vague popular sovereignty doctrine with which he had won the presidency, and both sides were demanding that he clarify that principle in his inaugural address. The issue was so divisive, however, that several prominent Democrats hoped Buchanan could avoid it. The Supreme Court might make the statement for him, they pointed out, thereby saving him from a politically risky statement.[49] Considering the "great object" of his administration "to destroy the dangerous slavery agitation and thus to restore peace to our distracted country," Buchanan agreed that a Court decision would achieve this end much more readily than any declaration he might make.[50] Accordingly, on February 3 Buchanan wrote his friend Catron, asking whether the Court would reach a decision before his inauguration. Catron replied on February 6 that the case had not yet come up in consultation, but he promised to let Buchanan know as soon as there were any developments. On February 10 Catron informed Buchanan that although the case still had not been discussed, he thought its decision probably would not help Buchanan. "Some of the Judges will not touch the question of power, and others may," Catron wrote, "but that it will settle nothing, is my present opinion." On February 19 Catron wrote again; but during this nine-day interval occurred the dramatic change in the Court's direction. Accordingly Catron now informed Buchanan that he could avoid any controversial statements in his inaugural address and "safely" say that the constitutionality of congressional control over slavery in the territories soon would be determined by the Supreme Court.[51]

Within the Court, meanwhile, extraordinary pressures were being exerted to influence individual justices. When Catron informed Buchanan that the Court would deal with the slavery issue, he indicated uncertainty about which way Grier would go on the constitutionality of the Missouri Compromise. "Will you drop Grier a line," Catron asked Buchanan, "saying how necessary it is—and how good the opportunity is, to settle the agitation by an affirmative decision of the Supreme Court."[52] Buchanan wrote to Grier, but unfortunately the contents of that letter are unknown, for no copy exists. But Buchanan must have said something convincing, for on February 23 Grier wrote back that now he would join the majority in declaring the Missouri Compromise unconstitutional.[53]

In fact Grier determined to go even further. He knew, from opinions expressed in the consultations, that the majority agreed on remanding Dred Scott to slavery, but that they disagreed on the reasons why. Nelson, for instance, thought it was because of the law of Missouri; the others believed it was because the Missouri Compromise was unconstitutional, regardless of the law of Missouri; and within that group, each had different reasons for the unconstitutionality of the Missouri Compromise. Grier feared that this lack of unanimity might weaken the majority decision, especially if the dissents were as powerful as he expected them to be. Grier had still another concern: if he and Nelson remained silent on the constitutionality of the Missouri Compromise (as they both contemplated doing), the division on that particular issue would be five southerners against two northerners. Fearing the repercussions of a geographic lineup, and knowing, too, that some southern members of the Court were preparing "rather extreme views," Grier sought to avoid a sectional decision and at the same time unify the Court's reasoning. He discussed this with Taney and with Wayne, and they came up with a possible solution: the chief justice should deliver the Opinion of the Court, as the majority had already decided he should, but the rest of the majority should merely concur with him without writing separate opinions. In that way, Grier hoped, "if the question must be met, there will be an opinion of the *court* upon it, if possible, without the contradictory views which would weaken its force."[54] In the end, though, Grier failed to influence his colleagues, for each eventually delivered his separate opinion. With the exception of Grier, who merely concurred in the opinions rendered by the chief justice and Nelson, each arrived at his conclusions by different means, just as Grier had feared.

Meanwhile, the air of expectancy became more and more pronounced. One correspondent described the situation as one of "great interest and some impatience."[55] On February 25, the *New York Daily Tribune* reported "with indisputable certainty" that the Court had definitely determined to declare the Missouri Compromise unconstitutional and to deny to Congress the right either to sanction or to prohibit slavery in the territories. Three days later the same journal declared that the decision

of the Court could be expected within a few days; and on March 2 it
repeated a similar notice.

But before the decision was announced, James Buchanan was inaugu-
rated as president of the United States, on Wednesday, March 4, 1857.
The ceremony occurred on the east portico of the Capitol, on a delight-
ful day, before a large crowd. Waiting for the festivities to begin, Chief
Justice Taney and the president-elect engaged in a short whispered conversation about the procedure of the ceremony; and when all was ready,
Buchanan repeated after Taney the oath of office prescribed in the Constitution.[56] Then the new president delivered his inaugural address. Buchanan had prepared his address very diligently, conferring with many
close friends and advisers. He had rewritten several drafts, and by the
time he arrived in Washington on the day before his inauguration he was
satisfied with everything except the portion about slavery in the territories. He spent March 3 at the National Hotel, conferring with friends
and advisers, and it was only that evening that he finally inserted the
final comments about the question then pending in the Supreme Court.[57]
As he read his inaugural address, Buchanan reviewed the question of
slavery in the territories, showing how the principle of popular sovereignty, the will of the majority, had been the basis for his party's victory
and his election. Then he came to that critical point, the differences between northern and southern views over the interpretation of that principle:

> A difference of opinion has arisen in regard to the point
> of time when the people of a Territory shall decide this
> question for themselves.
> This is, happily, a matter of but little practical importance.
> Besides, it is a judicial question, which legitimately belongs
> to the Supreme Court of the United States, before whom it
> is now pending, and will, it is understood, be speedily and
> finally settled. To their decision, in common with all good
> citizens, I shall cheerfully submit, whatever this may be.[58]

A great deal was written about Buchanan's address in newspapers all
over the country; but strangely enough, considering that the *Dred Scott*
decision was so eagerly awaited, there was very little editorial comment on

Buchanan's reference to it. Perhaps the most critical, as might be expected, was the *New York Daily Tribune:*

> You may cheerfully submit—of course you will—to whatever the five slaveholders and two or three doughfaces on the bench of the Supreme Court may be ready to utter on this subject; but not one man who really desires the triumph of Freedom over slavery in the Territories will do so.
>
> We may be constrained to obey as law whatever that tribunal shall put forth; but, happily, this is a country in which the People make both laws and judges, and they will try their strength on the issue here presented.[59]

On Thursday morning, March 5, the day following the inauguration, a large crowd assembled in the Supreme Court chamber, hoping to hear the decision in the *Dred Scott* case. Expectation had been stirred by the president's inaugural address as well as by rumor that the decision would be rendered that day. But the audience was disappointed; no decision was read. Instead, following the regular session, the Court met for a final consultation, and Taney read to his colleagues the opinion he had prepared. All the preliminaries were now completed. The news spread rapidly throughout Washington that the anticipated decision was about to be announced. Meanwhile, the aged chief justice remained in his rooms the remainder of that day making last-minute corrections and revisions. The following morning the Supreme Court rendered its long-awaited decision.[60]

PART IV

THE *DRED SCOTT* DECISION

Chapter 15

Taney:
Opinion of the Court

ON FRIDAY MORNING, March 6, 1857, the Supreme Court chamber was filled to capacity. Many were turned away because of the lack of space. The traditional "Oyez! Oyez!" opened the proceedings, and tension mounted as all nine justices solemnly took their seats. The chief justice announced prosaically that two cases already argued would be continued to the next term.[1] Then the clerk called *Dred Scott* v. *John F. A. Sanford*, and the chief justice began to read the long-awaited Opinion of the Court. He spoke for two and one-half hours, from 11:00 a.m. to 1:30 p.m., in a solemn voice that was very low and often "almost inaudible." The audience listened throughout with intense and profound attention, and although the chamber was crowded and uncomfortable, no one left until the chief justice had concluded.[2]

Whether Roger Brooke Taney's opinion was in fact the Court's opinion has been for a long time a matter of controversy. If an "Opinion of the Court" reflects the collective reasoning of the majority, valid questions can be raised about whose thinking and what majority Taney spoke for. Undoubtedly a majority concurred in the basic judgment that Dred Scott did not have the right to sue, and in that respect Taney did indeed speak for the Court. But beyond that, Taney's colleagues differed markedly in the reasons *why* Scott could not sue, and for none of those reasons was there an indisputable concurring majority. Indeed, within three months after the decision was announced, two prominent Boston attorneys, John Lowell and Horace Gray, published a widely read article in which they delineated with scholarly thoroughness a "box score" of which justices agreed on which issues.[3] Their analysis was followed by many others, some agreeing, some disagreeing, resulting in prolonged confusion for more than a century about exactly what the Court ruled.[4] Today, however, qualified analysts generally hold that Taney did not accurately reflect the reasoning of a majority and that his "Opinion of the Court" was in fact not that at all. Nevertheless the fruitless exercise of determining and analyzing what the Court "really" said has continued. It is time we recognize—if we are better to understand the passions that brought on the Civil War—that despite this controversy, Taney's opinion rightly or wrongly still has been viewed as the Court's opinion. In a sense, then, what the Court *really* decided is moot; more important is what contemporaries *thought* the Court had decided.

A further significant matter is that the opinion the chief justice read differed markedly from what was published in the official reports of the Supreme Court. Taney revised his opinion at least twice before it was published in May 1857 by Supreme Court Reporter Benjamin C. Howard. According to Court regulations, all opinions were to be given "forthwith" to the clerk to be recorded "immediately on the delivery thereof." This rule had never been stringently enforced and opinions were often revised before being officially printed. Invariably, though, changes were minor and did not affect the reasoning or principles in the opinions. But Taney's alterations may have been more extensive.[5] Taney later admitted to revisions, but he insisted they had no bearing on the principles he had enunciated in Court. He did not insert anything new, he maintained; he merely corrected "gross misunderstandings" and "misrepresentations" that the oral opinion had received in the press.[6] Yet shortly after the opinion appeared in its official form, Justice Benjamin Curtis wrote:

> I have no doubt of the correctness of my memory on this subject. I heard the opinion read twice—once in conference and once from the bench. I listened to it with attention and believe I know where and in what it was changed. These additions amount to upwards of eighteen pages. No one can read them, without perceiving that they are *in reply* to my opinion.[7]

Unfortunately there is no way to determine how accurate Curtis's observation was and exactly what changes the chief justice made. The original copy of the Taney opinion was later destroyed in a fire; and the Court did not then employ stenographers to record what was said.[8] The only contemporary record comes from those who were in the chamber on that day, and the fullest is an Associated Press account that was printed in newspapers all over the country in the next few days.[9] Being the only detailed record of the opinion until the official report was published several months later, this Associated Press dispatch was the basis upon which reactions to the decision were made all over the United States. How accurate the reporter was in hearing Taney's low and sometimes "inaudible" voice and in transcribing accurately what the chief justice said is impossible to determine. There is no dispute about the general principles; all agree on those. But in comparing the Associated Press account with the later official version, one finds discrepancies in phraseology that proved to be very important. Were they the fault of the reporter? Of an unidentified telegrapher or printer? Were these syntactical changes deliberate? Or, on the other hand, is what Taney was reported to have said actually what he did say on that fateful morning? Because the original opinion no longer exists, we shall probably never know. What is important, however, is what so many people believed Taney said; after all, there is much to the adage that history often is shaped not by what is the truth as by what is thought to be the truth.[10] Therefore, inasmuch as the first reaction of the country was based upon the Associated Press report, the following analysis and quotations are from that account, unless otherwise indicated, with the important revisions in the official published version indicated where they were made.[11]

This analysis does not intend to use twentieth-century moralism or historical hindsight to achieve some new or novel interpretation of the *Dred Scott* decision. An axiom of historical writing is that each generation of historians interprets events of the past through its own eyes. Unfortunately many modern historians, in their determined strivings for interpretive originality, too often have neglected the classic Von Ranke injunction to first narrate history as it actually happened (*"wie es eigentlich gewesen ist"*). If we are to understand why the *Dred Scott* decision contributed so much to the polarization that led to the Civil War, we must view it as the people of that time viewed it. We must read it as they read it, from the same newspaper reports they read, whether those reports were accurate or not. What is important is not how later generations analyze and interpret the contents of the Taney opinion, but what contemporaries read and what they thought and how they reacted. As Raoul Berger has written, quoting British historians H. G. Richardson and G. O. Sayles: "'We must learn, not from modern theorists, but from contemporaries of the events we are studying.' We should not impose 'upon the past a creature of our own imagining.'"[12]

American historical literature abounds with many lucid and scholarly interpretive analyses of the *Dred Scott* decision. Excellent though these are, they are markedly deficient on two counts. First, many writers tinged their interpretations with personal biases. They presented the decision not so much objectively as rather something either good or evil, depending of course upon their own views toward the issues. Second, all published scholarly legal and historical analyses and interpretations are based on the official version, 19 Howard 393-633—the *revised* version— not on the text that was read by the populace of 1857 and that was the basis for the initial, and often lasting, reactions to the decision. What is needed to correct those two fundamental shortcomings and to understand better the atmosphere of pre-Civil War America is an objective analysis of what the newspapers reported, augmented appropriately by the changes made later in the revised official version.

It must also be pointed out that the decision did not come as a great surprise. True, the Court could have avoided conflict by sticking to its original plan (the Nelson opinion); but once it decided to deal with the controversial issues, the outcome was not unexpected. Considering the makeup of the Court—a seven to two majority of southerners and moderate (on slavery) northerners—and especially in view of the Court's judicial record on slavery matters, the real surprise would have been had the Court decided favorably for Dred Scott. After all, as Professor Harold Hyman has posited, one of the tragic dilemmas of the nineteenth-century struggle for human freedom was that the proslavery forces did have the law of the land on their side.[13] In fact, abolitionists did not even wait for the decision. Anticipating its proslavery bent, their press launched its assault well before the decision was even announced and then merely intensified its attack afterward. It is almost as though abolitionists were trying to force a confrontation and the Court obliged. But what no one could anticipate was the reasoning and the wording the Court would use. Herein lies the unique significance of the press reports of what Taney said. Whether accurate or not, whether worded deliberately or unintentionally, the phraseology in the press reports completely transformed what some hoped the *Dred Scott* decision would accomplish. Instead of laying to rest the controversy over slavery, it brought to focus the explosive issue abolitionists were so eager to exploit— the place of blacks in white American society, or, as Taney so opportunely stated it for them, whether Negroes were "beings of an inferior order" with "no rights which white men were bound to respect." Even after wide-spread distribution of the revised opinion attempted to correct any mis-understandings of what the aged chief justice may or may not have stated, the damage had already been done: the blatant racism of the Taney pro-nouncement had already been openly broadcast, and this could not be undone. Even had the Supreme Court not expected to arouse both white supremacists and egalitarians, there is no question that this is precisely what did happen. Ironically, considering the nature of the times and the emotionalism of the slavery issue, these passions probably would have erupted anyway, as, of course, they did. After all, neither slavery nor racism was new; the hatreds they engendered had already for years been eroding American society. But there can be very little doubt that that eruption at the very least was hastened by the singularly questionable wording of the press accounts of Chief Justice Taney's "Opinion of the Court" in the *Dred Scott* case.[14]

Taney opened with a brief observation that the case had been argued at the previous term, but "owing to the difference of opinion existing among members of the court," it had been reargued "in order to give the subject more mature deliberation." Two questions had to be decided: whether the lower court had jurisdiction and, if so, whether the decision there on the merits was correct.

Summarizing the facts of the case, Taney turned to a discussion of jurisdiction.[15] Although the explicit adjudicative issue was Negro citizen-ship, implicitly involved was the racist creed injected earlier in the brief of Lyman D. Norris and in the majority opinion of Justice William Scott in the Missouri Supreme Court phase of *Dred Scott* v. *Irene Emerson*. Now, though, Taney approached the matter more legalistically, express-ing the unique doctrine of dual citizenship. (Taney had no way of know-ing, of course, that a later Court would exploit this concept, in the *Slaughterhouse* cases, to open the door for a century-long negation of civil rights of blacks.) There were two distinct types of citizenship, Taney declared, state citizenship and United States citizenship. Each state could establish its own qualifications for state citizenship, but being a citizen of a state did not *ipso facto* make one also a citizen of the United States. Furthermore, no state could confer upon anyone the rights of United States citizenship unless that person was entitled to those privileges under the Constitution.[16] The critical question here was whether the Constitution, in dealing with rights of citizens, included the Negro. To answer that question—and here Taney took a very narrow approach—it was necessary to determine who were citizens of the several states when the Constitution was adopted, for all persons who were then citizens of the states also had become citizens of the new national state.

Taney then posited that Negroes were not considered citizens of the states at that time. Starting with the Declaration of Independence, Taney maintained that "they were not recognized or intended to be included in that memorable instrument." The terminology Taney reportedly used to explain this point evoked perhaps the most acrimonious reaction associated with this decision:

> It is difficult at this day to realize the state of public opinion respecting that unfortunate class with the civilized and enlightened portion of the world at the time of the Declaration of Independence and the adoption of the constitution; but history shows they *have*, for more than a century, *been regarded* as beings of an inferior order, and unfit associates for the white race, either socially or politically; and *had* no rights which white men were bound to respect; and the black man might be reduced to slavery, bought and sold, and treated as an ordinary article of merchandise. This opinion, *at that time,* was fixed and universal with the civilized portion of the white race. It was regarded as an axiom in morals, which no one thought of disputing, and every one habitually acted upon it, without doubting for a moment the correctness of the opinion.[17]

There is no doubt that the chief justice was referring to public opinion at the time of the Declaration of Independence and the adoption of the Constitution. Yet one phrase was lifted from this excerpt, the tense of another phrase was transferred to it, and Taney was accused of saying that Negroes, under the Constitution, "have" no rights that white men were bound to respect. Incredulously, in the very newspapers where this accusation was made (Horace Greeley's *Tribune* being in the forefront), the phrase "had no rights" appeared correctly in the lengthy reprints of the Associated Press dispatch, but in the editorial commentaries it was made to read "have" no rights.[18]

It is very clear that the entire passage was devoted to describing public opinion at the time of the Declaration of Independence and the adoption of the Constitution. Nevertheless certain newspapers garbled the meaning of these sentences and accused Taney of speaking in the present rather than in the past tense. One can only speculate why they did this, but it raises legitimate questions about the credibility of a portion of the American press at a critical time in our history when truth and objectivity may have been subverted to self-seeking partisanship and political self-interest.

Whether as a result of these misrepresentations, or to correct a possible error in the Associated Press dispatch, or perhaps to change what he had originally actually said, Taney reworded this passage in the revised official version to read as follows:

> It is difficult at this day to realize the state of public opinion in relation to that unfortunate race, which prevailed in the civilized and enlightened portions of the world at the time of the Declaration of Independence, and when the Constitution of the United States was framed and adopted. But the public history of every European nation displays it, in a manner too plain to be mistaken.
>
> They *had* for more than a century *before* been regarded as beings of an inferior order; and altogether unfit to associate with the white race, either in social or political relations; and so far inferior, that they *had* no rights which the white man was bound to respect; and that the negro might justly and lawfully be reduced to slavery for his benefit. This opinion was at that time fixed and universal in the civilized portion of the white race. It was regarded as an axiom in morals as well as in politics, which no one thought of disputing, or supposed to be open to dispute; and men in every grade and position in society daily and habitually acted upon it in their private pursuits, as well as in matters of public concern, without doubting for a moment the correctness of this opinion.[19]

Taney then turned to history to support his position. Quoting the "life, liberty, and the pursuit of happiness" clause of the Declaration of Independence, he stated that these words "would seem to embrace the whole human family; and if used in a similar instrument at this day, would be so understood."[20] But, Taney continued, "it is too clear for dispute that the enslaved African race were not intended to be included," for this would be "flagrantly against the principles" the framers of the Declaration of Independence asserted. "They . . . knew that in no part of the civilized world were the negro race, by common consent, admitted to the rights of freemen. They spoke and acted according to the practices, doctrines, and usages of the day."

The status of the Negro was the same, continued Taney, when the Constitution was framed in 1787 and adopted in 1789. The preamble indicated not only the purpose of that document, but also for whom it was framed —"to ourselves and our posterity." That phrase, Taney maintained, meant only those who were citizens of the original states and their descendants, but did not include Negroes. He readily admitted that the Constitution did not specify that only white people were citizens; it spoke in general terms of *citizens* and *people*, without defining these terms. Nevertheless, Taney continued, there were two statements in the Constitution that indicated conclusively that Negroes were a separate class not regarded as citizens. One was the clause that allowed the importation of slaves until 1808; the other was the provision for the return of fugitive slaves. Thus the Constitution clearly recognized and sanctioned—in 1789 at least— the privilege of a master to hold property rights in his Negro slave. Obviously, the chief justice reasoned, the rights of liberty and citizenship that were conferred upon a master would not be granted equally to his Negro slave.

Taney maintained, furthermore, and in very broad terms, that just as the national government had not conferred national citizenship upon Negroes, neither had any states granted them state citizenship. (Curtis disagreed sharply, pointing out in his dissent that "all free native-born inhabitants of the States of New Hampshire, Massachusetts, New York, New Jersey and North Carolina, though descended from African slaves, were . . . citizens of those States . . . on equal terms with other [white] citizens.") Taney conceded that some state laws protected Negroes, but this was merely an exercise of the police function for the benefit of the entire state population and in no way indicative of a grant of citizenship to Negroes. On the contrary, said Taney, far more important than these few privileges was the fact that in no state did blacks have the right to bear arms, to vote, or to serve as jurors or witnesses in cases concerning white litigants.[21] He added, too, that every law of naturalization conferring citizenship was restricted specifically only to white people.[22]

On the basis of all these observations, declared the chief justice,

> . . . we have come to the conclusion that the African race who came to this country, whether free or slave, were not intended to be included in the constitution for the enjoyment of any personal rights or benefits; and make it the duty of the government to protect them as such. Hence, the court is of opinion, from the facts stated in the plea in abatement, that Dred Scott is not a citizen of Missouri, and is not, therefore, entitled to sue in the United States courts.

It is difficult to agree with Taney's conclusions regarding citizenship. There is no doubt—unhappily—that he accurately appraised the "place" of blacks in America at the time of the Declaration of Independence and the adoption of the Constitution. But the "place" of blacks in the social and economic structure of society is quite different from their "place" in the political or legal spectra of society. Taney's rejection of the undeniable fact that blacks had the right to vote in some states—especially slave states— is utterly appalling; it was a blatant falsification of the truth. After all, at issue here was not whether Dred Scott had the right to eat in the same restaurant or ride on the same vehicle as a white person—those "civil" rights that became the object of many Fourteenth Amendment and other due process litigations in later years. At issue, by Taney's own guidelines that the Constitution must be interpreted restrictively in terms of what it meant in 1789, was the irrefutable truth that in 1789 *some* states *did* allow *some* blacks to exercise *some* rights of citizenship. Yet Taney disavowed this completely. His subsequent denial of citizenship and jurisdiction must therefore elicit serious questioning and raise considerable legal doubt.[23]

Having declared that the Court lacked jurisdiction, Taney proceeded anyway to consider the case on its merits. According to the Associated

Press dispatch, as well as to all other contemporary reports, the chief justice launched directly into the merits without any explanation.[24] But in the revised official report Taney very methodically justified why this portion of his opinion was not, as he expected many would refer to it, *obiter dictum,* or extrajudicial. "There can be no doubt as to the jurisdiction of this court to reverse the judgment of a circuit court," he stated, "and to reverse it for any error apparent on the record, whether it be the error of giving judgment in a case over which it had no jurisdiction, or any other material error." The entire record of the case in the lower court had been transmitted to the Supreme Court, and "the correction of one error in the court below does not deprive the appellate court of the power of examining further into the record, and correcting any other material errors which may have been committed by the inferior court."[25] So justified, Taney proceeded to the merits and a discussion of the critical issue of slavery in the territories.

As is well known, one of the major controversies about this decision is whether what Taney said about slavery in the territories was *obiter dictum.* Many have argued that it was, many that it was not. One need only glance at any of the scholarly legal interpretations of this decision or at its numerous citations in later Supreme Court cases to recognize the enigma. In deference to Taney, he was not alone in discussing the merits after stating first that the Court lacked jurisdiction. Three of his concurring colleagues (Wayne, Daniel, and Campbell) did the same, as did Curtis in his dissent—and all under the "entire record" principle. Curtis at least concluded that the Court did have jurisdiction, and so no one ever faulted him for proceeding to the merits. Nelson, Catron, Grier, and McLean held that the plea in abatement was not even an issue; so their discussing the merits also could not be criticized. The debate has raged for more than a century, but Professor Kent Newmyer is correct in concluding that scholars by now generally agree that Taney was justified in going ahead on the "entire record" principle and that it therefore was not *obiter dictum.*[26]

After reading the agreed statement of facts, Taney declared that it raised two questions. The first was whether Dred Scott and his family were free in Missouri because of their residence at Fort Snelling. If they were not, Taney declared, the next question was whether they were free because of their residence in Illinois.

Taking up the first question, the chief justice pointed out that

Scott's claim to freedom by virtue of residence at Fort Snelling was based upon the act of Congress of March 6, 1820, which prohibited slavery in that portion of the Louisiana Purchase territory north of 36°30' not included within the boundaries of Missouri. "The difficulty which meets us at the threshold," he warned, "is, whether Congress is authorized to pass such a law under the powers granted to it by the constitution." Scott's attorneys had argued that Congress did have such a power; it derived from Article IV, Section 3, of the Constitution, which gave Congress the power to make "all needful Rules and Regulations respecting the Territory or other Property belonging to the United States." But, disagreed the chief justice, "this provision has no bearing on the present controversy. The power there is confined to the territory which then belonged to the United States, and can have no influence on territory which was acquired from foreign governments."

Taney thereupon reviewed the history of the land cessions made to the United States in the 1780s by the various states, maintaining that the only object of those cessions was to end existing controversies and to enable Congress to dispose of those lands for the common benefit. Furthermore, the Congress that accepted the lands did so as the agent for the thirteen independent and sovereign states, mutually associated for their own general welfare. Those thirteen sovereign states could govern the territory as they pleased. Accordingly, in 1787, acting as their agent, Congress enacted an ordinance prohibiting slavery in some of the territory belonging in common to all. This act was unquestionably within its powers and rights.

But, Taney continued, the situation changed when the Constitution was adopted. When the thirteen states dissolved the Confederation and surrendered a portion of their power to the newly created national government, they found it necessary to make some express provision that the new government could carry out the objective for which the western lands had been ceded earlier to the Congress of the Confederation. That objective, Taney declared, was to sell the land to pay the war debt incurred during the Revolution. However, before that land could be sold, government-owned military supplies began to accumulate and people began to emigrate there. It became necessary, therefore, for the new national government to be additionally empowered to do something about all this government-owned land and property until it was finally sold. This, Taney declared, was the purpose behind the "Rules and Regula-

tions respecting the Territory" clause in Article IV, Section 3, of the
Constitution—to give to Congress the authority to legislate with respect
to the *land*, so Congress could sell it and the public property on it to
pay off the debt incurred during the Revolution. But nothing in the Constitution gave Congress the authority to concern itself with the property
of any state or especially of any private individuals. On the contrary,
Taney maintained, the Constitution explicitly prohibited Congress from
any such action, for that same Article IV, Section 3, stated specifically
that nothing in the Constitution was to be so construed as to prejudice
any claims of the United States *"or of any particular State."* Hence, the
chief justice declared, whereas the Congress of the Confederation, as the
agent of thirteen sovereign states, could legislate with regard to slavery in
the common territories, the Congress under the Constitution, whose
powers were expressly delegated and limited by that document, did not
have the power to do so. When, therefore, in 1789 Congress reaffirmed
the Northwest Ordinance, it had the authority, under Article IV, Section 3,
to approve those sections that applied to the land and public property
in the Northwest Territory, but it did not have the constitutional power
to legislate over slaves that were private property. Thus, concluded Taney,
Article IV, Section 3, could not be the authority for Congress to prohibit slavery in the Louisiana Purchase territory north of $36°30'$.

Taney then turned to the power of Congress over territories acquired
since 1789, which of course included the Louisiana Purchase territory.
Although the Constitution did not stipulate the powers that Congress
might exercise over territory, there was no doubt that territory could be
acquired and that the ultimate goal was co-equal statehood. In the
interim, however, some sort of territorial government was necessary. But
since the Constitution did not specify what form that government should
be, that had to be left to the discretion of Congress. But in using this
discretionary power Congress still was restricted by explicit limitations
with regard to persons and private property. For instance, Congress could
not pass any law violating personal rights protected in the Bill of Rights,
such as freedom of religion or freedom of speech. But also in the Bill
of Rights were specified the rights of property—that Congress cannot
deprive a citizen of the United States of life, liberty, or property without due process of law. Expanding on the Fifth Amendment substantive
due process concept which Reverdy Johnson had expounded in his oral
argument, the chief justice maintained that this protection applied not

only in the states but also in the territories; after all, if Congress was prohibited from doing something, so was a territorial legislature created by Congress also prohibited from doing that same thing. It followed, therefore, that neither Congress nor a territorial legislature could pass any law depriving a citizen of his rights of property.[27]

But, asked the chief justice, was a slave property? If so, was he different from any other species or classification of property? To the first Taney answered "yes"; to the second, "no." The Constitution not only recognized the right of a master to his slave, but it also did not differentiate between slaves and other property. Indeed, Taney pointed out, property rights in slaves were even explicitly affirmed in the Constitution.[28] As a result, he concluded, neither Congress nor a territorial legislature could pass any law depriving a citizen of the United States of his rights in his slave:

> It is . . . the opinion of this court that the Act of Congress which prohibits citizens from holding property of this character north of a certain line is not warranted by the Constitution, and is therefore void; and neither Dred Scott nor any of his family was made free by their residence in Illinois [Fort Snelling?].[29]

Taney then very briefly took up the second question raised by the merits, whether Dred Scott was free by virtue of his residence in a free state, Illinois. Relying on *Strader* v. *Graham,* that a slave who resided in a free state was not permanently emancipated by residence there if he returned to a slave state, Taney concluded that when Dred Scott returned to Missouri, he was restored to slavery by the law of Missouri regardless of his status in Illinois.

Speaking for the Court, then, Chief Justice Taney declared that Dred Scott was not a citizen of the United States because he was both a Negro and a slave. He therefore did not have the right to sue in the federal courts. Consequently the lower court had no authority to adjudicate this litigation in the first place. It had therefore erred procedurally by deciding that Dred Scott was still a slave. The case would have to go back to the lower federal court for proper action, namely, the dismissal of Dred Scott's suit for lack of jurisdiction.

Chapter 16

Concurring Opinions

THE DECISION WAS BY a seven to two majority. Roger Brooke Taney's opinion, viewed as the Opinion of the Court, became the target of acrimonious criticism, and his Jacksonian judicial reputation, described as one that "had passed, for two decades, as a humanitarian concern for the poor against their commercial exploiters, and a consequent championing of regulatory state laws," now was viewed as "competitive sectionalism, a loyalty to the South which encompassed a scorn for the North."[1] Similar recriminations were directed at the majority for whom the chief justice spoke. However, because of questions raised about that "majority," it is necessary to go beyond Taney and to examine the concurring opinions. Did they actually concur? If so, in what?

It is not within the scope of this study to undertake a detailed legal analysis of the decision. To do so would duplicate what has been done many times and transcend the purpose to unravel the unique history of this remarkable litigation.[2] Nevertheless, the curtain cannot come down without at least a brief summary of the other opinions to determine wherein they compromised the "majority" that Taney spoke of.

As soon as the chief justice concluded, Samuel Nelson delivered his concurring opinion. It will be recalled that the Court first had decided not to discuss citizenship or the constitutionality of the Missouri Compromise, and that Nelson had been designated to write the Opinion of the Court. Then the Court reversed itself. Having already written that opinion, Nelson submitted it—even retaining the pronoun *we* throughout—as his concurring opinion. He thereby avoided the controversial issues and more than any of his colleagues demonstrated judicial restraint to steer clear of the political passions of the time.[3]

Justice Samuel Nelson had come to the Court in 1845 under tangled political circumstances that did little to enhance the prestige of that body. When Associate Justice Smith Thompson died in 1843, President John Tyler proposed at least six others before the choice finally fell, almost by default, to Nelson. Yet Nelson brought to the Court a broad and extensive knowledge of commercial and admiralty law, having been for fourteen years on the highest tribunal of New York, the last seven as its chief justice. His judicial record on slavery and other matters has led Professor Frank Gatell to describe Nelson as a "constitutionally conservative northern Democrat." In light of that record Nelson's stance in the *Dred Scott* case was not unpredictable.[4]

In contrast to the lengthy and detailed Associated Press report of Taney's opinion, the account of Nelson's was a brief summary of the main points. There is no reason to believe that Nelson revised his opinion materially, if at all, after it was read; the official published version agrees with the principles reported by all correspondents who were present. What follows, therefore, is based upon Nelson's opinion as it appears in the published Supreme Court Reports.[5]

Nelson pointed out that the Court had quickly dismissed the plea in abatement. "In the view we have taken of the case," he stated, "it will not be necessary to pass upon this question, and we shall therefore proceed at once to an examination of the case upon its merits." This, of course, had been the Court's attitude when Nelson wrote the opinion, but obviously not when he read it.

The first issue, Nelson proceeded, was whether Scott was free in Missouri by virtue of his residence in Illinois. "The question is one which belongs to each State to decide for itself," Nelson asserted, and "except in cases where the power is restrained by the constitution of the United States, the law of the State is supreme over the subject of slavery within its jurisdiction." Citing *Strader* v. *Graham,* Nelson adhered to the principle that federal courts follow the interpretation of state law as interpreted by the state itself. The Supreme Court of Missouri, he continued, in *Dred Scott* v. *Irene Emerson*, had clearly indicated what the law was with regard to slaves returning to Missouri after living in a free state.

If Scott was not free by virtue of residence in Illinois, what was the effect of his residence at Fort Snelling? Without broaching the constitutionality of the Missouri Compromise, Nelson declared that *Strader* v. *Graham* applied here, too: Scott's status in Missouri after living in free territory also depended upon Missouri law. Again Nelson returned to *Dred Scott* v. *Irene Emerson* as the precedent the federal courts were "bound to follow." Dred Scott was still a slave, then, because Missouri law said so. On both counts Nelson had avoided any controversial issues—and this, it is worth noting, is what would have been a bland and probably widely unnoticed *Dred Scott* decision had not the developments in conference changed the course of history.

When Nelson concluded, Justice John Catron read his concurring opinion. Appointed to the Court in 1837 on the last day of his term by Andrew Jackson (and confirmed only a few days later in Martin Van Buren's administration), Catron had served under Old Hickory in the War of 1812 and later became chief justice of the highest court in Tennessee. A moderate on states' rights, Catron had been a strong ally of Jackson's in the struggles against nullification and the bank, and on the bench he wrote numerous opinions favorable to Jacksonian policies. Historian Frank Gatell describes Catron as even more a "Jacksonian jurist" than Taney. Like fellow Tennesseean Andrew Johnson, Catron would later remain loyal to the Union even though his state would secede, and for it he would suffer the agony of being driven from his home in Nashville by a local citizens' committee. On judicial problems concerning slavery, Catron consistently upheld federal authority, but insisted as a proper Jacksonian that state laws should stand as long as they did not conflict with federal statutes.[6]

After reviewing the facts of the case, Catron guardedly rebuked his colleagues for going into the merits after having apparently first declared that the Court lacked jurisdiction. He, though, would not even discuss citizenship and jurisdiction; they were not at issue.

According to all contemporary reports, those were the opening remarks Catron read aloud in Court.[7] But in his revised published opinion, Catron eliminated his chastising comments. He now stated simply that the question of jurisdiction was not, in his opinion, before the Court for review, and that therefore he would discuss the merits only. Exactly why Catron made this change is not indicated; one might surmise that it was to eradicate from the record a statement some might seize upon to add to the already mounting criticism of the Court. This was the only major alteration, for all contemporary reports about Catron's opinion, brief though they were, coincided with the principles contained in the final printed version. Consequently, the analysis that follows is based upon the much more detailed revised opinion as published in the Supreme Court Reports.[8]

The first issue, said Catron, was whether Scott was free by virtue of residence in Illinois. Catron disposed of this briefly, stating that even if Scott had acquired freedom in that state, he remanded to slavery upon his return to slave soil. He did not cite precedents; he referred instead to the opinion just read by Nelson "with which I not only concur, but think his opinion is the most conclusive argument on the subject within my knowledge." (Curiously he did not similarly applaud Taney's legal reasoning, perhaps because of their difference over jurisdiction.)

The next question, continued Catron, was whether Scott was free by residence where slavery had been prohibited by the Missouri Compromise. First, though, it was necessary to determine whether Congress even had the power to enact such a prohibition. No, said Catron, because it violated the treaty by which the United States had acquired the Louisiana Purchase. The crucial point here was the sanctity of contractual obligations, a point on which Catron had maintained judicial consistency. Congress clearly had the authority to govern the territories, Catron agreed, but that authority was limited by any contractual obligations between the United States on the one hand and the sovereign power that ceded that territory on the other. Thus Congress could prohibit slavery in the territory north of the Ohio River, but at the same time could not interfere with slavery in the territory to the south. (In both instances the ceding powers were sovereign states under the Articles of Confederation.) As to the territory west of the Mississippi River, the same principle demanded the honoring of Article 3 of the act of cession of the Louisiana Purchase: that until an area achieved statehood, no law could deprive the people there of their property—and slave property was widely prevalent.

According to Catron, then, Dred Scott was still a slave for two reasons: first, because as Nelson had held, Missouri law said so; and second, because the Missouri Compromise slavery prohibition that purportedly had freed him was instead an unconstitutional assumption of power by Congress and therefore null and void—all this after having stated first (although it was expunged from the final printed version) that the Court had already agreed that it lacked jurisdiction.

The Taney, Nelson, and Catron opinions were the only ones read on Friday, March 6, because of their cumulative length. The remaining opinions, both concurring and dissenting, were left for the following day. But suddenly a procedural dispute erupted. The justices had agreed earlier that all concurring opinions would be delivered first, and the dissents would follow. Campbell and Daniel now proposed a change. They wanted to speak last, according to the correspondent of the *Boston Evening Transcript,* so they could refute statements they expected McLean and Curtis to expound. McLean and Curtis objected, and a special meeting was called for Saturday morning, March 7, just before the opening of Court. Exactly how much dissension existed over this issue is not clear; obviously it was settled in that one morning. When the Court convened—before another packed throng—McLean was first on the agenda, followed by Curtis. They took five hours. The remaining opinions of Wayne, Grier, Daniel, and Campbell, already written out, were merely filed as concurring opinions.[9] Since they were not presented orally, there is no contemporary account of what they "said," except for very brief one-or-two sentence generalizations that they concurred with the chief justice.[10] The only record of those four opinions, therefore, is what appears in the official printed Supreme Court Reports, from which the following analyses are made.

Justice James Moore Wayne's opinion was very short. Indeed, in view of his role in projecting political issues into the final decision, his opinion is more a justification of that action than the legal dissertation one might expect from a Supreme Court opinion. Yet Wayne was anything but a fire-brand Southern states' rights radical. The plantation-bred, Princeton-educated Georgia judge and Congressman was an ardent Democratic unionist. A stalwart backer of Jackson in both the nullification and bank issues, Wayne's principles and practices made him popular with Jacksonians and earned for him wide support for appointment to the Supreme Court in 1835, even before Taney. The last survivor of the Marshal Court, Wayne remained on the bench throughout the Civil War, loyal to the Union to the day he died in 1867. Although advocates of extreme states' rights often accused him of abandoning "southern" principles, they had no quarrel with him on questions involving the black man and slavery. As state and national legislator and judge, Wayne consistently held to his convictions of the inferiority of the black man and of the property rights of slaveholders. (By the mid-1850s Wayne had sold his plantation, but still owned nine slaves.) So staunch were his views on slavery that one writer has even suggested that Wayne may have written certain portions of Taney's opinion. The allegation lacks verification; but there never was any doubt about Wayne's attitude toward blacks and slavery.[11]

Wayne declared at the very outset that he concurred entirely with the opinion read by the chief justice, "without any qualifications of its reasoning or its conclusions." In fact, the opening sentence reveals that Wayne had prepared a much fuller opinion dealing at length with the issues, "prepared when I supposed it might be necessary and proper for me to do so." But in light of what Taney had propounded, Wayne stated, it was no longer necessary to file that opinion.[12] He especially supported Taney in deciding on the merits after having first declared against jurisdiction. The Court had to dispose of the citizenship question first because that was the only way to determine jurisdiction. But even if the Court decided it did not have jurisdiction, Wayne argued, the record had already come up; and if an error was discovered in any part of the record, the Court was obliged to correct it. There was an error—the lower court should have decided on the merits against jurisdiction rather than remand Scott to slavery by the law of Missouri—and the appellate court was justified in correcting that error. Hence, Wayne concluded, Taney was correct on the merits as well as on the questions raised in the plea in abatement.[13]

Justice Robert Cooper Grier presented the shortest opinion of all. Appointed to the Court by President James Knox Polk (after James Buchanan had turned down the "Pennsylvania" seat for the third time), Grier was a conservative Democrat whose judicial attitude toward slavery is described by historian Frank Gatell as "conform[ing] to the standard pattern of most northern Democrats of his era": toleration of (although not necessarily favoring) slavery where established by law, support of federal fugitive slave laws, and noninterference with legal state slave authority. Grier's relative pedestrian service on the Court ended in 1870 when he finally yielded to a combination of liberalized retirement benefits and repeated requests by his colleagues that he resign. Testimony to his bequest to American jurisprudence is the fact that he is probably best remembered, along with his *Prize Cases* opinions (1863), for the singular circumstances leading to his retirement and for the role he played, along with Catron, in leaking to President-elect Buchanan information about the *Dred Scott* decision before the Court's public announcements.[14]

Without giving any reasons, Grier merely stated that he concurred in Nelson's conclusion that Dred Scott was still a slave because Missouri law said so. Grier then stated, again without comment, that he concurred with Taney that the slavery prohibition of the Missouri Compromise was unconstitutional and that Dred Scott therefore could not sue in the federal courts as a citizen of Missouri. He indicated also that it made no difference whether the judgment of the lower court was affirmed or if the case was ordered dismissed for want of jurisdiction, for in either event the effect upon the parties would be the same. Grier naively overlooked the considerable differences in legal ramifications.[15]

Justice Daniel's concurring opinion was filed next. Peter Vivian Daniel was appointed to the Court by President Martin Van Buren. The last of the "Jacksonians" to be appointed, Daniel long had been an active and powerful member of the "Richmond Junto" (Virginia's ruling Democratic elite), abetted no doubt by his marriage in 1810 to Lucy Randolph, daughter of the famed Edmund Randolph. Several decades as a successful lawyer-politician in Virginia, during which time Daniel emerged as one of that state's leading Jacksonian Democrats, culminated first in a lower-court judgeship (1835) and finally, in the waning days of Van Buren's administration, in appointment to the Supreme Court (1841). Daniel came to the court the product of the New York-Virginia political axis that long had advocated Jeffersonian Republicanism and Jacksonian Democratic unity. But during the 1840s and 1850s, as slavery became more and more a political issue, Daniel withdrew into a position of rabid Southern sectionalism. He became "the Court's extreme agrarian, the sworn enemy of consolidation, corporations, and banks; the extreme sectionalist and radical partisan in the slavery question."[16] One could anticipate that his opinion in *Dred Scott* would contain highly partisan proslavery doctrine. It did.

Disagreeing with Nelson, Catron, and Grier, Daniel denied that Sanford had waived jurisdiction by answering over to the merits. He asserted, as Wayne had, that the entire record of a case was open for review.[17] Daniel proceeded, therefore, to examine the citizenship of Negroes and their right to sue in the courts of the United States. The crux of his argument matched or surpassed Taney's for blatant racism:

> ... that the African Negro race never have been acknowl-
> edged as belonging to the family of nations; that as amongst
> them there never has been known or recognized by the in-
> habitants of other countries anything partaking the character
> of nationality, or civil or political polity; that this race has
> been by all the nations of Europe regarded as subjects of
> capture or purchase; as subjects of commerce or traffic; and
> that the introduction of that race into every section of this

country was not as members of civil or political society, but as slaves, as *property* in the strictest sense of the term.[18]

Even though a Negro slave had been manumitted, Daniel continued, his freedom did not qualify him as a citizen of the United States. Any individual state, if it desired, might so recognize that black person, but that did not make him a citizen of the national state. That, Daniel asserted, existed only with those who were "peers" in forming the new government in 1789, and neither black freemen nor black slaves were considered the equal of the white man when the Constitution was framed. As a result, he concluded, Negroes were not and could not be citizens of the United States.

At this point, Daniel explained, the normal procedure would be to dismiss the case for want of jurisdiction and disregard the merits completely. But, he continued,

> . . . as these questions are intrinsically of primary interest and magnitude, and have been elaborately discussed in argument, and as with respect to them the opinions of a majority of the court, including my own, are perfectly coincident, to me it seems proper that they should here by fully considered, and, so far as it is practicable for this court to accomplish such an end, finally put to rest.[19]

Daniel turned, therefore, to a review of the merits, with no further explanation why what followed should not be considered *obiter dictum*. The first question was whether residence in free Illinois emancipated Dred Scott. Daniel maintained that it did not. Rather than rely on the sounder legal principle of *Strader* v. *Graham* as others had, Daniel argued that a slave was an item of property, recognized as such by the law of the land, and he posited the questionable credo that a person's right to his property could not be removed by any law inferior to the national law. Furthermore, Daniel declared, again standing on shaky legal grounds, the law of an individual state applied only to the citizens of that state, but could not confiscate property of citizens of other states. He did not (or could not) cite precedential decisions, either state or federal, to support these extreme proslavery declamations.

The next issue raised by the merits, continued Daniel, was whether Scott was emancipated by residence in the Louisiana Purchase territory

north of 36°30'. To determine this, he explained, it was necessary first
to ascertain the constitutionality of the slavery prohibition of the Missouri
Compromise. Analyzing discussions in Congress when the Missouri Compromise act was passed, Daniel asserted that those legislators thought they
had the constitutional power to legislate only over land and public property, but not over the private property of any citizens. But they compromised that view, sacrificing constitutional principle for political expediency. A truly sound construction of the Constitution, declared Daniel
—echoing Taney's extreme proslavery doctrine—recognized that slaves were
private property protected by the Constitution, no matter where in the
national domain. For those who considered the reaffirmation of the Ordinance of 1787 a valid precedent for the slavery prohibition of the Missouri Compromise, Daniel maintained that it, too, was a violation of the
spirit and language of the Constitution.

Accordingly, Daniel concluded, the judgment of the lower court on the
merits—that Dred Scott was still a slave—was correct, because the Missouri
Compromise was unconstitutional. Where the lower court had erred was
in sustaining the demurrer. To correct that error "the decision of the Circuit Court should be reversed, and the case remanded to that court, with
instructions to abate the action, for the reason set forth and pleaded in
the plea in abatement," namely, that Dred Scott could not be a citizen
having the right to sue because he was a Negro of African descent.

The last of the concurring opinions was that of Justice John Archibald
Campbell.[20] Campbell was the junior member of the Court, having been
appointed in 1853 by President Franklin Pierce. Although he lacked judicial experience, he was widely reputed as an outstanding courtroom lawyer and expert in both civil and common law. Twice he turned down
tendered nominations to the Alabama supreme court. In an incident as
unique and self-assertive as it was unprecedented, the entire member-
ship of the Supreme Court wrote to Pierce, when a vacancy occurred in
1852, urging him to appoint Campbell, and Chief Justice Taney even
deputized Catron and Curtis personally to the president to convey that
sentiment. A strict constructionist of the Constitution vis-à-vis property
and contract rights, Campbell opposed secession in 1860-61 and was
one of the commissioners who attempted to negotiate a peaceful settlement of the Fort Sumter crisis. Failing, he resigned from the Supreme
Court and sadly returned to Alabama, where he reluctantly supported
his state in its futile struggle against the Union. As a member of the Taney
Court, Campbell was a strong advocate of states' rights, yet insistent

upon enforcement of federal law against filibusterers and slave smugglers. But his earlier expressions on slavery presaged what his opinion might be in the *Dred Scott* case: at the Nashville Convention in 1850, as Alabama's delegate-at-large, Campbell had condemned the Wilmot Proviso and hoped that Congress would recognize and protect the right of slaveowners to bring their slave property into federal territories.[21]

Campbell concurred at the very outset with the chief justice that Dred Scott was not a citizen and that the case should be dismissed for want of jurisdiction. But in contrast with Taney, it had nothing to do with Scott being a black man of African descent. "My opinion in this case," Campbell stated, "is not affected by the plea to the jurisdiction, and I shall not discuss the questions it suggests." His concern was whether Scott was entitled to freedom by virtue of residence in a free state or territory.

Campbell discussed first the effect of residence in Illinois upon the status of a slave. Citing numerous authorities, especially the Mansfield and Stowell decisions in the famous *Somerset* and *Grace* cases, Campbell declared that the only law that could affect a slave was the local law where he was then residing. In this instance, it was Missouri law, and according to it Scott was still a slave.

What of Scott's residence in Wisconsin Territory, under the law of the United States? Was that sufficient claim to freedom? Campbell disagreed. As had Taney and Daniel, Campbell stressed that slaves were property and protected as such. He dealt at length with Article IV, Section 3, of the Constitution, the provision authorizing Congress to make rules and regulations for the territories. Distinguishing between public property of the United States and private property of individuals, he maintained that Congress could legislate only over the former. He bolstered his argument throughout by detailing the overriding penchant of earlier generations for the protection and inviolability of private property, which, he maintained, always included slave property. Consequently, Campbell reasoned, the slavery prohibition in the Missouri Compromise, as well as any similar acts having as their basis the power of Congress to legislate over the territories, was a violation of the Constitution and therefore null and void.

As a result, concluded Campbell, Dred Scott could not have been freed by residence in Wisconsin Territory. Since slaves could not be citizens, Scott could not sue in the federal courts as a citizen of Missouri. The judgment of the lower court should be affirmed, therefore, on the grounds that it did not have jurisdiction.

Chapter 17

Dissenting Opinions

FOR ALL PRACTICAL PURPOSES the case was decided once the majority had spoken. But two more justices were yet to be heard, and their ringing dissents vociferously challenged the legal views and interpretations of the majority.

John McLean's dissent was the first to be delivered to the standing-room crowd on Saturday morning, March 7. McLean had been Andrew Jackson's first Supreme Court appointee, in 1829, an appointment intended to serve political as well as judicial purposes. McLean did not disappoint Jackson; he has often been described as the epitome of the politician on the Supreme Court. Born in New Jersey, he grew up in Ohio where he was elected to Congress in 1812. His record and associations bore considerable fruit, as his almost insatiable political ambitions led him to a judgeship on the Ohio Supreme Court and to appointments as commissioner of the General Land Office and then postmaster general of the United States. Devoted service and loyalty to Jackson culminated in McLean being named to the Supreme Court in 1829. He served there credibly for over thirty-one years, transposing into judicial credo much of the political democracy characteristic of the era. Most of the time he neither disguised nor abandoned hope for the highest political office of all. Four times he was a candidate for the presidency. As slavery and free-soilism grew into a political issue, McLean gravitated more and more toward a political posture that reflected his strong antislavery philosophy. Long before the *Dred Scott* case came before the Supreme Court, McLean's antislavery bent already was evident in *Prigg* v. *Pennsylvania*, 16 Peters 539 (1842), in *Jones* v. *Van Zandt*, 5 Howard 215 (1847), and in *Strader* v. *Graham*, 10 Howard 82 (1850).[1]

Because the Republican press was especially interested in what McLean was expected to say, it seems surprising that no detailed account of his remarks was reported as in the case of the chief justice. The Associated Press dispatches were but a scanty three paragraphs in length, summarizing McLean very briefly. (The same dispatches were equally brief on what Benjamin Curtis said.) But it soon became apparent why. Delivered on Saturday, March 7, McLean's full opinion was filed with the Court on Monday, March 9, to be printed officially. That official opinion, along with the other official opinions, was not published until May.[2] But on Tuesday, March 10, McLean's dissent was printed in full in the *New York Daily Tribune*, and within a few days it appeared in many other anti-slavery newspapers throughout the country.[3] Except for typographical and other minor word changes, McLean's opinion as it appeared in the press and in the final official printed version were exactly the same. The press did not get a copy from the Court; Roger Brooke Taney had given strict instructions to both Court Reporter Benjamin C. Howard and to Clerk of the Court William Carroll that no copies of any of the opinions were to be given to anyone without his (Taney's) permission.[4] Apparently there was considerable substance to accusations that McLean furnished an advance copy of his opinion to friendly newspapers so his views could be quickly and accurately spread throughout the country.[5] The following summary of McLean's dissent is based upon the official opinion as it appears in the printed Supreme Court version. It is the same text that appeared in the Republican and abolitionist press in the few days following the pronouncement from the Court, while at the same time all that was available of Taney's opinion was the inaccurate and much-to-be-revised Associated Press account.[6]

McLean dealt first with jurisdiction, even though he insisted it was not at issue. The decision of the lower court on the plea in abatement was in favor of the plaintiff Scott, he pointed out, and the only one who could appeal from this decision was the defendant Sanford. But Sanford chose instead to defend himself on the merits, and since that decision was in his favor, he had no reason to appeal. It was the plaintiff Scott who appealed to the Supreme Court, not to seek a reversal of the decision on the plea in abatement that had been in his favor, but to seek a reversal on the merits that was against him. Consequently, McLean held, any questions raised in the plea in abatement were not even applicable when the writ of error was issued.[7]

But even assuming that the plea in abatement could be reviewed as a part of the entire record, McLean maintained that there still was not sufficient reason to deny jurisdiction. The only grounds for refusing jurisdiction was Sanford's statement about Scott being a Negro of African descent. Never before had that been an acceptable reason. True, blacks had been disqualified from some privileges, but in none of those instances were blacks declared not to be citizens. McLean defined citizenship as being a "freeman . . . having his domicil in a State." (He tacitly conceded here that a *slave* was not a citizen.) Disagreeing with Taney, he maintained that citizenship derived from state citizenship, and any black person who was a citizen of a state also had the right to sue in the federal courts. Whether or not a Negro was an "agreeable member of society" was "more a matter of taste than law"; it had nothing to do with citizenship. Nor did Scott being "a Negro of African descent" have any bearing on his citizenship. There was absolutely no doubt that the Court had jurisdiction.

Turning to the merits, McLean listed six points that he considered to be the main issues:

1. The locality of slavery, as settled by this court and the courts of the States.
2. The relation which the Federal government bears to slavery in the States.
3. The power of Congress to establish territorial governments, and to prohibit the introduction of slavery therein.
4. The effect of taking slaves into a new State or Territory, and so holding them, where slavery is prohibited.
5. Whether the return of a slave under the control of his master, after being entitled to his freedom, reduced him to his former condition.
6. Are the decisions of the Supreme Court of Missouri, on the questions before us, binding on this court, within the rule adopted?[8]

McLean discussed the first issue rather briefly, punctuating it with numerous legal precedents. He denounced in very strong terms the common-law doctrine claimed by some that slavery was justified by usage or custom, and he maintained that slavery could exist only where it was authorized "by positive law of a municipal character."

On the second point, McLean declared emphatically that slavery was a state institution. Analyzing in detail the debates in the Constitutional Convention, he concluded that the Constitution construed slavery as a uniquely state-oriented institution. The only concern of the federal government was its obligation to enforce the fugitive slave provision in the Constitution. Otherwise, the protection or abolition of slavery rested entirely with the states themselves. If they wanted slavery, they could have it; if they did not want slavery, they could abolish it.

His stress on the local character of slavery was undoubtedly one of the strongest points of McLean's dissent. Yet it was not new. As Eric Foner points out, the "freedom national" principle of the Republican party had been expressed by McLean and others, especially Salmon P. Chase and William H. Seward, at least as early as the Buffalo Free Soil platform of 1848. It was what antislave advocates expected McLean to say, and he did not disappoint them.[9]

But what of slavery in the territories? As did Taney and Campbell, McLean went into considerable detail on the powers of Congress to "dispose of" and "make needful rules and regulations" for the territories as prescribed in Article IV, Section 3, of the Constitution. But where his colleagues focused almost exclusively on the protection of property rights, McLean elaborated on the nature of government and "sound national policy," punctuating his dissertation with supportive court precedents. From both philosophical and practical points of view, he concluded, Congress clearly had the authority to legislate over slavery in the territories, whether to protect it or to abolish it. The nature of government itself gave Congress the power to legislate; "sound national policy" determined whether that legislation should be to protect or to abolish slavery.

McLean next discussed the effect of taking a slave into a free state or territory, what happened when that person returned to a slave state, and how binding a state court decision was on the United States Supreme Court. He conceded that a fugitive slave could legally be recovered; but a slave who went into that same locality with his master's consent undeniably was emancipated by the local law of that free state or territory. McLean cited precedent after precedent in slave state court decisions, emphasizing especially the long string of Missouri rulings before *Dred*

Scott v. *Irene Emerson*. He analyzed in detail both the majority and minority opinions in that case, and decried a politically inspired decision that reversed many years of comity toward the laws of other states. Still the majority of the United States Supreme Court had accepted *Dred Scott* v. *Irene Emerson* at face value as the law of Missouri, and bolstered by *Strader* v. *Graham* had viewed it as the precedent they were "bound" to follow. McLean disagreed. He argued adamantly that *Strader* v. *Graham* did not prescribe that the Supreme Court should accept the interpretation of a state's high court. That decision, he insisted, had been to dismiss for want of jurisdiction; anything beyond that in *Strader* was *obiter dictum* and of no authority.[10] The binding principle instead was *Pease* v. *Peck* (18 Howard 555), only recently promulgated (1856), that the Court had to determine for itself which construction to accept if a state's highest court rendered conflicting interpretations.[11] For McLean, it meant accepting the long-standing precedents that *Dred Scott* v. *Irene Emerson* had purportedly overthrown.

In the course of his lengthy arguments that Dred Scott was free by virtue of residence in Illinois and Wisconsin Territory, McLean openly denounced what the majority had said on this subject as *obiter dictum:*

> Nothing that has been said by them, which had not a direct bearing on the jurisdiction of the court, against which they decided, can be considered as authority. I shall certainly not regard it as such. The question of jurisdiction, being before the court, was decided by them authoritatively, but nothing beyond that question. A slave is not a mere chattel. He bears the impress of his Maker, and he is amenable to the laws of God and man.[12]

It was an ominous and defiant paragraph, which would provide both legal and rhetorical grist for partisan attacks on the decision.

Immediately after McLean concluded, Curtis delivered his dissenting opinion. The scion of a heritage whose family lines went back to 1632 Puritan Massachusetts, Benjamin Robbins Curtis was educated at Harvard and was the disciple in both philosophy and law of the great Joseph Story.[13] A Daniel Webster nationalist and conservative Boston Whig, Curtis attained a reputation for legal excellence that merited his appointment, by President Millard Fillmore in 1851, to the "New England chair" of the Supreme

Court left vacant by the death of Levi Woodbury. Curtis served on the bench only until September 1, 1857, when he resigned because of differences with Chief Justice Taney over publication of the *Dred Scott* opinions, although there were other contributing factors. But in the six years he was on the Supreme Court, Curtis served with distinction.[14] His major contributions were in the field of commercial law, and his restrictions of "due process" to procedural limitations were to conflict with Taney's broader substantive interpretation. Although strongly opposed to slavery, Curtis stood up to derisive denunciations by New England abolitionists as "the slave-catcher judge" by his judicial courage in upholding the hated fugitive slave law. But enforcing fugitive slave legislation was different from accepting Taney's interpretations of the law in the *Dred Scott* case, and Curtis's vigorous and searing dissent left no doubts of his disagreement with the majority.

Like McLean's opinion, Curtis's opinion was lengthy;[15] the reading of the two dissents took about five hours. Also, as with McLean's remarks, no detailed account of Curtis's remarks was recorded, although numerous correspondents reported in general on what he said. On March 9, as did McLean, Curtis filed his opinion with the clerk of the court. But at the same time, in spite of long-time Court practice and Taney's specific admonitions to the contrary, Curtis gave a copy to a Boston newspaperman, and on March 11 excerpts began to appear in the *Boston Courier*.[16] The next day the opinion was printed fully in *The Boston Daily Atlas*. The following two days, March 13 and 14, it appeared in two installments in the *New York Daily Tribune* and then in others.[17] As with McLean's opinion, an examination of the newspaper accounts of the Curtis opinion shows them to be the same as the official version published later, except for insignificant typographical errors or minor wording changes. Thus, until the official versions were published in May, the general public had complete and accurate accounts of Curtis's as well as McLean's dissents, whereas all that was available of the other side was that much-to-be-revised Associated Press account of Taney's opinion and the extremely sketchy newspaper reports of the concurring opinions.[18]

Curtis dealt first with the issue of Negro citizenship.[19] Like a law professor lecturing his students, he discoursed on the technical aspects of a plea in abatement and a writ of error, concluding that "upon a writ of error the *whole* record is open for inspection," and if *any* error be found, the Court could reverse it.[20] Furthermore, if any litigant questioned a court's right to hear a particular case, that court was obligated to make certain that it was not overstepping its authority. The first issue in this case therefore had to be jurisdiction.

The specific substantive point, of course, was whether "a person of African descent, whose ancestors were sold as slaves in the United States, can be a citizen of the United States." The way to answer that question, Curtis declared, was to establish who were citizens of the individual states when the Constitution was adopted, because citizens of those states were also citizens of the United States. This was the same logic Taney had used; but Curtis's results were different. In a lengthy and detailed analysis of constitutional and statutory provisions, court decisions, and political practices in New Hampshire, Massachusetts, New York, New Jersey, and North Carolina, Curtis developed "in a manner which no argument can obscure, that in some of the original thirteen States, free colored persons, before and at the time of the formation of the Constitution, were citizens of those States."[21] Curtis did not contend that *all* blacks were considered citizens. At the same time, though, the plea in abatement had claimed flatly that *no* Negro of African descent could be a citizen. That plea was incorrect, Curtis maintained, because *some* Negroes could be and indeed were citizens. The judgment of the lower court overruling the plea in abatement therefore was proper, and the case should be decided on its merits.

Before going on to the merits, however, Curtis reprimanded the majority for their "grave assumption of authority," despite "all settled practice," in going to the merits after denying jurisdiction. "I do not hold any opinion . . . binding, when expressed on a question not legitimately before it." He did not use the term *obiter dictum*, but his meaning was clear. He, on the other hand, was perfectly justified in discussing the merits, for unlike the majority, he had concluded that the Court did have jurisdiction.

Curtis confined himself only to questions raised by Dred Scott's residence in Wisconsin Territory. The reason, he explained, was that Harriet would be included in any discussion concerning residence in the territory, whereas only Scott was affected by residence in Illinois.

Curtis looked first at the law of Wisconsin Territory. This led him into a pedantic dissertation on different kinds of slavery prohibitions: those that completely terminated a master-slave relationship; those that did not necessarily abolish that relationship but consisted merely in the absence of laws under which a master might control his slave (Stephen A. Douglas undoubtedly took note of this!); and those that distinguished between temporary sojourn and permanent residence. The law of Wisconsin Territory was the first type, Curtis asserted, effecting a complete break in the master-slave relationship between Dr. Emerson and Dred and Harriet Scott. Curtis rejected the notion that military personnel were accorded any unique interpretation of the law. Owning a slave was not a military obligation, and military personnel, even under orders, came under the civil law of the territory in a situation involving slavery.

But what happened when Scott returned to Missouri? Did Missouri have to recognize freedom acquired outside that state? No, said Curtis, it was not mandatory. But unless there was positive legislation instructing Missouri's courts otherwise—and there was none—"the will of every civilized State must be presumed to allow such effect to foreign laws as in accordance with the settled rules of international law." Curtis then analyzed in detail the "rules of international law" and comity vis-à-vis recognition accorded by one state to changes wrought by laws of another state and concluded that Missouri always had recognized freedom acquired under the laws of another state or territory.[22]

Nevertheless, Curtis continued, some of his colleagues had accepted a contrary view propounded by the Missouri Supreme Court in *Dred Scott* v. *Irene Emerson.* Curtis refused to accept that decision as policy forming. Using the same reasoning and citing essentially the same precedents as had McLean, and quoting at great length from Gamble's dissent in *Dred Scott* v. *Irene Emerson,* Curtis asserted that the established rule in Missouri was the long list of precedents before 1852 that showed comity to the laws of other states.

All of this, Curtis continued, was predicated upon the assumption that the law in Wisconsin Territory that emancipated Dred Scott was constitutional in the first place. An assumption, however, was insufficient; the validity of that law must be proved before it could have a binding force.

The basic factor here, Curtis asserted, was the source and nature of the power of Congress over the territories. In a detailed and scholarly analysis of Article IV, Section 3, of the Constitution, he examined the many views of congressional authority over territories as seen in legislation, acts of cession, and debates at the Constitutional Convention, and he concluded that Congress had unequivocal authority to legislate over the territories.

That still left one critical question unanswered: was Negro slavery an exception to the general power of Congress over the territories? No, asserted Curtis; nothing in the Constitution prevented Congress either from prohibiting slavery or from protecting it in the territories. Again adopting a pedantic and almost patrician attitude, he discussed the various views toward the power of Congress over slavery in the territories: the extreme proslavery position that slaves were property and as such protected by the Constitution; the theory of popular sovereignty giving the people the right to determine whether or not to have slavery; and the abolitionist stance that Congress should prohibit slavery as a social and moral wrong. Curtis dismissed these as political theories, having no weight of judicial precedence. The only proof he could accept was an express provision in the Constitution. There was none. In the absence of such proof, Curtis declared, no objection could be raised against the constitutionality of any act of Congress either prohibiting or protecting slavery in the territories. Sound law prescribed that Dred Scott should be free.[23]

Chapter 18

The Verdict

THE SUPREME COURT HAD spoken. But what had it decided? There was no common agreement within the legal profession, in the press, in the political arena, or in the nation as a whole. One reason was that it was not clear exactly what the nine justices had said. Four opinions had not even been read in Court. The only information the nation had in the crucial few weeks immediately following the decision was what was reported in the press. And what the press reported, especially in those journals that were doctrinaire toward slavery, and what the justices actually said, were not exactly the same.[1] The official versions were not available until May, and as pointed out, critical portions of some of the opinions as read in Court were revised or deleted before publication. Furthermore, even after the official version was published, there continued to be disagreement about what the Court really decided. What made this especially confusing was that Taney's opinion was viewed *a priori* as the Opinion of the Court, synonymous with its decision. But was it that?

The *Dred Scott* decision dealt with three major issues: (1) the citizenship of Scott and his right to sue in a federal court; (2) the constitutionality of prohibiting slavery in the territories, and especially the constitutionality of the Missouri Compromise; and (3) the effect on a slave of returning to a slave state after having lived in free territory. Only on the first is there no doubt what the Court said: seven justices, McLean and Curtis dissenting, agreed that Scott was not a citizen of the United States with the right to sue in the federal courts. Furthermore, all seven agreed that the reason he was not a citizen was that he was a slave. This was a clear and undeniable majority.

But beyond that there was considerable disagreement about why Scott was a slave. It is especially important here to differentiate between what Taney said in his "Opinion of the Court" and what a majority held. According to Taney, one reason Scott was still a slave was that he was a Negro of African descent, the point raised in the plea in abatement. That aspect of the case—Scott's color and ancestry—was involved only in the question of jurisdiction; it was never raised anywhere in the discussion on the merits. Of the majority seven, only Wayne and Daniel agreed with Taney on the plea in abatement. The other four—Nelson, Catron, Grier, and Campbell—disavowed the plea in abatement as an issue and did not even discuss it. McLean, of the minority, agreed that it was not before the Court, but he discussed it anyway to show that if it were, the Court still would have jurisdiction. Thus only four believed that Scott being a Negro even related to citizenship, and one of those four held that it did not deprive him of that citizenship. It is quite clear, then, that Taney's "Opinion of the Court" on that issue was not a Court opinion; it was the opinion of only three. Yet many incorrectly accepted it as the majority decision, abetted undoubtedly by a vociferous portion of the press that was quick to praise or denounce a "majority" that actually did not exist for having rendered a decision it in fact had not rendered.

Equally discomfitting is what the Court said about the constitutionality of the Missouri Compromise slavery prohibition and the effect on a slave of returning to a slave state after having lived in a free state or territory. These judgments were based upon a consideration of the merits. All nine discussed the merits in one way or another, some very fully and some, like Wayne and Grier, merely expressing concurrence with opinions expressed by others. Six—Taney, Wayne, Daniel, Grier, Catron, and Campbell—concluded that Dred Scott was still a slave because the slavery prohibition of the Missouri Compromise was unconstitutional; Nelson avoided the Missouri Compromise completely. Normally there would be no question that those six constituted a majority. But in this instance, three of the six—Taney, Wayne, and Daniel—had already declared that the Court did not have jurisdiction in the first place. A fourth, Catron, may have done the same, for although he held that the Court did have jurisdiction, he also averred that since the majority had already decided against jurisdiction, that should have ended the deliberations and the merits should not have been taken up; and then he proceeded to do so anyway. If, as Mc-Lean and Curtis and many others charged, these declarations against jurisdiction precluded further discussions, anything Taney, Wayne, Daniel, and Catron went on to say about the merits could be considered *obiter dictum* and of no legal binding force. Anticipating this charge, Taney, Wayne, and Daniel, at least, included in their opinions reasons why, having already declared against jurisdiction, anything they said further on the merits remained justifiable.

As is well known, one of the major controversies about the decision has been that *obiter dictum* charge.[2] That it may not have been justified (see below) is immaterial; what is important is that many believed it and that it was repeatedly made. Indeed, recent scholarship indicates that it even became part of Republican and abolitionist strategy attacking the decision.[3] Undoubtedly this strategy was facilitated by press accounts of Taney's opinion that reported him going into the merits immediately after finding against jurisdiction, without any explanatory remarks, for many could view this as arrogant declamation of extrajudicial proslavery doctrine from the bench.

But a careful reading of the opinion—whether the original Associated Press version or the revised official version—indicates that Taney's discussion of the merits was actually a continuation of his canvass of citizenship and jurisdiction. Having declared that Scott was not a citizen because he was a Negro, Taney then asked whether Scott might be a citizen anyway because of his sojourn in free territory. This led him to the examination of slavery in the territories. But throughout his inquiry the basic question still was whether Dred Scott was a citizen, and Taney's answer was in the negative. The final judgment said nothing about slavery in the territories. It stated instead that the Court lacked jurisdiction—because Scott was not a citizen for two reasons: first, because he was a Negro of African descent (based upon the plea in abatement discussion) and second, because he was still a slave (based upon the discussion of the merits). Thus, Taney's whole opinion focused on jurisdiction.[4] Unfortunately, though, he did not say so. What came through instead—and then only in the final revised opinion—was the "entire record" doctrine, that the Court could examine the territorial issue as part of the entire record forwarded from the lower court. This is what opened the door to the *obiter dictum* charge. Simply by refuting the "entire record" doctrine one could maintain that the decision violated fundamental procedural principles. Opponents could thereby challenge the decision and still champion the rule of law.[5] Had Taney stated explicitly that the entire opinion focused on jurisdiction, perhaps there may never have been an *obiter dictum* charge.

Thus the "entire record" principle became the focal point of the *obiter dictum* argument.[6] A few months after the decision John Lowell and Horace Gray proffered a veiled suggestion that Taney may have been canvassing jurisdiction throughout, but they still concluded that the issue was determined by the findings on the plea in abatement.[7] Aside from that one instance, those who discussed the *obiter dictum* issue focused primarily on the "entire record" doctrine. It was not until half a century later, in 1911, that Edward S. Corwin finally showed what analysts had theretofore overlooked, that Taney's discussion of slavery in the territories was indeed a canvassing of jurisdiction and therefore not *obiter dictum.*[8] Unfortunately, though, Corwin's landmark scholarship did not end the controversy. Scholars such as James B. Thayer, Frank H. Hodder, Richard R. Stenberg, Helen T. Catterall, and Don E. Fehrenbacher still argued *obiter dictum,* and Corwin found support from scholars such as Elbert W. R. Ewing, Horace H. Hagan, Charles Warren, and Carl Brent Swisher.[9] Some of the best scholars of the period, including Allan Nevins and David M. Potter, have deftly avoided the issue.

It is time at long last to lay the *obiter dictum* matter to rest.[10] It should suffice that the weight of legal justification supports the "entire record" argument. It should suffice that Taney's examination of the merits was a continuation of his canvass of jurisdiction. It should suffice that no known controlling rule of the Court barred a continuation on the merits, imprudent and impolitic though it may have been. Finally, only three justices had denied jurisdiction on the plea in abatement. That was far short of a majority. At that point, then, the *Court* had not yet decided against jurisdiction. If the Court was to render a judgment, it had no recourse but to go to the merits. And the Court still included Taney, Wayne, and Daniel. Being outvoted on the jurisdictional issue did not disqualify them from participating in a decision. Even if one argues that it did preclude their discussion of the merits, under no circumstances can that be applied to the other six, themselves a clear majority. Four of those six then decided that Scott was not a citizen and that the Court should not have accepted jurisdiction in the first place—but that came only after they had examined the merits. These four, added to the three who denied jurisdiction on the plea in abatement, for the first time formed a legitimate majority against jurisdiction. It was only then that Taney's assertion about Scott not having the right to sue accurately reflected the Court—but not because Scott was a Negro of African descent as only three judges had said but rather because he was still a slave as a majority of seven said.

Disagreement and misunderstandings may have existed over the "entire record" doctrine, but there should never have been any doubts about the process by which the decision was reached. Regardless of any other issues, the c rt had every right to go into the merits after a minority had failed to suppress the writ of error on the plea in abatement. The problem was created, however, by the substance of the ultimate decision on the merits—that the Court should not have had jurisdiction in the first place. It was precisely the legal enigma that Roswell M. Field and Judge Robert W. Wells had feared earlier (although in relation to the fugitive slave laws)—the problem created by determining only after the merits are heard whether or not jurisdiction existed in the first place. This is a legal quagmire from which often there is no escape and which by its very nature engenders conflict. The dilemma is compounded by the relative facility of an *obiter dictum* accusation.

So it was with the *Dred Scott* decision. The fact that the Court was correct procedurally in discussing the merits was distorted by the ultimate decision that it lacked jurisdiction because Scott was still a slave. Taney did not help in an "Opinion of the Court" that was misleading and inaccurate. N r did McLean and Curtis help by allowing their political biases about an admittedly reprehensible and abhorrent decision to overshadow the fact that at least the process by which it came about was valid and legal. The press, both prodecision and antidecision, contributed by its prejudicial and predetermined attitudes without becoming fully knowledgeable about what the Court really said and did. Above all, despite the pressures brought upon them, one must question the lack of judicial restraint and political acumen of those nine men on the bench for not anticipating the Pandora's box they were opening. American constitutional history records instances when the Court boldly forged ahead to new vistas; it records other instances when the Court astutely refrained from being drawn into issues that rightly should be determined by other political processes. Bernard Schwartz was too kind in calling it merely a "mistake" on the Court's part "to imagine that a flaming political issue could be quenched by calling it a 'legal' question."[11] It was not a mistake; it was a tragedy.

Nevertheless, if the Court was at fault, it can share the blame. If the disposition of slavery in the territories was an issue to be resolved by the political process, neither the nation nor Congress was able or even willing to exercise that function. Historians of the period have documented how considerable sentiment had been mounting, in Congress and in the public at large, that the question of slavery in the territories "should be left to the ultimate decision of the courts, . . . [that it was] a purely judicial decision" best solved by the courts.[12] Even Abraham Lincoln expressed that notion, although he shortly would be one of the severest critics of its outcome. "The Court's fault," writes Wallace Mendelson, "lay in accepting the buck which Congress and the statesmen had passed, and in failing to anticipate the partisan, political use which its efforts could be made to serve."[13]

Arguments of counsel also deserve attention. From the very beginning Roswell M. Field and Montgomery Blair had employed arguments, especially with regard to *Strader* v. *Graham,* to circumvent a jurisdictional question and virtually force the Court to deal with the merits. True, they did not consider the Missouri Compromise to be involved, nor was it at first. But once Sanford's counsel injected it into arguments, it is expecting too much judicial restraint for the Court to ignore it, considering the overpowering pressures for a judicial solution to the territorial question. Yet they still could have exercised that restraint; indeed, they were within the proverbial whisker's width of avoiding those issues. But they chose otherwise. The judgment of history is that they chose wrongly.

But that is the judgment of history, with the advantage of hindsight and more than a century of analyses of what the different members of the Court said. Unfortunately those benefits were not available in 1857. All that contemporaries had were the distorted press reports of Taney's opinion and the full reports of McLean's and Curtis's dissents, including their denunciations of purported *obiter dicta.* Even though all the official opinions were published fully only two months later, the damage was done. If scholars have been in disagreement for so long, is it any wonder that contemporaries found it difficult to comprehend or agree?[14]

Thus we find that of the six who declared the Missouri Compromise unconstitutional, the validity of what three said—Taney, Wayne, and Daniel—was challenged as *obiter dictum.* Two—Grier and Campbell—maintained throughout that the plea in abatement was not before the Court; they did not confound their conclusions by a prior disclaimer on citizenship, and so even their harshest critics conceded their right to discuss the constitutionality of the Missouri Compromise on the merits. Catron could have been placed in either group; he reached his decision on the merits alone, as did Grier and Campbell, but only after having acknowledged that the Court lacked jurisdiction, as did Taney, Wayne, and Daniel. But because he did not actually discuss the plea in abatement and did not declare against jurisdiction on that point, he is logically grouped with Grier and Campbell. Of the remaining three, Curtis and McLean concluded that the Missouri Compromise was constitutional and legal; Nelson said nothing about it one way or the other. Thus, that two (or three, if we count Catron) declared the Missouri Compromise unconstitutional could not be denied; but that *six*—a majority—had done so was widely and vociferously disputed. That dispute need no longer exist. Substantively the Court committed an infamous error in failing to exercise a restraint that could have avoided those explosive issues. In procedural terms, however, there was no *obiter dictum*; the Court properly spoke to the merits when it declared the Missouri Compromise unconstitutional.

Similar misunderstanding presents itself in the decision that a slave who was emancipated by residence in free territory nevertheless was remanded to slavery when he returned to a slave state. This was the conclusion on the merits by seven justices, McLean and Curtis dissenting. Three of the seven—Nelson, Grier, and Campbell—held that Scott be remanded to slavery according to Missouri law, in spite of having been freed by Illinois law, because that was the interpretation by the Missouri Supreme Court in *Scott* v. *Emerson*. Those three based their decision upon the merits alone; to them the issue of jurisdiction was not even before the Court, and their conclusions on the merits were not challenged. But three more—Taney, Wayne, and Daniel—reached the same conclusion on the merits only after having first denied jurisdiction on the plea in abatement. Catron, as seen, might be placed in either group, although more probably with the first. Were any of these *obiter dicta*? Again, as in the instance of the Missouri Compromise, there has been considerable disagreement. That three (or four, if Catron is included) made a legitimate decision on this issue could not be disputed; but that it could also be considered a valid decision for Taney, Wayne, and Daniel, thus forming a majority of seven, was a matter of controversy. As seen, though, a discussion of the merits was in order once the Court lacked a majority against jurisdiction, and the charge of *obiter dictum* cannot hold.

To many contemporaries, though, the only indisputable principle the Court declared was that slaves could not be citizens of the United States, a principle, incidentally, that was not even necessary because no one had claimed that slaves were citizens. The validity of the other declarations about the citizenship of Negroes, about the constitutionality of the Missouri Compromise, and about the effect of living in a free state or territory upon a slave who returned to a slave state—those were widely disputed. Substantively they were reprehensible to the concept of human equality; but legally they were not *obiter dicta*. They were now, sadly, the law of the land.

But they had become the law of the land in a unique way and time. They were declared by the Supreme Court, not by the elected representatives of the people. Considering the composition of the Court, any expectation for a reversal was futile. Considering the political picture in Congress and the states, prospects for legislative reversal were extremely thin. Considering the time and the bitter divisiveness of the long-standing and discordant slavery issue, the *Dred Scott* decision now left little hope to those who were determined to end slavery in the United States. The proslavery forces clearly had the law of the land on their side, with the way now open, perhaps, to legalize slavery everywhere. What before had been no more than stump and pulpit antislavery rhetoric now loomed as an appalling probability. As posited by Eric Foner and others, Republicans and abolitionists now became convinced that a "slave power conspiracy" was forcing slavery onto the entire nation, with "slavery national" overwhelming "freedom national."[15] Despite the efforts of calmer heads, unless one side or the other gave in—and there was no indication of this— *Dred Scott* would propel the nation perceptibly closer to the tragedy of 1861.

The official judgment of the Supreme Court said nothing about these controversial issues. Based upon the concurrence of a majority of seven justices that Dred Scott was not a citizen having the right to sue in the federal courts, Chief Justice Taney issued the following ruling at the conclusion of his Opinion of the Court:

> [I]t is now here ordered and adjudged by this court that the judgment of the said Circuit Court in this cause be and the same is hereby reversed for the want of jurisdiction in that court, and that this cause be and the same is hereby remanded to the said Circuit Court with directions to dismiss the case for the want of jurisdiction.[16]

But the federal court in St. Louis never did dismiss the case because a mandate ordering it to do so never was issued by the Supreme Court.[17] Considering the nationwide notoriety of the litigation, the reason the Court did not issue the mandate seems ludicrous; it was simply that the court costs were not paid. A rule of the Supreme Court provided that no mandate implementing its decision would be issued until all the costs were taken care of.[18] On May 11, 1857, Montgomery Blair paid costs amounting to $63.18 charged to the plaintiff-in-error Dred Scott.[19] That money was furnished to Blair by Gamaliel Bailey, editor of the Washington, D.C., *National Era,* who had assured Blair back in 1854 that he, Bailey, would provide the money necessary for the incidental expenses incurred during the litigation. Bailey, in turn, had solicited $2.00 each from seventy-five Republican members of Congress, and he contributed the remainder, to pay the $63.18 for the court costs and $91.50 for the printing of briefs, a total of $154.68.[20] But the costs charged to the defendant-in-error John F. A. Sanford, amounting to $29.97½, never were paid. A bill for that amount was sent to Henry S. Geyer on April 29, 1857, but neither Geyer nor anyone else paid it.[21] Why is not known. The court costs not being paid, the Supreme Court never issued its mandate to the lower court, and the lower court, therefore, did nothing. Indeed, the original verdict of the Circuit Court of the United States for the District of Missouri, rendered on May 15, 1854, and then appealed to the Supreme Court of the United States, remains unchanged to this day in the records of that lower federal court. Furthermore, neither were the court costs ever paid there.[22]

But in the Circuit Court of St. Louis County, the state court where Dred Scott had originated his legal battles on April 6, 1846, and where his litigation had been continued since 1852 pending the outcome of the suit in the federal courts, the original case of *Dred Scott* v. *Irene Emerson* was finally closed out. On March 18, 1857, less than two weeks after the United States Supreme Court announced its decision, the following notation was made in the records of the Circuit Court of St. Louis County:

> Now at this day come the parties aforesaid by their respective attorneys, and waiving a Jury, submit to the Court, and the Court doth find that the defendant [Irene Emerson] is not guilty in manner and form as in the

> plaintiff's declaration alleged. It is therefore, considered
> and adjudged by the Court that said plaintiff take nothing
> by his said suit in this behalf, but that said defendent go
> thereof without day [sic] and receive of said plaintiff
> her costs and charges herein expended and have thereof
> execution.[23]

Other than that one notation, there is no evidence who the attorneys were who appeared in St. Louis for either side or how the case even happened to be called up for final disposition. It will be recalled that on March 22, 1852, the Supreme Court of Missouri had ordered that the judgment of the lower court freeing Dred Scott be "reversed, annulled, and for nought held and esteemed," and that the case be "remanded to the said Circuit Court for further proceedings . . . according to the opinion of this court herein delivered"—namely, that Dred Scott should be remanded to slavery. The lower court instead had continued the suit pending the outcome of the new case being instituted in the federal courts. Now that action was concluded, and there was no legal alternative left. After eleven years of litigation, from April 6, 1846, to March 18, 1857, the *Dred Scott* case finally was closed out in the court where it had originated—and Dred Scott was still a slave.

Epilogue

THE REPERCUSSIONS TO THE *Dred Scott* decision were of the greatest magnitude. The press and the pulpit, the political stump and the halls of Congress, all reverberated with scathing condemnations as well as vigorous defenses of the Court's pronouncements. Sectional differences, serious enough before March 6, 1857, now became more pronounced and more polarized as the impact of this decision added still more to those divisive forces already leading the nation inexorably toward civil war. Forces intent on ridding the nation of slavery now mounted an unprecedented assault upon the Court, determined to reverse *Dred Scott* before the unthinkable next step could occur—the legalizing of slavery everywhere. By a quirk of circumstance, the *Dred Scott* case and Chief Justice Roger Brooke Taney had demonstrated how it could be done. Both drove home traumatically what some had already been advocating, the power of a broad neo-Hamiltonian interpretation of the Constitution and federalism that the proslavery Calhoun states' rights agrarian South had abandoned as sectional differences gradually had multiplied. How ironic that Taney, a states' rights proslave agrarian, had used the national institutional machinery to strengthen slavery. If that machinery was strong enough to legalize slavery throughout the nation (as some feared it now would), was it not also strong enough to *destroy* slavery throughout the nation? If Republicans could just hold the line on slavery, all they had to do was gain control of that national machinery *without weakening it institutionally*; they could then use it to reverse whatever gains agrarianism and slavery had made. (After all, slavery was not the only concern of the new Republican party.) The key was governmental and judicial power centralized more in the national government as opposed to traditional

Jeffersonian Democratic decentralization and states' rights. Gaining control of the executive and legislative branches had to come first; "proper" appointments to the Supreme Court would eventually follow, along with a reorganization of the entire federal judiciary to ensure "proper" judges. Republicans were not unaware that they could legally elect a minority president under the unique nature of the electoral college system. In the meantime, the Court must be prevented from legalizing slavery nationally by reducing its prestige and influence—but not its institutional decision-making power. That was done through an *obiter dictum* campaign that attacked Taney's legal reasoning and the reasoning of the majority, thereby undermining confidence in those judges to make unbiased judgments in certain types of cases. At the same time, Republicans and abolitionists heightened the fear of a national "slave conspiracy" that purportedly included even members of the Supreme Court. The *Dred Scott* decision made it possible to bring all this into focus. Once that decision was promulgated, Republicans and abolitionists faced limited options. They could acquiesce in slavery—which was out of the question. They could resort to violence or secession—which only a few extremists advocated. Or they could mount an unprecedented assault on the Court as the spearhead of a furious political campaign to gain control over the national government and then run the government under a centralized-power philosophy that Taney unwittingly had shown could bring about their ends. A decision that might have destroyed the Republican party even after it came so close to winning in 1856 now instead gave it the occasion and impetus to take the offensive. Three and one-half years later Lincoln was elected.[1]

Neither of the parties to this famous suit lived to witness the bloody orgy they were so instrumental in bringing about. Already insane and institutionalized at the time the decision was announced, John F. A. Sanford died in New York on May 5, 1857; and about one and one-half years later, on September 17, 1858, the now famous Dred Scott passed away in St. Louis.[2]

But despite the decree of the Supreme Court of the United States, Scott died a free man. Shortly after the Court rendered its decision, it became known that Scott's real owner was not Sanford after all, but Dr. Calvin Clifford Chaffee, the Republican Congressman from the Tenth Congressional District of Springfield, Massachusetts, who had married Irene Emerson. This information was revealed to the public within a week after the Supreme Court's decision by the Springfield (Mass.) *Argus.* Where this newspaper got its information is not known, but being a Democratic journal, it took the occasion to accuse the Republican and former Know-Nothing physician of complicity and collusion and publicly chided the abolitionist congressman for owning slave property. Even people friendly to Dr. Chaffee became concerned.[3] On March 14 the *Springfield* (Mass.) *Daily Republican,* a politically sympathetic newspaper, published a lengthy anonymous letter that strongly suggested Chaffee had some explaining to do. That expanation was quickly forthcoming, in a reply the *Republican* published on March 16. Recognizing that the circumstances appeared spurious, Chaffee declared in no uncertain terms his opposition to slavery and his abhorrence of the decision of the Court. But in the case of Dred Scott, he stated, "the defendent [Sanford] was and is the only person who had or has any power in the matter, and neither myself nor any member of my family were consulted in relation to, or even knew of, the existence of the suit till after it was noticed for trial, when we learned of it in an accidental way."[4] When Mrs. Chaffee (then Mrs. Emerson) had moved from St. Louis, she simply had left Scott and his family there on their own. Chaffee was totally unaware that they even existed. Then in February 1857 he was suddenly and surprisingly informed (but how and by whom is unknown) that the Dred Scott who was the central figure in the great law suit going on in the Supreme Court was actually the slave of Mrs. Chaffee's deceased first husband. It was the first inkling he had of any possible association with this suit—and this was only a month before the final decision was to be announced.[5] "Possessed of no power to control—refused all right to influence the course of the defendant in the cause," Chaffee was advised by his legal counsel that he could do nothing in Dred Scott's behalf until after the case had been decided by the Supreme Court.[6] Now that time had come.

Stimulated by the adverse publicity in the opposition press all over the country, Chaffee now took measures to pave the way for Scott's freedom.[7] First he executed a quitclaim in which he, his wife, and his stepdaughter gave up any and all rights or interest they might have had in Dred Scott and his family.[8] At the same time they also transferred these rights to Taylor Blow, back in St. Louis, one of those who had been supporting Scott's case for such a long time. This was necessary because according to Missouri law a slave could be emancipated there only by a citizen of that state.[9] Accordingly, on May 26, 1857, Dred and Harriet Scott appeared in the Circuit Court of St. Louis County with Taylor Blow, who formally freed them. The emancipation papers were drawn up by Arba N. Crane, the lawyer who worked in Roswell M. Field's office and who had befriended the Scotts in the latter stages of their court action. The papers were duly acknowledged by Taylor Blow before Judge Alexander Hamilton, in whose court eight years earlier, coincidentally, the Scotts had had a tantalizingly brief taste of freedom.[10] But now, after eleven years of frustrating court litigation and despite the adverse decision of the Supreme Court of the United States, Dred Scott and his family—his wife, Harriet, and their daughters Eliza and Lizzie—were all finally free.

The nationwide publicity given to his case made Dred Scott a famous man. Newspapers all over the country carried accounts of the developments in the Supreme Court as well as brief biographical sketches of the *dramatis personnae*. Whenever a news item or a vignette appeared in one newspaper, it was readily reprinted in many others all over the country, and depending upon whether the newspaper represented a proslavery or an antislavery bent, the story was given either a complimentary or a derogatory slant. Scott was portrayed sometimes as a bright, alert, hard-working and conscientious person, sometimes as an illiterate and ignorant dolt.[11]

Despite this publicity, there is no clear picture of just what Scott did. It will be recalled that he had been employed by Charles Edmund La-Beaume in 1851 and apparently still was when he attained his freedom. Certainly he was under no physical restraints and was free to come and go at will.[12] None of the contemporary accounts give any clear indication of how Scott earned his living, either as a slave or as a freeman, although one article indicated that Harriet was a washerwoman and that her husband "employs himself in carrying to and fro the clothes his wife washes."[13] Apparently he worked also as a porter in some of the hotels, at least one of which was the locally famous Barnum's Hotel, on Second and Walnut streets. There he did all sorts of odd jobs, but he was especially just there, an attraction for hotel guests, who could claim later that they had once seen and talked to the famous Dred Scott.[14]

Perhaps the most important thing that happened to him after he became free—important to posterity, that is—was that his portrait was taken. In the course of an interview for *Frank Leslie's Illustrated Newspaper*, the correspondent convinced the Scotts to sit for a daguerrotype. Harriet was dubious at first, for she had heard rumors that several promoters were seeking to entice her husband on a tour through some portions of the North, probably to make political capital of his newly found notoriety, and she wanted none of this. Finally convinced that the newspaper's purpose was completely different, she agreed to be photographed, and the result was that Dred, Harriet, and both daughters had their pictures taken by one of St. Louis' finest photographers, J. H. Fitzgibbons. Those portraits appeared in the June 27, 1857, issue of *Frank Leslie's Illustrated Newspaper* and are the only known photographs ever made of the Scott family. Some time later, after Scott was dead, Mrs. Theron Barnum, wife of the proprietor of the hotel in which Scott had worked, engaged a St. Louis portrait painter, Louis Schultze, to copy that photograph onto canvas, and that painting, reproduced in countless history books, is the widely known picture of the famous ex-slave.[15]

On Friday, September 17, 1858, after an illness of several weeks, and after less than a year and a half of legal freedom, Dred Scott died in St. Louis of what some called consumption and others referred to as tuberculosis. His name by now known throughout the land, Scott's death was noted in newspapers all over the country. Although most of the accounts were confined to mentioning the mere fact of his death, some newspapers took the occasion once again to editorialize on the political implications of the Supreme Court's decision.[16] Scott was buried in the Wesleyan Cemetery, located about two miles west of the then city limits of St. Louis (today it is the intersection of Grand and Laclede avenues, in the heart of the city). Nine years later, in 1867, as the city spread westward, the cemetery was abandoned and the bodies disinterred and relocated elsewhere. Through the efforts of Taylor Blow, Scott was reburied on November 27, 1867, in Section 1, Lot No. 177, of Calvary Cemetery, in what is now the northern part of St. Louis. Blow had become a Catholic in 1865, and the cemetery's rules allowed a church member to purchase graves for family servants, regardless of color. There Scott was buried, in an unmarked grave.[17]

That grave remained unmarked and unnoticed for ninety years, until 1957. In that year, the one hundredth anniversary of the famous decision, the Reverend Edward J. Dowling, S. J., of St. Louis, began to raise funds for a tombstone. A local amateur historian in the north St. Louis community of Baden, Father Dowling had become interested in the *Dred Scott* case and was especially concerned that the last resting place of so important a figure in American history lacked even a common marker. On March 6, 1957, on the occasion of a locally sponsored centennial commemorative ceremony conducted at the gravesite, Father Dowling announced that Mrs. Charles C. Harrison, Jr., of Villa Nova, Pennsylvania, a granddaughter of Taylor Blow, had donated a stone marker, and that the funds he was raising would be used for some other graveside decoration. A two-and-one-half-foot granite headstone was duly installed on July 24, 1957, and two months later, on September 17, on the ninety-ninth anniversary of Dred Scott's death, the ceremonial unveiling took place. The headstone was formally dedicated, along with a bronze floral container, the gift of Father Dowling and the New Baden Society.[18]

Most of his life a slave who was denied both freedom and citizenship, Dred Scott went to his final resting place a free man. Today he rests in Calvary Cemetery with at least the common amenity accorded so many fellow free men and free citizens—a decent grave marked with a simple but dignified headstone. It is inscribed on one side:

DRED SCOTT
BORN ABOUT 1799
DIED SEPT. 17, 1858

and on the other:

DRED SCOTT
SUBJECT OF THE DECISION OF
THE SUPREME COURT OF THE
UNITED STATES IN 1857 WHICH
DENIED CITIZENSHIP TO THE
NEGRO, VOIDED THE MISSOURI
COMPROMISE ACT, BECAME
ONE OF THE EVENTS THAT
RESULTED IN THE CIVIL WAR

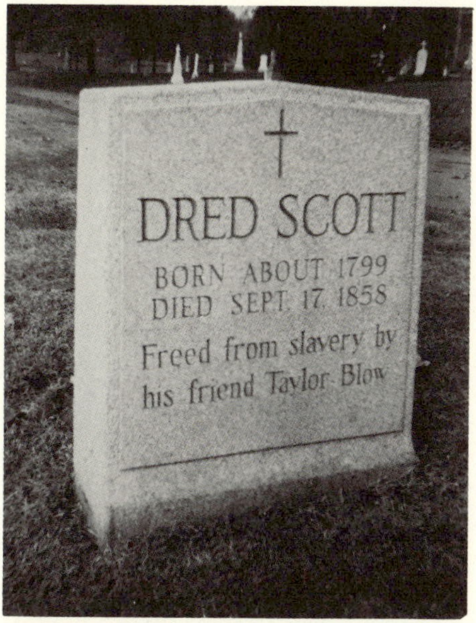

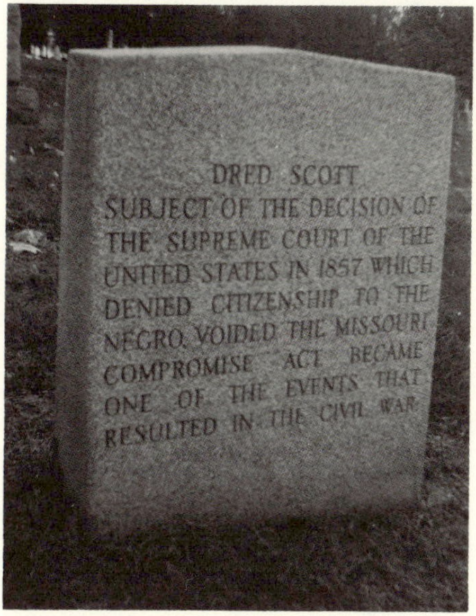

Dred Scott's Grave, Calvary Cemetery, St. Louis

Appendixes

Appendix A

THE "MISSING" COURT RECORDS

THE MAIN REASON THE history of the *Dred Scott* case has been so obscure for so long is that many of the court records that could have answered essential questions have disappeared. For many years one could remove records from the Circuit Court in St. Louis merely upon a personal receipt. Sometime around 1900 George W. Taussig, a St. Louis lawyer and son of one of Henry Taylor Blow's close friends, withdrew the Dred and Harriet Scott files, evidently intending to write something about the case. Taussig died in 1905 before he got around to it. His widow moved to California, but his papers were boxed up and deposited with a storage company in St. Louis. In 1907, when Frederick T. Hill did his study of the case, all he could find in St. Louis court archives was Taussig's receipt. Since no one knew what Taussig had done with them, the documents were presumed to be lost. About a year later, Taussig's nephew decided it was too costly to store his deceased uncle's papers, and so he withdrew them from storage to destroy those not worth saving. He took the boxes into the basement of his home, removed the papers from the boxes, and tossed those he thought worthless into the furnace. Suddenly something on one small bundle caught on the lip of the furnace got his attention—a faded pink ribbon and the words "Dred Scott, a man of color, vs. Irene Emerson." Recalling stories he had heard about "lost papers" and thinking these might be they, he pulled them from the furnace and returned them to the circuit court. The frayed and burned edges are still visible on those documents. They are all that remain of the original papers filed in the *Dred Scott* case. What happened to the rest is unknown; probably they were destroyed in that furnace before anyone realized what they were. With them presumably disappeared forever the evidence needed to document the full truth behind the *Dred Scott* case.

But there was one more possible source. Because the case was appealed to the Missouri Supreme Court, a transcript was made of the lower court proceedings and forwarded to the higher court. In that transcript were *copies* of most of the original documents, at least those containing the testimony in the lower court as well as the documentation of the principles and points of law raised there by attorneys. When I began to research my doctoral dissertation in 1947, like so many fledgling doctoral candidates I knew very little of my subject, mostly from secondary materials. Happening to be in Jefferson City, where the Missouri Supreme Court is located, I decided on an impulse to look into the records there, knowing that eventually I would have to examine them anyway. (At the time I had not yet even seen the materials in the lower court.) The only person in the clerk's office at the time was a young secretary who graciously permitted me to work in the basement archives where the records were stored. I located the files easily—they were arranged chronologically—and copied the information onto note cards. Later, after I had gone through the lower court's decimated files as well as some of the published materials on the case, I realized the singular importance of the information I had found in the Missouri Supreme Court. It was duly noted in my doctoral dissertation.

Several years later I had occasion to reexamine those documents. I was now informed by the clerk of the court—not a subordinate secretary this time—that the Dred Scott files had been missing for decades and that numerous efforts to locate them in the past had all proved futile! This was incredible, for I had located the papers myself only a few years earlier, with no difficulty at all. The clerk and I thereupon searched the basement archives, but to no avail. Why no one had been able to find them before is difficult enough to understand; but how the files could have been lost again was an even greater mystery, especially since I was certain I had replaced them exactly where I had found them. (In deference to the court, I recall that some "housecleaning" had been going on, replacing the old wooden files with fireproof metal cabinets, with some resultant rearranging.) Nevertheless, the clerk was sure the papers had been missing for the decade he had been with the court, and an elderly janitor recalled that they had been missing when he had been employed there some forty years earlier! Both of them, they said, had searched for the papers on numerous occasions, but in vain. Needless to say, I was completely dumbfounded. I was determined to find those papers again, for now the credibility of my doctoral dissertation was at stake. With the clerk's permission and, indeed, with his help and cooperation, I undertook a systematic file-by-file and drawer-by-drawer search of the basement archives. I was a high school teacher at the time, and the only opportunities I had to go to Jefferson City were during vacations and on occasional weekends. Five years later the search came to a successful conclusion. On August 21, 1956, I found the missing papers, a scant few feet from where they should have been in the first place. No one knows how they were misplaced, either the first time or the second time. The papers were turned over to the chief justice, who placed them in the court vault for safekeeping.

Appendix B

AGREED STATEMENT OF FACTS UPON WHICH THE CASE OF *DRED SCOTT* V. *JOHN F. A. SANFORD* WAS TRIED IN THE CIRCUIT COURT OF THE UNITED STATES AND IN THE SUPREME COURT OF THE UNITED STATES

In the Circuit Court of the United
States for the District of Missouri

Dred Scott
vs
John F. A. Sanford

The parties above named agree on the following statement of facts: —

In the year 1834, the plaintiff was a negro slave belonging to Doctor Emerson who was a surgeon in the army of the United States. In that year, 1834, said Dr Emerson took the plaintiff from the State of Missouri to the military post at Rock Island in the State of Illinois and held him there as a slave until the month of April or May 1836. At the time last mentioned, said Dr Emerson removed the plaintiff from said military post at Rock Island to the military post of Fort Snelling, situate on the west bank of the Mississippi River in the Territory known as Upper Louisiana acquired by the United States of France and situate north of the latitude of 36 degrees 30 minutes north & north of the State of Missouri. Said Dr Emerson held the plaintiff in slavery at said Fort Snelling from said last mentioned date until the year 1838.

In the year 1835 Harriet, who is named in the second count of the plaintiff's declaration was the negro slave of Major Talliaferro who belonged to the army of the United States. In that year 1835, said Major Taliaferro took said Harriet to said Fort Snelling a military post situate as herein before stated & kept her there as a slave until the year 1836 and then sold and delivered her as a slave at said Fort Snelling unto the said Dr Emerson herein before named. Said Dr Emerson held said Harriet in slavery at said Fort Snelling until the year 1838.

In the year 1836, the plaintiff and said Harriet at said Fort Snelling, with the consent of said Dr Emerson, who then claimed to be their master and owner, intermarried and took each other for husband and wife. Eliza and Lizzy named in the third count of the plaintiffs declaration are the fruit of that marriage. Eliza is about 14 years old and was born on board the Steamboat Gipsy north of the north line of the State of Missouri & upon the River Mississippi. Lizzy is about seven years old and was born in the State of Missouri at the military post called Jefferson Barracks.

In the year 1838 said Dr Emerson removed the plaintiff and said Harriet & their daughter Eliza from said Fort Snelling to the State of Missouri where they have ever since resided.

Before the commencement of this suit, said Dr Emerson sold and conveyed plaintiff, said Harriet, Eliza & Lizzy to the defendant as slaves, and the defendant has ever since claimed to hold them & each of them as slaves.

At the times mentioned in the plaintiff's declaration the defendant claiming to be the owner as aforesaid laid his hands upon said plaintiff, Harriet, Eliza & Lizzy & imprisoned them, doing in this respect however no more than what he might lawfully do if they were of right his slaves at such times.

Further proof may be given on the trial for either party.

> [signed] R. M. FIELD for pltff
> [signed] H. A. GARLAND for deft

[Appended to this document is the following:]

It is agreed that Dred Scott brought suit for his freedom in the Circuit Court of St. Louis County, that there was a verdict & judgment in his favor, that on on [sic] a writ of error to the Supreme Court the judgment below was reversed and the cause remanded to the Circuit Court, where it has been continued to await the decision of this case.

> [signed] FIELD for plff
> [signed] GARLAND for deft

Notes

ABBREVIATIONS USED IN NOTES

CCStL	Circuit Court of St. Louis County, Circuit Court, St. Louis
HSPa	Historical Society of Pennsylvania, Philadelphia
LC	Library of Congress
MinnHS	Minnesota Historical Society, St. Paul
MoHS	Missouri Historical Society, St. Louis
MoSC	State of Missouri Supreme Court, Jefferson City
NA	National Archives
PCStL	Probate Court, St. Louis
USCCStL	Circuit Court of the United States for the District of Missouri, St. Louis
USSC	Supreme Court of the United States
WiSHS	Wisconsin State Historical Society, Madison

Dred Scott Papers
    Dred Scott Papers, Missouri Historical Society, St. Louis

Dred Scott v. *Emerson,* CCStL
    Dred Scott v. *Irene Emerson,* Case No. 1, November Term, 1846, Circuit Court of St. Louis County, Circuit Court, St. Louis

Emerson File, AGO Archives
    File of John Emerson, Asst. Surg., U.S.A. (1832-42), Records of the Adjutant General's Office, National Archives

Emerson Letters, AGO Archives
    File of John Emerson, Asst. Surg., U.S.A., Letters and Reports (1835-42), Records of the Adjutant General's Office, National Archives

Emerson v. *Scott,* No. 14, March Term 1848, MoSC
    Irene Emerson v. *Dred Scott,* Case No. 14, March Term, 1848, State of Missouri
    Supreme Court, Jefferson City

Harriet Scott v. *Emerson,* CCStL
    Harriet Scott v. *Irene Emerson,* Case No. 2, November Term, 1846, Circuit Court
    of St. Louis County, Circuit Court, St. Louis

Letter Book, SGO Archives
    Letter Book, Surgeon General's Office (1833-43), Records of the Surgeon General's Office, National Archives

Letters Received, AGO Archives
    Letters Received, Adjutant General's Office (1833-43), Records of the Adjutant
    General's Office, National Archives

Letters Received, SGO Archives
    Letters Received, Surgeon General's Office (1833-43), Records of the Surgeon
    General's Office, National Archives

Scott v. *Emerson,* No. 137, October Term 1851, MoSC
    Dred Scott v. *Irene Emerson,* Case No. 137, October Term, 1851, State of Missouri Supreme Court, Jefferson City

Scott v. *Sanford,* No. 692, USCCStL
    Dred Scott v. *John F. A. Sanford,* Case No. 692, Circuit Court of the United
    States for the District of Missouri, St. Louis

Scott v. *Sanford,* No. 3230, USSC
    Dred Scott v. *John F. A. Sanford,* File No. 3230, Supreme Court of the United
    States

PROLOGUE

1. The correct spelling, used hereafter, is "Sanford," according to the signature
and other contemporary sources. The name was misspelled in court records, probably
through some clerk's error.

2. Among the best discussions of this period are Allan Nevins, *The Emergence of
Lincoln,* 2 vols. (New York, 1950); Carl Brent Swisher, *The Taney Period, 1836-64*
(New York, 1974), volume 5 of the Oliver Wendell Holmes Devise *History of the
Supreme Court of the United States;* and David M. Potter, *The Impending Crisis,
1848-1861* (New York, 1976).

3. Excellent works that include the resurgence of the Republican party both
nationally and locally are Joel H. Silbey, *The Transformation of American Politics,
1840-1860* (Englewood Cliffs, N.J., 1967); Michael F. Holt, *Forging a Majority:*

The Formation of the Republican Party in Pittsburgh, 1848-1860 (New Haven, 1969), and *The Political Crisis of the 1850s* (New York, 1978); Eric Foner, *Free Soil, Free Labor, Free Men: The Ideology of the Republican Party before the Civil War* (New York, 1970); and Ronald P. Formisano, *The Birth of Mass Political Parties: Michigan, 1827-1861* (Princeton, 1971).

4. "It was actually the catalyst for the civil conflict that soon followed. With it collapsed the practical possibility of resolving by political and legal means the issues that divided the nation. Thenceforth, extremists dominated the scene. Bloodshed alone could settle the issue of slavery and of the very nature of the Union, which that issue had placed in the balance." Bernard Schwartz, *From Confederation to Union: the American Constitution, 1835-1877* (Baltimore, 1973), p. 130.

5. Jefferson Davis, *A Short History of the Confederate States of America* (New York, 1890), p. 47. Recent studies indicate that the erosion of the Court's prestige was not as long-lasting as traditional histories have claimed. See especially Stanley I. Kutler, *Judicial Power and Reconstruction Politics* (Chicago, 1968), and William M. Wiecek, "The Reconstruction of Federal Judicial Power," *The American Journal of Legal History* 13 (October 1969): 333-59, and portions of R. Kent Newmyer, *The Supreme Court Under Marshall and Taney* (New York, 1968), and Harold M. Hyman, *A More Perfect Union: The Impact of the Civil War and Reconstruction* (New York, 1973). They point out that critics of the *Dred Scott* decision vented their fury not so much on the institution of the Court itself as on the individual judges who had debased that institution. Republicans and abolitionists wanted to control the Court, not destroy its influence. Attacks upon the Court aimed at "creative reform, not denunciation or destruction," observes Kutler (p. 11). Newmyer states (pp. 144-45) that frequent illnesses of several justices, plus deaths, resignations, and institutional reform (the move to create new circuits and thereby add new judges to the bench) "greatly reduced [the] efficiency and vitality" of the court. Nonetheless, the *short-term* effect of the decision on the Court's prestige was as Jefferson Davis noted. Before *Dred Scott* there was a willingness—even an eagerness—to look to the Court to solve constitutional problems of slavery in the territories (see ch. 18, *infra*); following *Dred Scott,* confidence in the Court on such issues evaporated. Foner asserts that "Republicans were apprehensive that the Supreme Court [now might] establish the right of transit of slaves through the free states" and thereby open the North to slavery. Foner, *Free Soil, Free Labor, Free Men,* pp. 97-98. Justice Benjamin R. Curtis resigned from the Court a few months after the decision; one reason was the mistrust and lack of confidence toward the Court resulting from its involvement in divisive political matters. (See ch. 17, *infra*.) Note, too, the conspicuous omission of the Court as a possible balance wheel in the various compromises proposed during the secession crisis. "The Supreme Court was discredited in the North," Hyman points out, "and had nothing more to say to the South. If sectional reconciliation was to come forth, its source had to be the White House." (Hyman, *A More Perfect Union,* p. 34.) But once secession became a reality, Lincoln and his party successfully "Republicanized" the Court, and its role during the Civil War and Reconstruction era was anything but insignificant. As Potter points out, during the 1850s antislavery forces conducted "a systematic assault" to "dis-

credit the federal courts." By the time of the Civil War they saw they "could attain their goals better by controlling the federal machinery than by resisting it." Potter, *The Impending Crisis, 1848-1861*, pp. 293-94, 295.

6. See, among others, Charles G. Haines and Foster H. Sherwood, *The Role of the Supreme Court in American Government and Politics, 1835-1864* (Berkeley, 1957), p. 393; Carl Brent Swisher, *Roger B. Taney* (New York, 1936), p. 522; William B. Hesseltine, *The South in American History* (New York, 1943), p. 351; Louis B. Boudin, *Government by Judiciary* (New York, 1932), p. 1; Daniel W. Howe, *Political History of Secession to the Beginning of the American Civil War* (New York, 1914), p. 346; Bernard Schwartz, *The Reins of Power* (New York, 1963), pp. 83-86; Wallace Mendelson, *Capitalism, Democracy, and the Supreme Court* (New York, 1960), p. 51; Walter Chandler, "The Centenary of Associate Justice John Catron of the United States Supreme Court," *Tennessee Law Review* 15 (1937): 48; "Hampton L. Carson on the Dred Scott Decision," *American Law Review* 36 (1902): 429.

7. The name is incorrectly spelled "Emmerson" in many court records, but the correct spelling, based upon signatures and other contemporary sources, is "Emerson." The correct spelling will be used hereafter.

CHAPTER 1
Before Dr. Emerson

1. Petition of Dred Scott, April 6, 1846, in file of *Harriet Scott* v. *Irene Emerson*, Case No. 2, November Term, 1846, Circuit Court of St. Louis County, *Ms.*, Circuit Court, St. Louis, Missouri (hereafter referred to as "*Harriet Scott* v. *Emerson*, CCStL, *Ms.*"). When the case was instituted in 1846, the city of St. Louis was a part of St. Louis County. When the two became separate political entities, records of the Circuit Court of St. Louis County remained with the city's courts, where they still reside.

2. The Blow family came originally from England to Southampton County, where they became landowning farmers. There, on May 10, 1771, Peter Blow was born, one of five children of Richard and Ann Blow. Mrs. J. A. Johnston to author, September 16, 1948 (letter in possession of author); Will of Richard Blow, December 19, 1785, in Will Book No. 4, Circuit Court, Southampton County, Virginia, *Ms.*

3. Elizabeth Taylor was born in Southampton County, Virginia, on April 21, 1785, the only child of Henry and Rebecca Tyson Taylor. Her parents died when she was an infant and she was raised by her paternal grandparents. For the Blow family, see John A. Bryan, "The Blow Family and Their Slave Dred Scott," Missouri Historical Society *Bulletin,* part 1 in 4 (July 1948): 223-31, and part 2 in 5 (October 1948): 19-33.

4. Vincent Hopkins, *Dred Scott's Case* (New York, 1951), p. 1. In later years Peter Blow was referred to as "Captain," but source materials do not clarify whether the rank was only titular or if he was indeed promoted.

5. Southampton County records indicate that the Blows left Virginia between October 20 and December 21, 1818. Southampton County Land Books (1801,

1812, and 1818), Southampton County Personal Property Books (1799, 1812, and 1818), and Southampton County Deed Book 16 (1818-20), *Ms.*, Virginia State Library, Richmond. See also *Daily Missouri Republican* (St. Louis), July 22, 1866; *St. Louis Dispatch,* July 23, 1866; and *The Missouri Republican* (St. Louis), August 21, 1869.

6. The Blow family had owned slaves for many years. When Peter Blow's father died in 1786, he bequeathed to his wife and children eleven slaves along with other property, and it was thus that fourteen-year-old Peter Blow became the owner of at least one slave, "a Negro boy Davey." Will of Richard Blow, December 19, 1785, in Will Book No. 4, Circuit Court, Southampton County, Virginia, *Ms.*, and Hopkins, *Dred Scott's Case,* p. 7. By 1818, when the Blows left Virginia for Alabama, Peter Blow was at least part owner with one Henry Moore of four slaves, three of whom were described in the Southampton County tax records simply as being over twelve years of age. Their names were not recorded nor is there any evidence when or how Blow and Moore obtained them. Nor is it clear just what happened to the Blow-Moore partnership or what disposition was made of those slaves. It seems reasonable to assume that the partnership was dissolved and that one or perhaps all four slaves remained with Blow, and that one of them was Dred Scott. Of course, it is possible that Blow disposed of all four and then obtained Scott. All that is certain is that Blow owned Dred Scott before leaving Virginia, that Scott was with the Blow family during the entire time they lived in Alabama, and that he was with the family when they arrived in St. Louis in 1830. Julia Webster Blow to Mary Louise Dalton, March 13, 1907, Dred Scott Papers, *Ms.*, Missouri Historical Society, St. Louis (hereafter referred to as "Dred Scott Papers"); *Frank Leslie's Illustrated Newspaper* (New York), June 27, 1857.

7. Richard Edwards and M. Hopewell, *Edwards's Great West and her Commercial Metropolis* (St. Louis, 1860), pp. 225, 341-43; *St. Louis Republican,* September 12, 1875; J. Thomas Scharf, *History of Saint Louis City and County* (Philadelphia, 1833), 1: 607; L. U. Reavis, *Saint Louis: The Future Great City of the World* (St. Louis, 1875), p. 351; Mrs. Dana O. Jensen, ed., "Stephen Hempstead, 'I At Home,' " Missouri Historical Society *Bulletin* 22 (July 1966): 441.

8. Joseph Charless, Sr., fled to the United States from Ireland, by way of France, coming first to New York in 1795. He lived briefly in Philadelphia, where he married and where he learned the printing trade in the employ of Matthew Carey, a fellow Irish exile. In 1800 he moved to Lexington, Kentucky, and there, on January 17, 1804, Joseph Charless, Jr., was born. In 1807 the family moved to St. Louis where, in 1808, Joseph, Sr., founded the *Missouri Gazette,* the first newspaper west of the Mississippi and one that advocated the abolition of slavery in the territory that later became the state of Missouri. This attitude undoubtedly influenced Joseph, Jr., who grew up in St. Louis, learned the printing trade in his father's shop, and apprenticed briefly in a law office. He went back to Lexington to complete his law training at Transylvania University and then returned to St. Louis to practice law. Meanwhile, Joseph, Sr., turned over his newspaper to another son, Edward, who renamed it *The Missouri Republican,* and Joseph, Sr., and Joseph, Jr., opened a wholesale drug and paint business, Charless and Company, which proved very success-

ful. Bryan, "Blow Family," pt. 1, p. 225; Edwards and Hopewell, *Great West*, pp. 584-87; Reavis, *Saint Louis*, p. 200.

9. *Daily Missouri Republican*, July 22, 1866; H. D. Pittman, ed., *Americans of Gentle Birth and Their Ancestors* (St. Louis, 1903), p. 383; Theodore A. Bingham, *Genealogy of the Bingham Family* (Harrisburg, 1898), p. 211; Edwards and Hopewell, *Great West*, 461-64; Scharf, *Saint Louis City and County*, 2: 647. The LaBeaumes were one of the few Protestant families among the French pioneers of St. Louis. Bryan, "Blow Family," pt. 1, pp. 228-29. A list of persons who in 1851 owned property within the city of St. Louis worth more than $20,000 included Joseph Charless, Jr., Henry Taylor Blow, Louis A. LaBeaume, and Charles Edmund LaBeaume. Scharf, *Saint Louis City and County*, 1: 685.

10. *Daily Missouri Republican*, May 20, 26, July 7, 1847; David D. March, "The Life and Times of Charles D. Drake" (Doctoral dissertation, University of Missouri-Columbia, 1949), pp. 28-36. Drake was to be one of the most prominent Radical Republicans in Missouri during the Reconstruction era.

11. Edwards and Hopewell, *Great West*, pp. 224-27; Scharf, *Saint Louis City and County*, 1: 607-8; Bryan, "Blow Family," pt. 1, p. 229. His oldest daughter was the famous Susan E. Blow, who founded the first public kindergarten in the United States.

12. Bryan, "Blow Family," pt. 1, pp. 230-31.

13. Ibid., pp. 225-27. See also various documents in file of Estate of Peter Blow (No. 976), PCStL, Ms.

14. *The Saint Louis Daily Evening News*, May 26, 1857.

15. Dalton, Notes, February 18, 1907, and Blow to Dalton, March 13, 1907, Dred Scott Papers; *Daily Missouri Republican*, October 19, 1862. The resurgence of black American history has resulted in the publication of many autobiographical sketches written by ex-slaves, including *The Narrative of William W. Brown, A Fugitive Slave* (Reading, Mass., edition, 1969). Brown was a slave in St. Louis while Scott was there, and although there is no mention of either Scott or the Blows in Brown's narrative, it at least gives some flavor of the life of a slave in St. Louis at that time.

16. Dalton, Notes, February 18, 1907, Dred Scott Papers.

17. Ibid.; Petition of Dred Scott, April 6, 1846, in *Harriet Scott v. Emerson*, CCStL, Ms.; Blow to Dalton, March 13, 1907, Dred Scott Papers; Frank H. Hodder, "Some Phases of the Dred Scott Case," *Mississippi Valley Historical Review* 16 (June 1929): 3.

18. Bryan, "Blow Family," pt. 1, pp. 225-28. John A. Bryan was the supervisor of the National Park Service museum in St. Louis' historic "Old Courthouse," advertised locally as "site of the Dred Scott case."

19. File of Estate of Peter Blow (No. 976), PCStL, Ms.

20. Petition of Dred Scott, April 6, 1846, in *Harriet Scott v. Emerson*, CCStL, Ms.

21. Testimony of Henry T. Blow, June 30, 1847, in Bill of Exceptions, March 4, 1848, file of *Dred Scott v. Irene Emerson*, Case No. 1, November Term, 1846, Circuit Court of St. Louis County, Ms., Circuit Court, St. Louis (hereafter referred to as "*Dred Scott v. Emerson*, CCStL, Ms.").

22. Bryan, "Blow Family," pt. 1, p. 228.

23. The name "Dred Scott" appeared for the first time in 1846, on the petition that instituted the case. Except for routine lists of cases, newspapers were not to mention the name again until the 1850s.

24. The Washington, D.C., *National Era* began to carry the novel in serial form on July 24, 1856. It had been written earlier and clearly bore no resemblance to the facts of Dred Scott's life.

25. *Springfield* (Mass.) *Daily Republican*, February 12, 1903.

26. "Dred Scott," T. W. Chamberlain Collection, *Ms.*, MoHs; John D. Lawson, ed., *American State Trials* (St. Louis, 1921), 13: 220.

27. Summons, August 8, 1833, in file of Estate of Peter Blow (No. 976), PCStL, *Ms.*

CHAPTER 2
With Dr. Emerson

1. John Emerson to Adjutant General, November 18, 1833, in Letters Received, Adjutant General's Office, *Ms.*, NA (hereafter referred to as "Letters Received, AGO Archives"); Charles E. Snyder, "John Emerson, Owner of Dred Scott," *Annals of Iowa* 15 (October 1938): 441.

2. Alexander Buckner to Lewis Cass, September 10, 1832; Samuel Merry to Cass, October 26, 1832; Thomas Hart Benton to Cass, December 17, 1832; Buckner to Joseph Lovell, December 20, 1832; Benton to Cass, July 12, 1833; Samuel Pettigrew et al. to Cass, February 14, 1835, in file of John Emerson, Asst. Surg., U.S.A. (1832-42), Records of the Adjutant General's Office, *Ms.*, NA (hereafter referred to as "Emerson File, AGO Archives"); Emerson to Thomas Lawson, November 24, 1837, in file of John Emerson, Asst. Surg., U.S.A., Letters and Reports (1835-42), Records of the Adjutant General's Office, *Ms.*, NA (hereafter referred to as "Emerson Letters, AGO Archives"). For more on Emerson's Missouri associates, see Floyd C. Shoemaker, ed., *Missouri and Missourians* (Chicago, 1943), 1: 408, 410-13; William Hyde and Howard L. Conard, eds., *Encyclopedia of the History of St. Louis* (New York, 1899), 3: 1456; J. Thomas Scharf, *History of Saint Louis City and County* (Philadelphia, 1883), 1: 654-55, 663-64, and 2: 1515-41; and Snyder, "John Emerson," p. 441.

3. Buckner to Cass, September 10, 1832; Henry Atkinson to J. B. Brant, September 28, 1832, Certificate of Capt. J. B. Brant, March 7, 1833, Order No. 17, Hq., Jefferson Barracks, June 5, 1833; and Emerson to Lovell, June 10, 1833, in Emerson File, AGO Archives. His salary was $100 per month.

4. See correspondence from October 1832 to October 1833, in Emerson File, AGO Archives; in Letter Book, Surgeon General's Office (1833-43), Records of the Surgeon General's Office, *Ms.*, NA (hereafter referred to as "Letter Book, SGO Archives"); and in Letters Received, Surgeon General's Office (1833-43), Records of the Surgeon General's Office, *Ms.*, NA (hereafter referred to as "Letters Received, SGO Archives").

5. Cass to Emerson, October 25, 1833, in Army Letters of Appointment (1829-45), vol. 1, Records of the Adjutant General's Office, *Ms.*, NA; Francis B.

Heitman, *Historical Register and Dictionary of the United States Army* (Washington, 1903), 1: 405. See also Emerson to Lovell, October 22, 1833, in Letters Received, SGO Archives; Lovell to Emerson, October 23, 25, 26, 1833, in Letter Book, SGO Archives; Emerson to Adjutant General, November 18, 1833, in Letters Received, AGO Archives.

6. Post Returns, Fort Armstrong (December 1833-April 1836), Records of the Adjutant General's Office, *Ms.*, NA; George W. Cullum, *Biographical Register of the Officers and Graduates of the U.S. Military Academy at West Point* (New York, 1868), 1: 19; Frederic L. Paxson, *History of the American Frontier* (Cambridge, 1924), pp. 180, 213-14.

7. Davenport to Adjutant General, August 1, 1835, in Letters Received, AGO Archives; Emerson to Lovell, August 7, 1835, in Letters Received, SGO Archives; Deposition of Miles H. Clark, May 13, 1847, in *Dred Scott* v. *Emerson*, CCStL, *Ms.*; John H. Hauberg, "U.S. Army Surgeons at Fort Armstrong," *Journal of the Illinois State Historical Society* 24 (January 1932): 619, describes the severity of the cholera.

8. Article VI, Section 1, Constitution of August 26, 1818.

9. Emerson to Lovell, January 26, 1834, Emerson to Cass, January 26, 1834, in Emerson File, AGO Archives; Emerson to Surgeon General, January 26, February 3, 1834, March 28, 1835, in Letters Received, SGO Archives; Davenport to Adjutant General, July 5, 1834, in Letters Received, AGO Archives; Emerson to Lovell, March 28, April 1, 1835, January 6, 1836, and George A. McCall to Emerson, October 8, 1835, in Emerson Letters, AGO Archives.

10. Emerson to Surgeon General, August 7, 1835, in Letters Received, SGO Archives; Davenport to Adjutant General, August 1, 1835, May 4, 1836, in Letters Received, AGO Archives; and Surgeon General to Emerson, January 29, 1836, in Letter Book, SGO Archives. An analysis of frontier troop movements is found in Helen Heideman, "The History of the United States Army during the Administration of Andrew Jackson, 1829-1837" (M.A. thesis, Washington University, St. Louis, 1948), pp. 60-61.

11. Emerson to Lawson, July 10, 1838, in Emerson Letters, AGO Archives; Desposition of Miles H. Clark, May 13, 1847, in *Dred Scott* v. *Emerson*, CCStL, *Ms.*; Snyder, "John Emerson," pp. 442-43. One feature of the Davenport, Iowa, centennial in 1936 was a mural by Helen Johnson Hinrichsen commemorating three periods in the city's history. In the panel depicting the Indian period is a doctor, assisted by a black man, dressing a soldier's wounds. The doctor is John Emerson, the black man is Dred Scott. Gladys E. Hamlin, "Mural Painting in Iowa," *The Iowa Journal of History and Politics* 37 (July 1939): 295.

12. Davenport to Adjutant General, May 4, 9, 1836, in Letters Received, AGO Archives.

13. Deposition of Miles H. Clark, May 13, 1847, in *Dred Scott* v. *Emerson*, CCStL, *Ms.*

14. Emerson to Surgeon General, May 13, 1837, in Emerson Letters, AGO Archives; Emerson to Surgeon General, August 22, 1836, in Letters Received, SGO Archives; Davenport to Adjutant General, June 3, 1837, and Davenport to

Emerson, October 4, 1837, in Letters Received, AGO Archives; Adjutant General
to Davenport, July 12, 1837, in Letters Sent, Adjutant General's Office (1833-
43), Records of the Adjutant General's Office, *Ms.*, NA; entries dated July 3, 21,
September 6, December 30, 1836, in Journal No. 10, Lawrence Taliaferro Papers,
Ms., MinnHS; Edward D. Neill, "Occurrences In and Around Fort Snelling, From
1819 to 1840," *Collections of the Minnesota Historical Society* 2 (1860-67): 131.

15. For more on Taliaferro, see Taliaferro's Autobiography and Journal No. 10,
Lawrence Taliaferro Papers, *Ms.*, MinnHS; Declaration of Eliza Taliaferro in Application for Bounty Land Based on Service of Lawrence Taliaferro, October 3, 1873,
Records of the Veteran's Administration, *Ms.*, NA; Taliaferro to William B. Lewis,
February 15, 1830, in Letters Received (1830-36), Records of the Office of Indian
Affairs, *Ms.*, NA; Heitman, *Historical Register*, 1: 943; Neill, "Occurrences," p.
115; Grace L. Nute, sketch in *Dictionary of American Biography*, vol. 18, 1935 ed.,
s.v. "Lawrence Taliaferro"; William B. Folwell, *A History of Minnesota* (St. Paul,
1921), 1: 140-45; Willoughby M. Babcock, "Major Lawrence Taliaferro, Indian
Agent," *Mississippi Valley Historical Review* 11 (December 1924): 358-75.

16. When the freedom suit was instituted in 1846, Harriet declared that Taliaferro
had brought her to Fort Snelling "about eleven years ago," which would be 1835.
She also stated that she had been at Fort Snelling "for about three years" when
Taliaferro sold her to Emerson; that would have her coming to Fort Snelling in late
1833 or 1834. Taliaferro went back to Virginia in each of those years, so any one
of them could be correct. Petition of Harriet Scott, April 6, 1846, in *Harriet Scott
v. Emerson*, CCStL, *Ms.* See also Taliaferro correspondence in Letters Sent (1830-
36) and Letters Received (1830-36), Records of the Office of Indian Affairs, *Ms.*,
NA, and in Letters Received, Secretary of War (1833-43), Records of the Office of
the Secretary of War, *Ms.*, NA. Taliaferro stated later that Harriet was seventeen
years old and Dred Scott forty when they were married. Unidentified newspaper
clipping in Lawrence Taliaferro Papers, *Ms.*, MinnHS.

17. "Autobiography of Maj. Lawrence Taliaferro; Written in 1864," *Collections
of the Minnesota Historical Society* 6 (1894): 234-35.

18. Ibid., p. 235. Italics mine.

19. Unidentified newspaper clipping in Lawrence Taliaferro Papers, *Ms.*,
MinnHS. Italics mine.

20. In his autobiography, Taliaferro gave the date simply as 1836. By the time
of the trials, Mrs. Thompson had remarried and signed her deposition "Catherine
A. Anderson." Deposition of Catherine A. Anderson, May 10, 1847, in *Dred Scott
v. Emerson*, CCStL, *Ms.* See also Post Returns, Fort Snelling (May 1836 through
September 1837), Records of the Adjutant General's Office, *Ms.*, NA.

21. Deposition of Catherine A. Anderson, May 10, 1847, in *Dred Scott v.
Emerson*, CCStL, *Ms.*; Petition of Harriet Scott, April 6, 1847, in *Harriet Scott v.
Emerson*, CCStL, *Ms.*

22. Emerson to Surgeon General, July 10, 1838, in Emerson Letters, AGO
Archives; Emerson to Surgeon General, October 18, 1837, in Letters Received,
SGO Archives; Post Returns, Fort Snelling (October 1837), Records of the Adjutant
General's Office, *Ms*, NA; Deposition of Catherine A. Anderson, May 10, 1847, in

Dred Scott v. *Emerson*, CCStL, *Ms.* Traveling by canoe down the Mississippi was not uncommon when steamboat transportation was not available. "Autobiography of Maj. Lawrence Taliaferro," 235; Babcock, "Major Lawrence Taliaferro, Indian Agent," p. 375.

23. Emerson to Lawson, November 24, 1837, in Emerson Letters, AGO Archives. Fort Jesup was located about twenty-five miles southwest of Natchitoches, Louisiana, on the dividing ridge between the Red and Sabine rivers.

24. Emerson to Surgeon General, November 24, December 9, 15, 1837, in Emerson Letters, AGO Archives; Surgeon General to Emerson, December 22, 1837, January 6, February 1, 1838, in Letter Book, SGO Archives.

25. Certificates of George Walker, October 10, 1850, and Mary Bainbridge, October 31, 1850, in Application for Bounty Land Based on Service of John Emerson, Assistant Surgeon, United States Army, No. 1920, November 2, 1850, Records of the Veterans' Administration, *Ms.*, NA. Eliza Irene Sanford was born in 1815 in Winchester, Virginia, one of five daughters of Alexander Sanford, an iron manufacturer whose family had been in Virginia since 1699. Her brother was John F. A. Sanford. Alexander Sanford moved to St. Louis while his children were still young, and it is possible that Emerson and Irene Sanford knew each other in the early 1830s when both were in St. Louis (although Irene was much younger), and that at Fort Jesup they renewed an old acquaintanceship. See also *Springfield* (Mass.) *Daily Republican*, February 12, 1903, and Snyder, "John Emerson," pp. 451-52.

26. In the petition instituting the case in 1846, Harriet stated that after Emerson had gone to Fort Jesup "and having married there, he had petitioner [Harriet] removed to that post from Fort Snelling." Petition of Harriet Scott, April 6, 1846, in *Harriet Scott* v. *Emerson*, CCStL, *Ms.* Dred's petition, however, made no mention of Fort Jesup. But there is substantial evidence that he did go. First is the testimony by Mrs. Anderson, who used the plural in referring to this incident: "Dr. Emerson left Fort Snelling, in the fall of 1837, but left these slaves hired out. They remained there until April, 1838, when they left for the South, for Fort Gibson, I think." Deposition of Catherine A. Anderson, May 10, 1847, in *Dred Scott* v. *Emerson*, CCStL, *Ms.* Even though she had the wrong destination, the rest of her statement is accurate and supported by other evidence. The Emersons returned to Fort Snelling on the steamboat *Gipsey* in October 1838. Also on that vessel was the Reverend Alfred Brunson, who later stated that he had met as passengers on the *Gipsey* Dr. and Mrs. Emerson "with the afterwards famous Dred Scott, as their slave." Steven R. Riggs, "Protestant Missions In the Northwest," *Collections of the Minnesota Historical Society* 6 (1894): 139-40.

27. There is no record in any St. Louis court of such a suit.

28. Contemporary St. Louis newspapers reported that the "Gipsey, Capt. Thos. Gray," arrived from Louisville on September 24, 1838, and departed two days later "for Saint Peter's." *Daily Missouri Republican*, September 24, 1838. Emerson also reported September 26 as the date he left St. Louis for Fort Snelling. Furthermore, Dr. and Mrs. Emerson and Dred Scott were identified as passengers on the *Gipsey*. Riggs, "Protestant Missions In the Northwest," pp. 139-40. Missionary records at Fort Snelling dated October 1838 state that "the steamer Gipsey came up to the Fort on the 21st with Chippeway goods." Neill, "Occurrences," p. 137. Emerson

reported to the Surgeon General that he arrived at Fort Snelling on October 21. Emerson to Surgeon General, October 22, 1838, in Emerson Letters, AGO Archives. Finally, in Captain Gray's own words: "In 1836 and for years thereafter I was captain of the Steamer Gipsey, a light-draughted boat which made frequent trips to the 'Head of the Hollow,' where we had to stop to chop our wood for fuel, and on one of these trips carried to Fort Snelling that famous Negro Dred Scott, whose case afterwards made such a noise in the law courts." *The Missouri Republican,* July 29, 1883.

29. Emerson to Lawson, November 1, 1838, May 21, 1839, February 18, 1840, in Emerson Letters, AGO Archives; Surgeon General to Emerson, January 25, April 12, June 18, 1839, in Letter Book, SGO Archives; Emerson to Surgeon General, May 29, 1840, in Letters Received, SGO Archives; notation dated May 3, 1839, in Journal No. 9, Lawrence Taliaferro Papers, *Ms.,* MinnHS; Snyder, "John Emerson," pp. 444-51; William J. Peterson, *Steamboating on the Upper Mississippi* (Iowa City, 1937), p. 116.

30. Agreed Statement of Facts, May 4, 1854, File of *Dred Scott* v. *John F. A. Sanford,* Case No. 692, Circuit Court of the United States for the District of Missouri, *Ms.,* Office of the Clerk, United States District Court, Eastern District of Missouri, St. Louis (hereafter referred to as "*Scott* v. *Sanford,* No. 692, USCCStL, *Ms.*"). See appendix B.

31. *Daily Missouri Republican,* May 20-June 30, 1840. Emerson was in Cedar Keys, Florida, by June 27. Emerson to Lawson, June 27, 1840, in Emerson Letters, AGO Archives.

32. Welsey F. Diem, "Steamboating on the Upper Mississippi, 1823-1845" (M.A. thesis, Washington University, St. Louis, 1932), p. 58.

33. Writ of Summons, June 24, 1847, in *Dred Scott* v. *Emerson,* CCStL, *Ms.*

34. Gray was not the only steamboat captain summoned to testify. Another was Thomas O'Flaherty, but he did not testify either. Perhaps he commanded the steamboat that carried the group downriver in 1840. Of course, he may have had knowledge of another trip, or, for that matter, his relationship with the case may have been something completely different. Unless additional data becomes available, O'Flaherty's role in the Dred Scott drama remains a mystery.

35. For Emerson's activities in Florida from June 27, 1840, to September 6, 1842, see *Ms.* records of the Adjutant General's Office and the Surgeon General's Office, National Archives.

CHAPTER 3
After Dr. Emerson

1. Petition of Harriet Scott, April 6, 1846, and Deposition of Adeline Russell, December 20, 1849, in *Harriet Scott* v. *Emerson,* CCStL, *Ms.;* Emerson to Adjutant General, February 28, 1842, in Letters Received, AGO Archives; Emerson to Surgeon General, April 27, 1842, in Letters Received, SGO Archives; *Daily Missouri Republican,* April 3, 1857; John W. Burgess, *The Middle Period, 1817-1858* (New York, 1904), pp. 450-51. The Sanford family owned an estate, "California," located

outside the city limits of St. Louis in what is now Bridgeton, Missouri. Mary Louise Dalton, Notes, February 22, 1907, Dred Scott Papers.

2. It was first reported in a biographical sketch of the slave in the *St. Louis Daily Evening News,* April 3, 1857, and then widely reprinted.

3. Italics mine.

4. The document is Agreed Statement of Facts, May 4, 1854, *Scott* v. *Sanford,* No. 692, USCCStL, *Ms.*

5. Testimony of Samuel Russell in Bill of Exceptions, March 4, 1848, in *Harriet Scott* v. *Emerson,* CCStL, *Ms.*

6. Emerson to Surgeon General, September 6, 1842, in Emerson Letters, AGO Archives; Silas Reed to Secretary of War John C. Spencer, November 28, 1842, Emerson to Surgeon General, December 14, January 1, March 27, 1843, in Emerson File, AGO Archives.

7. Emerson's unsuccessful efforts to remain in the service and to clear his name are detailed in Reed to Spencer, December 8, 1842; Emerson to Surgeon General, December 14, 1842, January 1, 1843; A. G. Marchand et al. to John Tyler, January 1843 [*sic*]; Emerson to Surgeon General, March 27, June 8, 1843, in Emerson File, AGO Archives; Surgeon General to Emerson, January 26, 1843; Surgeon General to Thomas G. Mowrer, June 28, 1843; Surgeon General to Emerson, May 13, August 12, 1843, in Letter Book, SGO Archives.

8. General Records (No. Y-4), pp. 445-47, Office of the Recorder of Deeds, St. Louis, *Ms.*

9. *The Davenport Gazette,* January 4, 1844; *Daily Missouri Republican,* January 15, 1844; Charles E. Snyder, "John Emerson, Owner of Dred Scott," *Annals of Iowa* 15 (October 1938): 452-53.

10. Will of John Emerson, December 29, 1843, in file of Estate of John Emerson (No. 1914), PCStL, *Ms.* It is very clear that all the property was left to Mrs. Emerson as her life estate and not, as some historians claim, to be held "in trust" for the daughter. The original of the will was filed in the Scott County Court House in Davenport, but since Emerson owned property in Missouri, too, an ancillary will was filed in the probate court in St. Louis. Sanford was Emerson's brother-in-law; the other executor, Davenport, owned land in Iowa adjacent to Emerson's and undoubtedly the two had become friends.

11. Certified Copy of Probate Proceedings, August 13, 1844, in file of Estate of John Emerson (No. 1914), ibid. The witnesses were all residents of Davenport: Gilbert C. R. Mitchell (later a mayor of Davenport), Joseph D. Learned, and Patrick Gregg.

12. Judge James W. Bollinger to Dalton, February 16, 1907, Dred Scott Papers.

13. See various documents in file of Estate of John Emerson (No. 1914), PCStL, *Ms.*

14. Bollinger to Dalton, February 16, 1907, Dred Scott Papers.

15. A legend has persisted in Davenport that Dred Scott had indeed been there (Snyder, "John Emerson," p. 455), but there is no substantiating evidence. There is ample evidence, though, that Emerson owned more slaves than the Scotts. When he was at Fort Jesup in 1838, he wrote that "one of my negroes in St. Louis has

sued me for his freedom." Emerson to Surgeon General, July 10, 1838, in Emerson Letters, AGO Archives. However, an examination of court records in St. Louis shows no evidence that such a suit ever was filed. He had at least one slave with him in Florida in 1841, a "bright mulatto" named William. Emerson to Surgeon General, July 21, 1841, in Letters Received, SGO Archives. Of course the inventory of the Emerson estate in Iowa cited the "several slaves" there.

16. Deposition of Adeline Russell, December 20, 1849, in *Harriet Scott v. Emerson*, CCStL, Ms.

CHAPTER 4
Issues and Lawyers

1. Among others see *The Daily Union* (Washington, D.C.), December 17, 1856; *The New York Journal of Commerce*, December 17, 1856; *Morning Courier and New-York Enquirer*, December 18, 1856; *The National Era* (Washington, D.C.), March 19, 1857; William C. Breckenridge to Eugene M. Violette, September 20, 1916, in James M. Breckenridge, *William Clark Breckenridge, His Life, Lineage and Writings* (St. Louis, 1932), pp. 200-201; Otto Gresham, *The Dred Scott Case* (Chicago, 1908), p. 3.

2. Frederick Trevor Hill, *Decisive Battles of the Law* (New York, 1907), pp. 116-18.

3. Frank H. Hodder, "Some Phases of the Dred Scott Case," *Mississippi Valley Historical Review* 16 (June 1929): 4-6; Vincent Hopkins, *Dred Scott's Case* (New York, 1951), pp. 10-12, 190.

4. See chapter 69, "An Act to enable persons held in slavery to sue for their freedom," in *The Revised Statutes of the State of Missouri, Revised and Digested . . . during the Session of Eighteen Hundred and Forty-four and Eighteen Hundred and Forty-five* (St. Louis, 1845), pp. 531-34.

5. Action in False Imprisonment, April 6, 1846, in *Harriet Scott v. Emerson*, CCStL, Ms.

6. For discovery of missing Dred Scott documents, see appendix A; also *St. Louis Post Dispatch*, August 22, 1956; *New York Times*, August 23, 1956; *Christian Science Monitor*, August 24, 1956.

7. John W. Burgess, *The Middle Period, 1817-1858* (New York, 1904), p. 451.

8. *Daily Missouri Republican*, April 3, 1857.

9. *The Saint Louis Daily Evening News*, April 3, 1857.

10. For a discussion of the origins of the case, see Walter Ehrlich, "Origins of the Dred Scott Case," *The Journal of Negro History* 59 (April 1974): 132-42.

11. Bill of Exceptions, March 4, 1848; Writ of Summons, December 22, 1849; Bond of C. Edmund LaBeaume and Henry T. Blow, April 9, 1851, in *Dred Scott v. Emerson*, CCStL, Ms.; Bond of Joseph Charless, July 2, 1847; Bond of C. Edmund LaBeaume and Louis T. LaBeaume, April 25, 1852, in *Harriet Scott v. Emerson*, CCStL, Ms.

12. Permanent Records, No. 26 (1856-57), p. 163, Circuit Court of St. Louis

County, *Ms.*, CCStL; *Daily Missouri Republican,* May 27, 1857. Burgess *(Middle Period,* p. 452) states that Taylor Blow also paid the state court costs for Scott. There are no existing records to either verify or disclaim this statement.

13. Summons in False Imprisonment, April 6, 1846, and Action in False Imprisonment, April 6, 1846, in *Harriet Scott* v. *Emerson,* CCStL, *Ms.*

14. The biographical sketch of Francis B. Murdoch is based upon the following: *San Jose* (Calif.) *Pioneer,* April 29, May 13, 1882; *History of Madison County, Illinois* (Edwardsville, Ill., 1882), p. 188; *History of Santa Clara County, California* (San Francisco, 1881), p. 721; Edward C. Kemble, *A History of California Newspapers* (Los Gatos, Calif., 1962), pp. 219-20; Henry Tanner, *The Martyrdom of Lovejoy* (Chicago, 1881), pp. 230-31; Frank H. Dugan, "An Illinois Martyrdom," in *Papers in Illinois History and Transactions for the Year 1938* (Springfield, Ill., 1939), pp. 149-52; J. F. Snyder, "Alfred Cowles," in *Transactions of the Illinois State Historical Society for the Year 1909* (Springfield, Ill., 1910), pp. 172-73; Peyton Hurt, "The Rise and Fall of 'Know Nothings' in California," California Historical Society *Quarterly* 9 (June 1930): 115-16; Benjamin B. Beales, "The San Jose *Mercury* and the Civil War," ibid., 22 (September 1943): 224.

15. George W. Stevens, *The History of the Central Baptist Church* (St. Louis, 1927), pp. 27, 33-34.

16. *History of Santa Clara County, California,* p. 721.

17. *Daily Missouri Republican,* May 26, 1847; David D. March, "The Life and Times of Charles D. Drake" (Doctoral dissertation, University of Missouri-Columbia, 1949), pp. 28-36; John D. Lawson, ed., *American State Trials* (St. Louis, 1921), 13: 226. Document files in various St. Louis courts show Drake as the Blows's attorney in several suits in 1846.

18. W. V. N. Bay, *Reminiscences of the Bench and Bar of Missouri* (St. Louis, 1878), pp. 165-71; Lawson, *American State Trials,* 13: 229-30; J. Thomas Scharf, *History of Saint Louis City and County* (Philadelphia, 1883), 2: 1477; Richard Edwards and M. Hopewell, *Edwards's Great West and her Commercial Metropolis* (St. Louis, 1860), p. 587.

19. Entry dated March 29, 1851, Edward Bates Diary, *Ms.*, MoHS, St. Louis.

20. For Field and Hall see *Daily Missouri Republican,* December 6, 1847; *St. Louis Daily New Era,* December 6, 1847; Frank E. Stevens, "Alexander Pope Field," *Journal of the Illinois State Historical Society* 4 (April 1911): 7-37; Horace White, *The Life of Lyman Trumbull* (Boston, 1911), p. 11; Frederick C. Pierce, *Field Genealogy* (Chicago, 1901), 2: 1123-26; *Green's St. Louis Directory* for 1847 and 1848; Lawson, *American State Trials,* 13: 227.

21. Fees Paid by Benoni S. Garland, December 13, 1859, in file of Estate of John F. A. Sanford (No. 5328), PCStL, *Ms.*

22. Bond of Alexander Sanford, August 13, 1844, in file of Estate of John Emerson (No. 1914), PCStL, *Ms.* Garland did the legal work.

23. Dalton to Hill, February 11, 1907, Dred Scott Papers; Bay, *Reminiscences of the Bench and Bar of Missouri,* p. 569; Lawson, *American State Trials,* 13: 226; Floyd C. Shoemaker, ed., *Missouri and Missourians* (Chicago, 1943), 1: 633; Scharf, *Saint Louis City and County,* 2: 1471-72.

24. For Garland and Norris see Lawson, *American State Trials,* 13: 227-28; James Grant Wilson and John Fiske, eds., *Appleton's Cyclopedia of American Biography* (New York, 1887), 2: 605; John Livingston, *Portraits of Eminent Americans Now Living* (New York, 1853), pp. 657-64; Hugh A. Garland, *The Life of John Randolph of Roanoke* (New York, 1850), pp. v-viii; Scharf, *Saint Louis City and County,* 2: 1484; Alexander N. DeMenil, "A Century of Missouri Literature," *Missouri Historical Review* 15 (October 1920): 83-84. Although they had the same last name, there is no evidence that Benoni S. Garland and Hugh A. Garland were related.

CHAPTER 5
First State Circuit Court Trial

1. 1 Missouri Reports 476 (1824).
2. 1 Missouri Reports 725 (1827).
3. 2 Missouri Reports 20 (1828).
4. 2 Missouri Reports 145 (1829).
5. 2 Missouri Reports 157 (1829).
6. 2 Missouri Reports 214 (1830).
7. 3 Missouri Reports 195 (1833).
8. 3 Missouri Reports 275 (1833).
9. 3 Missouri Reports 401 (1834).
10. 4 Missouri Reports 597 (1837). For discussion of these cases, see Helen T. Catterall, ed., *Judicial Cases Concerning American Slavery and the Negro* (Washington, 1937), 5: 113-17, 125, 128-30, 135-43, 148-51.
11. 4 Missouri Reports 354 (1837); Catterall, *Judicial Cases,* 5: 148.
12. Chapter 69, "An Act to enable persons held in slavery to sue for their freedom," *The Revised Statutes of the State of Missouri, Revised . . . during the Session of Eighteen Hundred and Forty-four and Eighteen Hundred and Forty-five* (St. Louis, 1845), pp. 531-34.
13. Petition of Dred Scott, April 6, 1846, and Petition of Harriet Scott, April 6, 1846, in *Harriet Scott* v. *Emerson,* CCStL, Ms. Those who have had access to the court records have managed to mix up the documents, for some are in the *Dred Scott* v. *Emerson* file, which should be in the *Harriet Scott* v. *Emerson* file, and vice versa.
14. Endorsements dated April 6, 1846, on Petition of Dred Scott and Petition of Harriet Scott in ibid.
15. Summons in False Imprisonment, April 6, 1846, and Action in False Imprisonment, April 6, 1846, in ibid.
16. The Return Docket of the Circuit Court of St. Louis County for the period up to 1847 has been lost, but an index indicates that these are the numbers. Identifying labels on case documents also show these numbers.
17. Stipulation, February 12, 1850, in *Harriet Scott* v. *Emerson,* CCStL, Ms.
18. Writ of Summons, April 6, 1846, in ibid.; Writ of Summons, April 6, 1846,

in *Dred Scott* v. *Emerson*, CCStL, *Ms.* This is the last appearance of Murdoch's name on any of the papers in the case. The absence of a bond for Dred might suggest that Murdoch supported only Harriet's bid for freedom. Yet Murdoch filed the petition for Dred as well.

19. George W. Goode to Dred Scott, April 8, 1846, in *Dred Scott* v. *Emerson*, CCStL, *Ms.*; Pleas, November 19, 1846, in *Harriet Scott* v. *Emerson*, CCStL, *Ms.*; Permanent Records, No. 17 (1845-46), p. 357, CCStL, *Ms.*

20. Deposition of Catherine A. Anderson, May 10, 1847, in *Dred Scott* v. *Emerson*, CCStL, *Ms.* It is not clear why Mrs. Anderson testified by deposition rather than personally in court. Perhaps it was in deference to her sex.

21. Deposition of Miles H. Clark, May 13, 1847, in *Dred Scott* v. *Emerson*, CCStL, *Ms.*; Muster Rolls, "G" Company, 1st Infantry (July 1834-August 1836), "D" Company, 1st Infantry (July 1836-April 1837), Records of the Adjutant General's Office, *Ms.*, NA.

22. James R. Lackland to Samuel Russle [*sic*], June 2, 1847, and Russell to Lackland, June 2, 1847, in *Dred Scott* v. *Emerson*, CCStL, *Ms.*

23. Permanent Records, No. 18 (1847-48), p. 10, CCStL, *Ms.* Judge John M. Krum, who handled the earlier proceedings of the suit, resigned early in 1847, and Hamilton replaced him just a few days before the April term commenced. *Daily Missouri Republican*, January 30, March 30, April 16, 1847. The "Old Courthouse," as it is now called, is one of St. Louis' historic monuments, standing alongside the world-famous Gateway Arch on the riverfront grounds of the Jefferson National Expansion Memorial.

24. Permanent Records, No. 18 (1847-48), pp. 8-10, CCStL, *Ms.*; *Daily Missouri Republican*, June 29, July 1, August 3, 1847.

25. Bill of Exceptions, March 4, 1848, and Writ of Summons, June 24, 1847, in *Dred Scott* v. *Emerson*, CCStL, *Ms.* The other witnesses were Thomas O'Flaherty, Thomas Gray, Adam D. Steuart, John F. Carter, and Stewart Carter. Gray and O'Flaherty were steamboat captains. Gray had commanded the *Gipsey,* which carried the Emersons and Scotts to Fort Snelling in 1838 and aboard which baby Eliza had been born; probably he was to testify about that. Perhaps O'Flaherty was to testify to another voyage. Major Steuart was an army paymaster stationed in St. Louis at the time. He had served at Fort Snelling when Emerson was there, and on at least one occasion he had accompanied Emerson on a trip from St. Louis to Rock Island. Presumably Steuart had personal knowledge of Dred Scott's having lived in free territory. What connection the Carters had with the case is unknown. Emerson to Surgeon General, January 1, 1843, in Emerson File, AGO Archives; Journal No. 10, May 12, 1836, Lawrence Taliaferro Papers, *Ms.*, MinnHS; *Daily Missouri Republican*, May 11, November 20, 1847.

26. Bill of Exceptions, March 4, 1848, in *Dred Scott* v. *Emerson*, CCStL, *Ms.* Goode had summoned one defense witness, Benoni S. Garland, but did not call on him.

27. Plaintiff's Instructions, n.d., and Defendant's Instructions, n.d., in ibid.

28. Brief of George W. Goode, April 3, 1848, in file of *Irene Emerson* v. *Dred*

Scott, Case No. 14, March Term, 1848, State of Missouri Supreme Court, *Ms.,* Jefferson City, Mo. (hereafter referred to as *"Emerson* v. *Scott,* No. 14, March Term, 1848, MoSC, *Ms."*). This file is part of the "missing" papers the author found in the Missouri Supreme Court. It contains, among other documents, copies of the attorneys' briefs with the points of law they were concerned with, information heretofore unknown to historians.

29. Permanent Records, No. 18 (1847-48), p. 10, CCStL, *Ms.*

30. *Daily Missouri Republican,* July 1, 1847. *Harriet Scott* v. *Irene Emerson* was not even listed in the newspaper, probably because it was not recorded in the official minutes of the Circuit Court until December 11, 1847, when the recorder somehow learned that he had completely overlooked this suit. Permanent Records, No. 18 (1847-48), p. 89, CCStL, *Ms.*

31. *Daily Missouri Republican,* June 30-July 5, 1847; *St. Louis Daily New Era,* June 30-July 5, 1847.

CHAPTER 6
First State Supreme Court Appeal

1. Permanent Records, No. 18 (1847-48), pp. 10, 74, CCStL, *Ms.;* Motion for New Trial, June 30, 1847, and Additional Reason for New Trial, July 1, 1847, in *Harriet Scott* v. *Emerson,* CCStL, *Ms.;* Affidavit of Plaintiff, July 24, 1847, in *Dred Scott* v. *Emerson,* CCStL, *Ms.*

2. Petition of Dred Scott, July 1, 1847, and Declaration of Field and Hall, November 18, 1847, in *Dred Scott* v. *Emerson,* CCStL, *Ms.;* Permanent Records, No. 18 (1847-48), pp. 38, 48, 187, CCStL, *Ms.*

3. Petition of Dred Scott, July 1, 1847, Writ of Summons, July 3, 1847, Statement of Field and Hall, November 15, 1847, Declaration of Field and Hall, November 18, 1847, in *Dred Scott* v. *Emerson,* CCStL, *Ms.;* Bond of Joseph Charless, July 2, 1847, in *Harriet Scott* v. *Emerson,* CCStL, *Ms.;* Permanent Records, No. 18 (1847-48), pp. 38, 48, 187, CCStL, *Ms.*

4. Frederick C. Pierce, *Field Genealogy* (Chicago, 1901), 2: 1124; Frank E. Stevens, "Alexander Pope Field," *Journal of the Illinois State Historical Society* 4 (April 1911): 22.

5. Bill of Exceptions, December 4, 1847, March 4, 1848, in *Dred Scott* v. *Emerson,* CCStL, *Ms.;* Permanent Records, No. 18 (1847-48), p. 91, CCStL, *Ms.;* Transcript, March 6, 1848, in *Emerson* v. *Scott,* No. 14, March Term, 1848, MoSC, *Ms.* A *bill of exceptions* is a written statement of objections to the decision of a court, made by a party to the cause, and properly certified by the judge or court who made the decision. The object of a bill of exceptions is to put the decision objected to on record for the information of the appellate court having cognizance of the cause in error. John Bouvier, *Bouvier's Law Dictionary and Concise Encyclopedia* (Kansas City, 1914), 1: 348. A *writ of error* is a writ issued by an appellate

to an inferior court, ordering the latter to send up the record of a particular litigation so an alleged error might be corrected. Ibid., 2: 3498.

6. Motion, March 14, 1848, in *Dred Scott* v. *Emerson,* CCStL, *Ms.;* Permanent Records, No. 18 (1847-48), pp. 205, 213, and Permanent Records, No. 26 (1856-57), pp. 163, 267, CCStL, *Ms.*

7. General Record (Jefferson City, 1847-57), p. 35, MoSC, *Ms.*

8. Brief of George W. Goode, April 3, 1848, in *Emerson* v. *Scott,* No. 14, March Term, 1848, MoSC, *Ms.*

9. Brief of Field and Hall, April 3, 1848, in ibid.

10. Opinion of Justice Scott, in file of *Irene Emerson* v. *Harriet,* Case No. 16, March Term, 1848, MoSC, *Ms.* See also 11 Missouri Reports 413 (1848). The decision was actually rendered in Harriet Scott's case, and all that was said about her husband's case was that since it was in "all respects similar, . . . a similar disposition is made of it." General Record (Jefferson City, 1847-57), p. 50, MoSC, *Ms.*

11. *Daily Missouri Republican,* April 14, July 6, October 27, 1848; *Saint Louis Daily Union,* July 6, 1848.

CHAPTER 7
Second State Circuit Court Trial

1. Writs of Summons, February 17, 25, April 28, May 1, December 8, 17, 22, 1849, in *Dred Scott* v. *Emerson,* CCStL, *Ms.;* Writs of Summons, May 28, December 8, 20, 1849, in *Harriet Scott* v. *Emerson,* CCStL, *Ms.; Daily Missouri Republican,* May 30, 1849, June 22, 25, 1850; *St. Louis Daily New Era,* June 1, 1849.

2. Permanent Records, No. 19 (1849-50), pp. 295-96, CCStL, *Ms.*

3. Bill of Exceptions, February 13, 1850, in *Dred Scott* v. *Emerson,* CCStL, *Ms.;* Deposition of Adeline Russell, December 20, 1849, in *Harriet Scott* v. *Emerson,* CCStL, *Ms.*

4. The additional witnesses were Joseph Charless, Taylor Blow, Captain Thomas O'Flaherty, Captain Thomas Gray, Major Adam D. Steuart, Colonel Joseph Plympton, John F. Carter, Stewart Carter, a Dr. Watts, John Loving, John F. Dars, and Dr. R. M. Jennings. Writs of Summons, February 25, May 1, December 17, 20, 22, 1849, in *Dred Scott* v. *Emerson,* CCStL, *Ms.* The relationship of Charless and Blow to Dred Scott has already been indicated, as is the probable relationship of the two steamboat captains, Gray and O'Flaherty. The army officers Plympton and Steuart had been stationed at various times at the same posts where Emerson and Scott had been. But who the others were and what knowledge they had of the facts of the case is unknown.

5. Bill of Exceptions, February 13, 1850, in ibid.

6. Instructions "A," February 12, 1850, in ibid.

7. Instructions "B," February 12, 1850, in ibid.

8. Permanent Records, No. 19 (1849-50), p. 295, CCStL, *Ms.*

9. *Daily Missouri Republican,* January 16, 1850.

CHAPTER 8
Second State Supreme Court Appeal

1. It was at this point, as already indicated, that the duplication of cases ended and only Dred's went forward, with the agreement that the decision in his case would be binding in Harriet's.

2. Permanent Records, No. 19 (1849-50), pp. 295, 307, 339, 340, CCStL, *Ms*; Motion for New Trial, January 17, 1850, in *Harriet Scott* v. *Emerson*, CCStL, *Ms.*; Bill of Exceptions, February 13, 1850, in *Dred Scott* v. *Emerson*, CCStL, *Ms.*; Writ of Error, March 8, 1850, in file of *Dred Scott* v. *Irene Emerson*, Case No. 137, October Term, 1851, State of Missouri Supreme Court, *Ms.*, Jefferson City (hereafter referred to as "*Scott* v. *Emerson*, No. 137, October Term, 1851, MoSC, *Ms.*"); Transcript, February 23, 1850, in ibid. The Missouri Supreme Court has no existing docket for this period, but notations on documents in the file indicate docket numbers.

Although Mrs. Emerson was the appellant in the supreme court litigation, the case was nevertheless officially docketed as "*Dred Scott* v. *Irene Emerson.*" Contributing to confusion is that some of the documents in the file are labeled "*Irene Emerson* v. *Dred Scott.*" There is no explanation for these discrepancies.

3. General Record (St. Louis, 1849-50), p. 63, MoSC, *Ms.*; *Daily Missouri Republican,* March 12, 19, 1849, March 22, 1850.

4. Mrs. Emerson appeared "personally" before the recorder of deeds of St. Louis County on March 28, 1849, to sell some of her deceased husband's land. General Records (No. Y-4), pp. 446-47, Office of the Recorder of Deeds, St. Louis, *Ms.* By October 10, 1850, she was in Springfield, Massachusetts, where she "personally appeared" before a justice of the peace to file a claim for bounty land. Certificate of George Walker, October 10, 1850, in Application for Bounty Land Based on Service of John Emerson, Assistant Surgeon, United States Army, No. 1920, Records of the Veterans' Administration, *Ms.*, NA. See also *Springfield* (Mass.) *Daily Republican,* February 12, 1903; Charles E. Snyder, "John Emerson, Owner of Dred Scott," *Annals of Iowa* 15 (October 1938): 458-60; Vincent Hopkins, *Dred Scott's Case* (New York, 1951), p. 29. The name "Chaffee" is pronounced "*Chay-*fee."

5. 3 Missouri Reports 401 (1834). Garland did not actually cite the case, but he used the principle contained therein.

6. Points made by appellant, in *Scott* v. *Emerson*, No. 137, October Term, 1851, MoSC, *Ms.*

7. Brief of appellee, in ibid. The reference to the Fort Jesup episode was the first made by any of the attorneys.

8. This brief resume of the Missouri senatorial campaign of 1850 comes primarily from the following: William N. Chambers, *Old Bullion Benton: Senator from the New West* (Boston, 1956), pp. 337-77; Benjamin Merkel, "The Antislavery Movement in Missouri, 1819-1865" (Doctoral dissertation, Washington University,

St. Louis, 1939), pp. 109-28; William M. Meigs, *The Life of Thomas Hart Benton* (Philadelphia, 1904), pp. 408-14; P. Orman Ray, *The Repeal of the Missouri Compromise* (Cleveland, 1909), pp. 27-66; Clarence H. McClure, "Opposition in Missouri to Thomas Hart Benton," *Bulletin of Central Missouri State Teachers College* 27 (December 1926): 120-218; and Richard R. Stenberg, "Some Political Aspects of the Dred Scott Case," *Mississippi Valley Historical Review* 19 (March 1933): 572-73.

9. Throughout this period Birch was suing Benton for slanderously calling him (Birch) a "wife-beater." Birch was known as "personally and politically a malignant enemy" of Benton's. For further attitudes of the judges toward Benton, see John F. Ryland to Major Bronaugh in *Lexington* (Mo.) *Chronicle,* September 12, 1851; *Daily Missouri Republican,* August 18, 1849, September 18, 1851, March 3, April 27, May 8, 18, June 16, 1852; McClure, "Opposition in Missouri to Thomas Hart Benton," pp. 130, 142, 157.

10. Diary of William B. Napton, p. 223, and Edward Bates Diary, October 26, 1850, *Ms.,* MoHS.

11. Edward Bates Diary, October 26, 1850, *Ms.,* MoHS; Stenberg, "Some Political Aspects of the Dred Scott Case," p. 573.

12. For instance, the Whig candidate Henry S. Geyer declared himself in favor of certain proslavery principles, despite the opposition of a number of prominent Whigs, and enough anti-Benton Democrats gave him sufficient support to defeat Benton. *Daily Missouri Republican,* January 20, February 21, 1851; Diary of William B. Napton, pp. 56-57, *Ms.,* MoHS; Chambers, *Old Bullion Benton,* pp. 368-77.

13. Diary of William B. Napton, p. 223, and Edward Bates Diary, October 26, 1850, *Ms.,* MoHS.

14. Diary of William B. Napton, p. 223, *Ms.,* MoHS.

15. The campaign was hotly contested, nine candidates running for the supreme court's three judgeships. Although partisan politics became involved, the *Dred Scott* case per se was never mentioned in the press. *Daily Missouri Republican,* March 4-August 10, 1851.

16. Apparently Field received no special consideration, for other cases not originally scheduled were also placed on the docket. *Daily Saint Louis Intelligencer,* December 12, 1851.

17. Brief of Lyman D. Norris in *Scott v. Emerson,* No. 137, October Term, 1851, MoSC, *Ms.;* General Record (St. Louis, 1849-54), p. 209, MoSC, *Ms.; Daily Saint Louis Intelligencer,* December 1, 1851.

18. Brief of Lyman D. Norris, in *Scott v. Emerson,* No. 137, October Term, 1851, MoSC, *Ms.*

19. The printed version of Norris's brief, which appears in 15 Missouri Reports 577-81 (1852), is not complete. Unless otherwise indicated, the excerpts from and analysis of the brief are based upon the original document discovered by the author in the Missouri Supreme Court.

20. General Record (St. Louis, 1849-54), p. 236, MoSC, *Ms.; Daily Missouri Republican,* December 25, 1851, January 23, February 16, 17, March 16, 1852.

From all indications Dred Scott's attorney continued to rely on his 1850 brief, as no other brief is in the files, nor is there any reference to any other.

21. Opinion of William Scott, March 22, 1852, in *Scott v. Emerson*, No. 137, October Term, 1851, MoSC, *Ms.* The opinion as printed in 15 Missouri Reports 582-87 (1852) is, except for minor changes in punctuation, otherwise exactly as the original.

22. 15 Missouri Reports 583.

23. Ibid., p. 584.

24. Ibid., p. 586.

25. For more on *Strader* v. *Graham*, see ch. 9, *infra*.

26. 15 Missouri Reports 586-87.

27. Opinion of Hamilton R. Gamble, March 22, 1852, in *Scott v. Emerson*, No. 137, October Term, 1851, MoSC, *Ms.* The opinion as published in 15 Missouri Reports 587-92 (1852) is the same as the original, except for some minor changes in punctuation.

28. Ibid., pp. 591-92.

29. Ibid., p. 576.

30. General Record (St. Louis, 1849-54), p. 236, MoSC, *Ms.*

31. *Daily Missouri Republican,* March 23, 1852.

32. *Daily Saint Louis Intelligencer,* March 23, 1852; *Morning Signal* (St. Louis), March 23, 1852. Among those that made no mention of the case at all were *The Western Watchman* (St. Louis), March 25, April 1, 8, 1852, and the *Liberty* (Mo.) *Weekly Tribune,* March 26, April 2, 9, 16, 1852, even though they printed news about the supreme court.

33. *Daily National Intelligencer* (Washington, D.C.), April 8, 1852.

34. Allan Nevins, *Ordeal of the Union* (New York, 1947), 2: 78-80.

35. Garland and Norris to Louis T. LaBeaume, March 23, 1852, and Motion, June 8, 1852, in *Harriet Scott* v. *Emerson*, CCStL, *Ms.;* Garland and Norris to Samuel Conway, March 23, 1852, and Motion, June 8, 1852, in *Dred Scott v. Emerson*, CCStL, *Ms.;* Permanent Records, No. 18 (1847-48), p. 213; No. 22 (1852-53), pp. 51-52, 111; No. 24 (1854-55), pp. 33, 407; No. 25 (1855-56), pp. 54, 228, 364; No. 26 (1856-57), pp. 30, 163, CCStL, *Ms.;* Agreed Statement of Facts, May 4, 1854, in file of *Scott v. Sanford*, No. 692, USCCStL.

CHAPTER 9
From State Case to Federal Case

1. See file of Estate of John Emerson (No. 1914), PCStL, *Ms.* No one was appointed to replace Alexander Sanford after he died in 1848. In 1849 Mrs. Emerson herself, and not an administrator, sold land that belonged to the estate. General Records (No. Y-4), pp. 446-47, Office of the Recorder of Deeds, St. Louis, *Ms.*

2. Missouri Revised Statutes, Annotated, I, 11. Italics mine.

3. Among contemporary references to Sanford as executor are Roswell M. Field to Montgomery Blair, January 7, 1855, Dred Scott Papers; Ransom H. Gillet to Caleb Cushing, November 16, 1857, Caleb Cushing Papers, *Ms.*, LC; unidentified newspaper article, n.d., in Samuel Latham Mitchell Barlow Miscellaneous Papers, *Ms.*, New York Public Library; *Morning Courier and New-York Enquirer,* December 19, 1856; *Springfield* (Mass.) *Daily Republican,* March 14, May 7, 1857; *New York Daily Tribune,* May 7, June 6, 1857; *The Saint Louis Daily Evening News,* May 8, 1857.

4. For more on Sanford see *Springfield* (Mass.) *Daily Republican,* February 12, 1903; *New York Daily Tribune,* May 7, 1857; *Daily Missouri Republican,* August 11, 1847; *The Saint Louis Daily Evening News,* May 8, 1857; Paul Beckwith, *Creoles of St. Louis* (St. Louis, 1893), p. 56; Charles E. Snyder, "John Emerson, Owner of Dred Scott," *Annals of Iowa* 15 (October 1938): 451.

5. Thomas C. Reynolds to Cushing, May 16, 1854, Caleb Cushing Papers, *Ms.*, LC; *Daily Missouri Republican,* October 31, 1854. See W. V. N. Bay, *Reminiscences of the Bench and Bar of Missouri* (St. Louis, 1878), pp. 236-41, for biographical sketch of Field. Field was the father of the famous poet Eugene Field.

6. Lee to Dalton, February 15, 1907, Dred Scott Papers; John W. Burgess, *The Middle Period* (New York, 1904), pp. 449-51. These accounts were confirmed by R. E. Bombauer in an address before the Missouri Bar Association memorializing Crane. *Proceedings of the Twenty-Fifth Annual Meeting of the Missouri Bar Association . . . December 12 and 13, 1907* (Kansas City, 1908), pp. 232-33.

7. *Frank Leslie's Illustrated Newspaper,* June 27, 1857, refers to Crane's "indefatiguable industry" in behalf of the Scotts.

8. John D. Lawson, ed., *American State Trials* (St. Louis, 1921), 13: 251.

9. Bond of C. Edmund LaBeaume and Henry T. Blow, April 9, 1851, in *Dred Scott v. Emerson,* CCStL, *Ms.*; notation dated April 25, 1852, on ibid.; *Green's St. Louis City Directory* for 1845, 1847, 1848, and 1851.

10. Field to Blair, January 7, 1855, Dred Scott Papers.

11. Permanent Records, No. 26 (1856-57), p. 263, CCStL, *Ms.*; *Daily Missouri Republican,* May 27, 1857.

12. Probate Proceedings in the Matter of the Estate of John F. A. Sanford, 1857, Office of the Commissioner of Records, Surrogate's Court, New York City, *Ms.*; file of Estate of John F. A. Sanford (No. 5328), PCStL, *Ms.*; W. W. Corcoran to Lawrence Riggs, February 7, 1857, Papers of W. W. Corcoran, *Ms.*, LC; *Morning Courier and New-York Enquirer,* December 18, 1856; *New York Daily Tribune,* May 7, 1857.

13. Petition of Samuel L. M. Barlow, July 23, 1857, in Probate Proceedings in the Matter of the Estate of John F. A. Sanford, 1857, Office of the Commissioner of Records, Surrogate's Court, New York City, *Ms.*; unlabeled newspaper clipping, Samuel Latham Mitchell Barlow Miscellaneous Papers, *Ms.*, New York Public Library. See also the Barlow and Sanford probate records.

14. Notation by Caleb Cushing, November 23, 1857, on Chaffee to Cushing, November 9, 1857, Caleb Cushing Papers, *Ms.*, LC; Gillet to Blair, November 16,

1857, ibid.; Chaffee to Editor, March 14, 1857, in *Springfield* (Mass.) *Daily Republican*, March 16, 1857; R. A. Chapman to Editor, n.d., in ibid., May 29, 1857. See also article in ibid., August 10, 1896, on occasion of Chaffee's death. The author deals with the question of ownership of Dred Scott in his article, "Was the Dred Scott Case Valid?" *Journal of American History* 55 (September 1968): 256-65. That title was ill-chosen; the focus of the article is on the genuineness of the case, not its validity. The legal relationship between Scott and Sanford did not affect the validity of the suit. As Potter correctly points out, a freedom suit could be brought against anyone *holding* a person as a slave, whether or not he was the legal owner, and Sanford did admit to holding the Scotts as slaves. David M. Potter, *The Impending Crisis, 1848-1861* (New York, 1976), p. 269 (footnote).

15. The "test case" possibility becomes especially plausible in light of the growing sentiment that the courts should settle the issue of slavery in the territories. See Wallace Mendelson, "Dred Scott's Case—Reconsidered," *Minnesota Law Review* 38 (1953): 16-28, and ch. 18, *infra*.

16. For LaBeaume see *St. Louis Daily New Era*, April 6, 1846, April 20, 1848; *Daily Missouri Republican*, May 31, 1858; Richard Edwards and M. Hopewell, *Edwards's Great West and her Commercial Metropolis* (St. Louis, 1860), p. 400; J. Thomas Scharf, *History of Saint Louis City and County* (Philadelphia, 1883), 1: 685; Vincent Hopkins, *Dred Scott's Case* (New York, 1951), p. 29.

17. *Morning Courier and New-York Enquirer*, March 16, 1857; 1856 Democratic Political Lists: Names of Active Workers in the Various States, Papers of William Learned Marcy, Ms., LC.

18. For example, see *The Daily Union* (Washington, D.C.), December 17, 1856; *The New York Journal of Commerce*, December 17, 1856; *Morning Courier and New-York Enquirer*, December 18, 1856; *The National Era* (Washington, D.C.), March 19, 1857.

19. Scharf, *Saint Louis City and County*, 2: 1884; Alexander N. DeMenil, "A Century of Missouri Literature," *Missouri Historical Review* 15 (October 1920): 83-84.

20. Field to Blair, December 24, 1854, Dred Scott Papers; Reynolds to Cushing, May 16, 1854, Caleb Cushing Papers, Ms., LC; *Daily Missouri Republican*, October 31, 1854; *Daily National Intelligencer* (Washington, D.C.), December 24, 1856; Burgess, *Middle Period*, p. 449.

21. Field to Blair, January 7, 1855, Dred Scott Papers. The publication is a twelve-page pamphlet entitled *The Case of Dred Scott in the Supreme Court of the United States, December Term, 1854*. It contains a copy of the proceedings in the United States Circuit Court, as well as a ringing appeal, over the signature (actually the mark) of Dred Scott, for financial and legal assistance. A copy of this rare pamphlet is in the Boston Public Library; another is in the Lawson Collection in the Law Library of the University of Missouri-Columbia.

22. Dalton, Notes, February 18, 1907, Dred Scott Papers.

23. Field to Blair, December 24, 1856, ibid.

24. Ibid., January 7, 1855.

25. *Strader* v. *Graham,* 10 Howard 82 (1850), at 86.

26. Field to Blair, December 24, 1856, Dred Scott Papers.

CHAPTER 10

U. S. Circuit Court

1. Declaration of Dred Scott, November 2, 1853, in *Scott* v. *Sanford,* No. 692, USCCStL, *Ms.*

2. According to the Judiciary Act of 1789. Original jurisdiction for diversity cases was transferred to district courts by congressional action in 1875. Samuel P. Orth and Robert B. Cushman, *American National Government* (New York, 1931), pp. 507-8; Arthur E. Sutherland, *Constitutionalism in America* (New York, 1965), p. 188.

3. Bond of C. Edmund LaBeaume and Taylor Blow, November 2, 1853, and Writ of Summons, November 2, 1853, in *Scott* v. *Sanford,* No. 692, USCCStL, *Ms.* The docket is no longer in existence, but notations on the papers indicate that this was the case number.

4. Law Record B, Circuit Court of the United States for the District of Missouri (1853-1854), *Ms.,* pp. 241, 254, Office of the Clerk, United States District Court, Eastern District of Missouri, St. Louis (hereafter referred to as "Law Record B, USCCStL, *Ms.* "); Plea in Abatement, April 7, 1854, in *Scott* v. *Sanford,* No. 692, USCCStL, *Ms.* ; John Bouvier, *Bouvier's Law Dictionary and Concise Encyclopedia* (Kansas City, 1914), 2: 7.

5. Demurrer, April 14, 1854, in *Scott* v. *Sanford,* No. 692, USCCStL, *Ms.;* Bouvier, *Bouvier's Law Dictionary,* 1: 837, 1697.

6. Law Record B, USCCStL, *Ms.,* 273; Field to Blair, January 7, 1855, Dred Scott Papers; Notes of Roswell M. Field, n.d., in *Scott* v. *Sanford,* No. 692, USCCStL, *Ms.*

7. Law Record B, USCCStL, *Ms.,* pp. 273, 276; Wells to Blair, February 12, 1856, Dred Scott Papers.

8. Field to Blair, January 7, 1855, Dred Scott Papers.

9. Law Record B, USCCStL, *Ms.,* pp. 287-88. Justice McLean, in his dissenting opinion in the United States Supreme Court, declared that at this point Garland might have done one of two things. One was to appeal immediately to the Supreme Court against the decision sustaining the demurrer; the other was to proceed, as Garland did, on the merits. 19 Howard 530-31 (1857). Justice Curtis, who also dissented, declared that Garland had no choice but to proceed as he did, on the merits. Ibid., p. 565. McLean's view is the more widely accepted. Louis B. Boudin, *Government by Judiciary* (New York, 1932), 2: 8.

10. Law Record B, USCCStL, *Ms.,* pp. 287-88.

11. Ibid., p. 295. Although this court was in the Eighth Judicial Circuit of Justice John Catron, he was not present at this term of the Circuit Court, and so, when the case came before the Supreme Court in Washington, he was not disqualified from hearing it. Ibid., pp. 241-98.

12. Reynolds to Cushing, April 24, 1854, Caleb Cushing Papers, *Ms.*, LC; *Daily Missouri Republican,* April 4, 1853, April 3, 30, 1854; *The St. Louis Intelligencer,* April 2, 1850.

13. Law Record B, USCCStL, *Ms.*, 295; Bill of Exceptions, May 15, 1854, Instructions for Plaintiff, May 15, 1854, Instructions for Defendant, May 15, 1854, in *Scott* v. *Sanford,* No. 692, USCCStL, *Ms.* For Wells's personal attitude toward slavery, see W. V. N. Bay, *Reminiscences of the Bench and Bar of Missouri* (St. Louis, 1878), p. 540.

14. Field to Blair, January 7, 1855, Dred Scott Papers.

15. Wells to Blair, February 12, 1856, ibid. Wells cited *Strader* v. *Graham* as the basis for this interpretation, again a misreading of that decision. He could have cited sounder precedents.

16. Verdict, May 15, 1854, Bill of Exceptions, May 15, 1854, and Motion for New Trial, May 15, 1854, in *Scott* v. *Sanford,* No. 692, USCCStL, *Ms.*

17. Bill of Exceptions, May 15, 1854, in ibid.; Law Record B, USCCStL, *Ms.,* p. 296. Considering how quickly Judge Wells implemented the appeals apparatus, and in light of some correspondence between Wells and Blair, one might speculate that perhaps Wells was privy, along with Field and Garland, to seeking a decision by the United States Supreme Court clarifying the law relative to slavery in the territories.

18. *Daily Missouri Republican,* April 4, 11, 20, May 15, 16, 1854; *The Saint Louis Daily Evening News,* May 15, 16, 1854; *Daily Saint Louis Intelligencer,* May 18, 1854.

19. *St. Louis Daily Morning Herald,* May 18, 1854.

20. Recollections of Thomas C. Reynolds, n.d., T. W. Chamberlain Collection, *Ms., MoHS.*

CHAPTER 11

U. S. Supreme Court: First Arguments

1. Transcript, May 23, 1854, in file of *Dred Scott* v. *John F. A. Sanford,* File No. 3230, Supreme Court of the United States, *Ms.,* Office of the Clerk, Supreme Court of the United States (hereafter referred to as "*Scott* v. *Sanford,* No. 3230, USSC, *Ms.*"); Docket (1854) and Docket (1855), USSC, *Ms.*

2. *Daily Missouri Republican,* October 15, 1854.

3. Reverdy Johnson to B. H. Richardson and others, March 6, 1858, in *The Washington Union,* March 18, 1858. Whether Garland would have continued with the case when it went to the Supreme Court is, of course, unanswerable; but undoubtedly his death brought in Geyer and Johnson. It is not clear which came in first. It is possible, since Geyer was from Missouri and already acquainted with Garland, that he (Geyer) may have had prior knowledge of the case ever since it had been in the Missouri Supreme Court, that he agreed to work on it, and that he was the "southern gentleman" who then brought in Johnson.

4. Bernard C. Steiner, *Life of Reverdy Johnson* (Baltimore, 1914), pp. iii, 37. See also *Biographical Register of the American Congress, 1774-1949* (81st

Cong., 2d sess., House Document 607, Washington, D.C., United States Printing Office, 1950), p. 1379. Accusations were made later, but never proved, that pro-slavery forces "hired" Johnson because of his influence over Taney. Not only were they old friends, but Johnson had led the Jackson forces in the Senate when Taney was confirmed as chief justice. *New York Weekly Tribune,* March 21, 1857.

5. For more on Geyer see W. V. N. Bay, *Reminiscences of the Bench and Bar of Missouri* (St. Louis, 1878), pp. 150-52; *Biographical Register of the American Congress, 1774-1949,* p. 1205; and John F. Darby, *Personal Recollections* (St. Louis, 1880), p. 371.

6. For Montgomery Blair see William E. Smith, *The Francis Preston Blair Family in Politics* (New York, 1933), 1: 380-82. See also Wells to Franklin Pierce, January 19, 1853; Ryland to Pierce, January 19, 1853; and Cushing to Blair, March 9, 1855, Gist Blair Collection, *Ms.,* LC; John J. Hayes to Governor Goodwin, n.d., Papers of Francis Preston Blair, Jr., *Ms.,* LC.

7. Samuel Simmons to Blair, October 31, 1854, Gist Blair Collection, *Ms.,* LC; Blair to Editors, n.d., *Daily National Intelligencer* (Washington, D.C.), December 24, 1856; Smith, *Blair Family,* 1: 385.

8. *The Case of Dred Scott, in the Supreme Court of the United States,* December Term, 1854, pp. 1-2.

9. Field to Blair, January 7, 1855, Dred Scott Papers; Blair to Editors, n.d., *Daily National Intelligencer* (Washington, D.C.), December 24, 1856.

10. Field to Blair, December 24, 1854, January 7, 1855, Dred Scott Papers; Gamaliel Bailey to Justin S. Morrill, May 8, 1857, Papers of Justin S. Morrill, *Ms.,* LC; Bailey to Lyman Trumbull, May 12, 1857, Papers of Lyman Trumbull, *Ms.,* LC; Smith, *Blair Family,* 1: 385-86. Bailey assumed this responsibility even though his newspaper was in severe financial straits. Lewis Tappan to Bailey, March 9, 1855, Lewis Tappan Letter Book (1854-1856), *Ms.,* LC; Bailey to Elihu Washburne, March 26, 1855, Papers of Elihu B. Washburne, *Ms.,* LC.

11. Docket G, p. 3388, USSC, *Ms.;* Docket (1854) and Docket (1855), ibid.

12. McLean to Blair, March 29, 1855, Papers of John McLean, *Ms.,* LC; *Daily Missouri Republican,* March 27, 1855.

13. Field to Blair, January 7, 1855, Dred Scott Papers.

14. Ibid.

15. Ibid., December 24, 1854.

16. Minutes (1855), December 3, 1855, USSC, *Ms.;* Docket (1855), ibid.

17. The analysis of Blair's brief is based on Montgomery Blair, *Brief of the Plaintiff, Dred Scott v. John F. A. Sanford, Supreme Court of the United States, December Term, 1855* (Washington, D.C., 1856).

18. 2 Haggard's Admiralty 29 (1827). With the famous *Somerset* v. *Stewart,* Lofft 1, 98 Eng. Rep. 499 (1772), this is one of the most important legal milestones in the gradual abolition of slavery in the British empire. For an excellent analysis of *Somerset, Grace,* and other slave cases, see William M. Wiecek, "*Somerset*: Lord Mansfield and the Legitimacy of Slavery in the Anglo-American World," *The University of Chicago Law Review* 42 (Fall 1974): 86-146.

19. The Virginia case was *Griffith* v. *Fanny*, Gilmer 143 (1820); the Mississippi case was *Harry et al* v. *Decker and Hopkins*, Walker 36 (1818); the Kentucky case was *Rankin* v. *Lydia*, 2 A. K. Marshall 467 (1820).

20. See *Scott* v. *London*, 3 Cranch 324 (1806); *Lee* v. *Lee*, 8 Peters 44 (1834); *Prigg* v. *State of Pennsylvania*, 16 Peters 539 (1842); *Williams* v. *Ash*, 1 Howard 1 (1843); and *Rhodes* v. *Bell*, 2 Howard 397 (1844).

21. *Le Grand* v. *Darnall*, 2 Peters 664 (1829).

22. Docket (1855), USSC, *Ms.* Evidently Geyer's brief was not printed in pamphlet form as was Blair's, for only printed briefs were bound and kept in the permanent files. The docket makes no mention of any separate brief filed by Reverdy Johnson.

23. Minutes (1855), February 11, 1856, USSC, *Ms.*

24. *The National Era* (Washington, D.C.), August 10, November 2, 1854; *Daily Missouri Republican*, July 25, 1855.

25. *Daily Missouri Republican*, January 11, February 16, March 3, 11, November 11, January 25, 1856.

26. *Congressional Globe*, 34th Cong., 1st sess.

27. *Washington Star*, February 13, 1856, as quoted in *New York Daily Tribune*, February 15, 1856. Justice McLean wrote about the possible ramifications of the case to John Teasdale, a fellow Ohioan and a newspaper editor, but Teasdale did nothing to publicize the approaching arguments. McLean to Teasdale, November 2, 1855, John McLean Letters, *Ms.*, Ohio State Archaeological and Historical Society, Columbus.

28. Minutes (1855), February 11, 1856, USSC, *Ms.* Aside from the chief justice, the others are named in the order of their appointment to the Court. McLean and Wayne were already on the bench when Taney was appointed in 1836. Recent biographies have been written about Daniel and Taney, as have some articles about Curtis, hopefully presaging a long-needed biography about that New England jurist. Standard biographies about McLean, Wayne, and Campbell are old but adequate. No biographies have been written yet on Nelson, Grier, and Catron. For brief but excellent biographical materials on all, see sections written by Frank O. Gatell and William Gillette in Leon Friedman and Fred Israel, eds., *The Justices of the United States Supreme Court, 1789-1969: Their Lives and Major Opinions*, vols. 1 and 2 (New York, 1969).

29. Minutes (1855), February 11, 12, 13, 14, 1856, USSC, *Ms.*; Docket (1855), ibid.

30. According to the clerk of the Supreme Court of the United States.

31. *Daily Missouri Democrat* (St. Louis), February 25, 1856. Among others that reported these highlights were *The Sun* (Baltimore), Feburary 15, 1856; *North American and United States Gazette* (Philadelphia), February 20, 1856; *New York Daily Tribune*, February 20, 1856.

32. *Washington Star*, February 13, 1856, *Boston Post*, February 16, 1856.

33. *New York Daily Tribune*, February 20, 1856; *North American and United States Gazette* (Philadelphia), February 20, 1856. There is no indication that they broached what the law should be if that return was not voluntary.

34. *Daily National Intelligencer* (Washington, D.C.), February 12, 13, 14, 15, 1856; *The Daily Globe* (Washington, D.C.), February 12, 13, 14, 15, 1856; *Washington Star*, February 13, 1856; *The Daily Union* (Washington, D.C.), February 12, 13, 14, 15, 1856.

35. The name was spelled "Drea Scott" and "Fred Scott" in many of these papers but the name was so unfamiliar that few readers were aware of the error. The St. Louis *Daily Missouri Republican's* correspondent made no mention of the case in dispatches he wrote from Washington on February 11, 13, and 14. The correspondent of another St. Louis newspaper, the *Daily Missouri Democrat,* wrote a lengthy dispatch to his home office on February 11 in which he discussed, among other things, Chief Justice Taney as a possible presidential candidate, but not one word about the *Dred Scott* case argued on that very same day.

36. *The National Era* (Washington, D.C.), February 21, 1856.

CHAPTER 12
The Court Consults

1. According to Swisher, newspaper correspondents "kept the story alive by recounting the various and conflicting rumors." Carl Brent Swisher, *Roger B. Taney* (New York, 1936), p. 488.

2. *Daily Missouri Democrat,* February 25, 1856.

3. *New York Daily Tribune,* February 18, 1856; Jeter A. Isely, *Horace Greeley and the Republican Party, 1853-1861* (Princeton, 1947), p. 226.

4. Joseph Blunt to McLean, May 2, 1856, Papers of John McLean, Ms., LC; Johnson to Richardson and others, March 6, 1858, in *The Washington Union,* March 18, 1858.

5. *Daily Missouri Republican,* February 21, 1856.

6. David M. Potter, *The Impending Crisis, 1848-1861* (New York, 1976), p. 276. Wallace Mendelson, "Dred Scott's Case—Reconsidered," *Minnesota Law Review* 38 (1953): 16-28, details this situation.

7. John Catron to James Buchanan, February 6, 1857, James Buchanan Ms., HSPa. Swisher suggests that it was McLean who leaked news to the antislavery press. Swisher, *Roger B. Taney,* p. 489.

8. John A. Campbell to Samuel Tyler, November 24, 1870, in Samuel Tyler, *Memoir of Roger Brooke Taney* (Baltimore, 1872), p. 382. Campbell's account is confirmed by Nelson. Samuel Nelson to Tyler, May 13, 1871, in ibid., p. 385. Campbell recalled the issue again in 1874 in a speech memorializing Justice Curtis. 20 Wallace x-xi (1875).

9. *New York Daily Tribune,* February 29, 1856. The same dispatch appeared on the same day in Philadelphia in the *North American and United States Gazette,* under the heading "Special Correspondence."

10. *New York Daily Tribune,* February 29, 1856; *North American and United States Gazette* (Philadelphia), February 29, 1856; *The Sun* (Baltimore), March 1, 1856; *Daily National Intelligencer* (Washington, D.C.), March 1, 1856; *The National Era* (Washington, D.C.), March 6, 1856.

11. One legislator may have had the case in mind. On March 27 Senator James Harlan of Iowa, arguing for congressional power to prohibit slavery in the territories, gave as one reason that "there is no adverse decision of the Supreme Court." *Congressional Globe*, 34th Cong., 1st sess., app., p. 273. Not once, though, did he advert to the case pending in which the Court might deliver such an "adverse decision." Ibid., pp. 273-76.

12. *New York Daily Tribune*, April 9, 1856. Similar observations appeared in the *North American and United States Gazette* (Philadelphia), April 9, 1856.

13. 20 Wallace *x-xi* (1875). This was Campbell's recollection, which was substantiated in all the opinions rendered later. Catron, Campbell, McLean, and Grier did not discuss the plea in abatement in their final opinions; Taney, Wayne, Daniel, and Curtis did.

14. Warren excuses this erroneous reporting as merely guessing by these reporters, rather than having any confidential information from any of the justices. Charles Warren, *The Supreme Court in United States History* (Boston, 1922), 3: 6.

15. *New York Daily Tribune*, April 9, May 15, 1856; Harvey to McLean, March 30, 1856, Papers of John McLean, *Ms.*, LC.

16. Francis P. Weisenburger, *The Life of John McLean* (Columbus, Ohio, 1937), p. 197; Jeter A. Isely, *Horace Greeley and the Republican Party, 1853-1861* (Princeton, 1947), p. 226; Swisher, *Roger B. Taney*, pp. 489-90. Despite his own strong desire for a decision dealing with slavery in the territories, Greeley realistically expected the Court to evade this controversial issue by denying jurisdiction.

17. Campbell to Tyler, November 24, 1870, in Tyler, *Memoir of Roger Brooke Taney*, pp. 382-83; Nelson to Tyler, May 13, 1871, in ibid., p. 385.

18. 20 Wallace *xi* (1875).

19. Campbell to George T. Curtis, October 18, 1879, cited in Vincent Hopkins, *Dred Scott's Case* (New York, 1951), p. 46.

20. Benjamin R. Curtis to George Ticknor, April 8, 1856, in Benjamin R. Curtis, ed., *A Memoir of Benjamin Robbins Curtis* (Boston, 1879), 1: 180.

21. Campbell to Curtis, October 18, 1879, cited in Hopkins, *Dred Scott's Case*, p. 46.

22. Apparently this was on April 12. The only consultations noted in the press were those of April 7, 9, and 12, but there may have been others not reported.

23. *New York Daily Tribune*, April 8-12, 1856. Similar views were to be found in the *North American and United States Gazette* (Philadelphia), April 8-12, 1856.

24. Minutes (1855), May 12, 1856, USSC, *Ms.*

25. *Congressional Globe*, 35th Cong., 1st sess., p. 617. Perhaps the most famous of these charges was the "Stephen, Franklin, Roger and James" accusation made by Abraham Lincoln in his 1858 senatorial campaign, and then echoed by others, that Douglas, Pierce, Taney, and Buchanan "all understood one another from the beginning, and all worked upon a common plan or draft drawn up before the first blow was struck." John G. Nicolay and John Hay, eds., *Complete Works of Abraham Lincoln* (New York, 1894), 3: 10.

26. *New York Daily Tribune*, May 15, 1856.

27. *Congressional Globe*, 40th Cong., 3d sess., app., p. 211, cited in Weisenburger, *Life of John McLean*, p. 197.

28. For some supportive views see Bernard C. Steiner, *Life of Roger Brooke Taney* (Baltimore, 1922), p. 405; Swisher, *Roger B. Taney,* p. 489; Alexander A. Lawrence, *James Moore Wayne, Southern Unionist* (Chapel Hill, N.C., 1943), p. 152; Frank H. Hodder, "Some Phases of the Dred Scott Case," *Mississippi Valley Historical Review* 16 (June 1929): 9; and Edward S. Corwin, "The Dred Scott Decision, in the Light of Contemporary Legal Doctrines," *American Historical Review* 17 (October 1911): 53.

29. McLean to Robert A. Parrish, March 3, 1855, Papers of John McLean, *Ms.,* LC; McLean to Teasdale, November 2, 1855, John McLean Letters, *Ms.,* Ohio State Archaeological and Historical Society, Columbus; McLean to Cass, May 13, 1856, in *The National Era* (Washington, D.C.), May 22, 1856; Joseph C. Hornblower to McLean, May 13, 1856, and McLean to Hornblower, June 6, 1856, in *Daily National Intelligencer* (Washington, D.C.), June 16, 1856. See also *St. Louis Daily New Era,* February 20, 1848; *Daily Missouri Republican,* February 5, 1847, April 15, June 20, 1856; *The Daily Union* (Washington, D.C.), April 5, May 17, 23, 1856; Weisenburger, *Life of John McLean,* p. 211; Swisher, *Roger B. Taney,* p. 491; William S. Myers, *The Republican Party* (New York, 1928), p. 64.

30. Campbell to Tyler, November 24, 1870, in Tyler, *Memoir of Roger Brooke Taney,* p. 383.

31. Contemporaries closely associated with McLean thought, as did Salmon P. Chase, that McLean was "reasonably sound on slavery, politically and personally, if not judicially." Robert M. Cover, *Justice Accused: Antislavery and the Judicial Process* (New Haven, 1975), p. 247.

32. *New York Daily Tribune,* May 15, 1856.

33. Blunt to McLean, May 2, 1856, Papers of John McLean, *Ms.,* LC.

34. Ibid. See *Lemmon v. The People,* 20 New York 562 (1860); also *The National Era* (Washington, D.C.), November 2, 1854, and *New York Morning Express,* May 6, 1857.

35. Minutes (1855), May 12, 1856, USSC, *Ms.* This did not limit the argument to just these two issues; it merely made sure that among the principles to be reargued these two would be thoroughly examined. There may have been yet another reason for a postponement, to await the decision in *Pease v. Peck.* This case had no connection with the slavery issues of *Scott v. Sanford*; it entailed instead a situation in which the Supreme Court was confronted with conflicting state precedents. The Court decided that given that problem, it would not necessarily accept the latest state decision as binding. According to Justice Grier, who wrote the opinion in *Pease v. Peck,* this decision was reached deliberately to create a precedent that would allow the Court to disregard the latest Missouri decision when it took up the *Dred Scott* case. But *Pease v. Peck* had not been announced yet; pending that, *Scott v. Sanford* was postponed. Curtis, *Memoir of Benjamin Robbins Curtis,* 1: 210. Two days after that postponement the Court announced *Pease v. Peck.*

36. *New York Daily Tribune,* May 15, 1856.

37. *North American and United States Gazette* (Philadelphia), May 15, 1856.

38. *Morning Courier and New-York Enquirer,* May 14, 1856, as quoted in *Boston Daily Advertiser,* May 15, 1856.

39. *Daily National Intelligencer* (Washington, D.C.), May 14, 1856; *The New York Herald*, May 14, 1856; *The Sun* (Baltimore), May 14, 1856; *The National Era* (Washington, D.C.), May 22, 1856.

40. This observation is based upon the author's examination of a great many newspapers, representing all parts of the country and political points of view, as well as a large number of manuscript collections, all covering this period and beyond.

CHAPTER 13
U. S. Supreme Court: Second Arguments

1. *Congressional Globe,* 34th Cong., 1st sess., app., p. 701.

2. Ibid., p. 995.

3. Ibid., pp. 725-26.

4. *Daily Pennsylvanian* (Philadelphia), October 27, 1856.

5. This observation is based upon an examination of many newspapers and manuscript collections of this period.

6. Allan Nevins, *Ordeal of the Union* (New York, 1947), 2: 516.

7. James D. Richardson, ed., *A Compilation of the Messages and Papers of the Presidents* (New York, 1897), 6: 2934.

8. *Congressional Globe,* 34th Cong., 3d sess., pp. 11, 15-16.

9. Ibid., pp. 34, 37, 85-93, 102; Nevins, *Ordeal of the Union,* 2: 518.

10. The Court convened on December 1, and *Scott* v. *Sanford* was now docketed as Case No. 7. Minutes (1956), December 1, 1856, USSC, Ms.

11. Henry S. Geyer, *Case for Defendant in Error, Dred Scott v. John F. A. Sanford, Supreme Court of the United States, December Term, 1856,* pamphlet, 12 pp. (Washington, D.C., 1856). There is no indication from any records that Reverdy Johnson filed a separate brief.

12. *Groves* v. *Slaughter,* 15 Peters 449 (1841); *Rankin* v. *Lydia,* 2 A.K. Marshall (Ky.) 467 (1820).

13. Docket (1856), USSC, Ms. The following analysis of his brief is based on Montgomery Blair, *Additional Brief of M. Blair, Dred Scott v. John F. A. Sanford, Supreme Court of the United States, December Term, 1856,* pamphlet, 8 pp. (Washington, D.C., 1857).

14. Blair's argument here was shallow and evaded an important issue.

15. A number of historians, including Donald O. Dewey, *Marshall versus Jefferson: The Political Background of Marbury v. Madison* (New York, 1970), have argued that most contemporaries really did not appreciate the full implications of Marshall's use of judicial review.

16. *New York Daily Tribune,* December 16, 17, 1856; *The National Era* (Washington, D.C.), December 18, 1856.

17. Minutes (1856), December 15, 1856, USSC, Ms.

18. According to the Washington correspondent of *The New York Herald,* Blair was turned down by eminent antislavery spokesmen such as Senators William H. Seward of New York, John P. Hale of New Hampshire, and William Pitt Fessen-

den of Maine "unless the dollars and cents were forthcoming." *The New York Herald*, December 17, 1856. The correspondent of the *New York Daily Tribune*, however, placed the blame for failure to obtain associate counsel on Blair himself, either for not asking some who were willing to help, or for procrastinating so long that others lacked time to prepare adequate arguments *New York Daily Tribune*, December 17, 1856. According to Blair himself, he first sought assistance "of one of the ablest men at the bar in the South," but this man declined. (The *New York Daily Tribune* said that this was former Senator George E. Badger of North Carolina, known to advocate the power of Congress to legislate over slavery in the territories. Ibid.) Blair then "applied to leading members of the profession in the North" (presumably Seward, Hale, and Fessenden), but with no success. Blair to Editors, n.d., *Daily National Intelligencer* (Washington, D.C.), December 24, 1856. Blair insisted, however, that none of them refused because of "mercenary motive[s]," but rather because they either had previous commitments or thought they did not have time to prepare adequate argument. Ibid. Abolitionist Lewis Tappan solicited William H. Seward's participation, but also in vain. Tappan to Seward, July 21, August 20, 1856, William H. Seward Papers, *Ms.*, University of Rochester. Curtis finally agreed to join Blair if the latter would handle the citizenship issue; Curtis felt well enough acquainted with the issue of slavery in the territories to make an argument on that subject even with only two or three days to prepare. George T. Curtis, *Constitutional History of the United States* (New York, 1896), 2: 272-73.

19. Although the Supreme Court was crowded with listeners, very few people wrote down what the lawyers actually said. Neither was there an official Court stenographer to record their remarks. A number of press correspondents summarized the arguments, the most complete being that of an unidentified Associated Press reporter, whose dispatch was telegraphed to member newspapers all over the country and then copied by others. The analysis of Blair's oral argument is based upon this report, which appears in, among other newspapers, the *New York Daily Tribune*, December 17, 1856, and the St. Louis *Daily Missouri Republican*, December 18, 1856.

20. When Blair made this presentation, he had to discuss all the issues, expecting to be the only counsel on his side. Curtis joined Blair only after the arguments of December 15.

21. There is no indication whether Blair made here the point he had included in his printed brief, that the authority of Congress over slavery in the territories was only for Congress to decide and was not even within the scope of the judicial branch for review.

22. *The Daily Union* (Washington, D.C.), December 17, 1856. Blair made a similar assertion shortly afterwards, in a letter that he wrote for newspaper publication. Blair to Editors, n.d., in *Daily National Intelligencer* (Washington, D.C.), December 24, 1856. The "portion of the press" to which both referred included at least the Washington correspondent of the abolitionist *Morning Courier and New-York Enquirer*, whose dispatches printed on March 16 and December 18, 1856, challenged the integrity of the case.

23. The only accounts of Geyer's oral argument were brief reports that appeared in the contemporary press. Two, however, were in more detail and are the basis for

the following analysis. One was by a reporter of the Washington, D.C., *Daily Union,* whose article appeared on December 17, 1856. The other was by the Associated Press reporter whose dispatch appeared in, among other newspapers, the *New York Daily Tribune,* December 17, 1856, and the *Daily Missouri Republican,* December 18, 1856.

24. Minutes (1856), December 17, 1856, USSC, *Ms.*; Docket (1856), ibid.; *New York Daily Tribune,* December 18, 1856.

25. The fullest account of Johnson's oral argument was the Associated Press report that appeared in, among other newspapers, the *New York Daily Tribune,* December 18, 1856, and the *Daily Missouri Republican,* December 20, 1856.

26. Many historians incorrectly credit Taney with this novel interpretation of substantive due process. Johnson used it in his argument, and Lyman D. Norris had suggested it earlier in the state case. The idea, however, was not completely new. It had been mentioned often in debates over slavery, but only recently had it been formulated in constitutional adjudication. Due process of law for centuries had been accepted as a procedural guarantee, insuring the accused a fair trial. Then in an 1856 case involving property rights in liquor (*Wynehamer* v. *New York*, 13 New York 378), the New York State Supreme Court expressed the modern concept of substantive due process under the Fifth Amendment. Undoubtedly Johnson was aware of the *Wynehamer* case, as was Taney, even though neither cited it. Among others, see Arthur Bestor, "State Sovereignty and Slavery: A Reinterpretation of Proslavery Constitutional Doctrine, 1846-1860," *Journal of the Illinois State Historical Society* 54 (Summer 1961): 172.

27. According to one report, Johnson spoke for the full three hours allotted on that day. *The Daily Union* (Washington, D.C.), December 18, 1856. Another correspondent reported that Johnson took only two hours. *Morning Courier and New-York Enquirer,* December 19, 1856. Three hours were allotted and Johnson was the only one who spoke that day.

28. The official minutes indicate that only Blair and Curtis addressed the Court on that day, but most newspaper accounts reported that Geyer and Johnson also spoke briefly.

29. The most complete account of Blair's closing argument, as well as Geyer's, which followed his, is the Associated Press dispatch of December 18 that appeared, among other newspapers, in the *New York Daily Tribune,* December 19, 1856, and the *Daily Missouri Republican,* December 21, 1856.

30. The analysis of Curtis's oral argument is based upon the Associated Press dispatch of December 18, upon the detailed report of the correspondent "Index" (James E. Harvey) of the *New York Daily Tribune,* and upon a revised copy of this speech, which was printed fully in a number of newspapers and which Curtis included later in a published constitutional history of the United States. *New York Daily Tribune,* December 19, 1856, *Daily Missouri Republican,* December 21, 1856; *Daily National Intelligencer* (Washington, D.C.), January 1, 1857; *Boston Daily Advertiser,* January 15, 1857; Curtis, *Constitutional History of the United States,* 2: 499-517. Curtis had his argument published in the contemporary press because, as he put it: "Two Senators, each of whom represented a slave-holding State, Mr. Crittenden of Kentucky and Mr. Badger of North Carolina, both of the highest rank as lawyers, Mr. Seaton,

the wise and accomplished editor of the *National Intelligencer,* and other friends, urged me to write out and publish my argument. I did so, and it was printed by Mr. Seaton in his paper. I mention this, not as proof of merit in the argument, but because I was convinced, by this and many other occurrences, that some of the ablest minds in the South, at that time, did not regard it as supremely important to their sectional interests to have it judicially proclaimed that the Missouri Compromise restriction was unconstitutional." Benjamin R. Curtis, ed., *A Memoir of Benjamin Robbins Curtis* (Boston, 1879), 1: 241.

CHAPTER 14
The Court Consults Again

1. Among the important newspapers that printed the Associated Press reports in full were: *Daily Missouri Republican* (St. Louis), December 18-21, 1856; *The Saint Louis Daily Evening News,* December 17, 18, 20, 1856; *Daily Missouri Democrat* (St. Louis), December 18, 22, 1856; *The Sun* (Baltimore), December 16-19, 1856; *The Daily Richmond Enquirer,* December 17-20, 1856; *The Charleston* (S.C.) *Mercury,* December 20, 21, 1856; *Boston Evening Transcript,* December 16-19, 1856; *Boston Post,* December 16-19, 1856; *Boston Daily Advertiser,* December 16-19, 1856; *The Daily Ohio Statesman* (Columbus), December 16, 1856; *The Providence* (R.I.) *Daily Post,* December 16, 17, 1856; *North American and United States Gazette* (Philadelphia), December 16-19, 1856; *Daily Pennsylvanian* (Philadelphia), December 16-19, 1856; *The New York Herald,* December 16-19, 1856; *The New York Journal of Commerce,* December 16-19, 1856; *The Daily Democratic Press* (Chicago), December 17, 1856.

Among those that published only parts of those dispatches were: *The Charleston* (S.C.) *Daily Courier,* December 22, 1856; *The Norwich* (Conn.) *Weekly Courier,* December 24, 1856.

Newspapers printing comments by their own Washington correspondents included: *The Sun* (Baltimore), December 16-20, 1856; *North American and United States Gazette* (Philadelphia), December 17, 20, 1856; *New York Daily Tribune,* December 16-20, 1856; *The New York Herald,* December 17, 19, 23, 1856; *The New York Journal of Commerce,* December 17-19, 1856; *Morning Courier and New-York Enquirer,* December 18, 19, 1856; *The Charleston* (S.C.) *Daily Courier,* December 20, 22, 1856.

Newspapers that carried reprints of the Associated Press dispatch or of correspondents' reports included: *Boston Daily Advertiser,* December 19, 1856; *Columbian Weekly Register* (New Haven, Conn.), December 27, 1856; *Bangor* (Maine) *Daily Whig and Courier,* December 24, 1856; *The Savannah Daily Republican,* December 19, 20, 1856; *New Hampshire Patriot and State Gazette* (Concord), December 24, 1856; *The Daily Pioneer and Democrat* (St. Paul, Minn.), January 7, 1857; *The Daily Constitutionalist* (Augusta, Ga.), December 21, 1856.

2. *Morning Courier and New-York Enquirer,* December 18, 1856.

3. Among others, see ibid., December 19, 1856; *The New York Journal of Commerce,* December 18, 1856; *The Sun* (Baltimore), December 18, 1856;

North American and United States Gazette (Philadelphia), December 17, 20, 1856; *New York Daily Tribune,* December 17, 22, 1856.

4. *New York Daily Tribune,* December 20, 22, 1856. Note the use of the term that was to be so widely used later.

5. *Morning Courier and New-York Enquirer,* December 18, 1856.

6. *North American and United States Gazette* (Philadelphia), December 22, 1856.

7. *Springfield* (Mass.) *Daily Republican,* December 18, 1856; *The Evening Post* (New York), December 22, 1856; *The National Era* (Washington, D.C.), December 25, 1856.

8. *Morning Courier and New-York Enquirer,* December 18, 1856.

9. Ibid., December 19, 23, 1856; *New York Daily Tribune,* December 19, 1856; *The Evening Post* (New York), December 22, 1856; *The New York Herald,* December 25, 1856. Partially to counter these false allegations as well as to explain his own role in the litigation, Blair wrote a lengthy letter to the editors of the Washington, D.C., *Daily National Intelligencer,* detailing how to his knowledge the case was genuine and that there had been no intention to involve it in politics. Blair to Editors, n.d., in *Daily National Intelligencer,* December 24, 1856.

10. *The New York Herald,* December 23, 1856.

11. *The New York Journal of Commerce,* December 17, 18, 1856.

12. This conclusion is based upon the author's examination of newspapers representing all parts of the country.

13. *Congressional Globe,* 34th Cong., 3d sess., pp. 151, 159.

14. Alexander H. Stephens to Linton Stephens, December 15, 1856, in Richard M. Johnston and William H. Browne, *Life of Alexander H. Stephens* (Philadelphia, 1883), p. 316.

15. Stephens to Stephens, January 1, 1857, in ibid., p. 318.

16. Robert J. Walker to Stephen A. Douglas, January 7, 1857, Stephen A. Douglas Papers, *Ms.,* University of Chicago.

17. See also James A. Hamilton to Hamilton Fish, January 19, 1857, Correspondence of Hamilton Fish, *Ms.,* LC; Blunt to McLean, January 22, 1857, Papers of John McLean, *Ms.,* LC; Martin Van Buren to Blair, January 31, 1857, Gist Blair Collection, *Ms., LC;* Blair to Van Buren, February 5, 1857, Papers of Martin Van Buren, *Ms.,* LC. Wallace Mendelson, "Dred Scott's Case—Reconsidered," *Minnesota Law Review* 38 (1953): 16-28, indicates how so many looked to the courts to decide the slavery issue.

18. *New York Daily Tribune,* January 3, 5, 9, 1857; *The New York Herald,* January 5, 1857; *New York Morning Express,* January 5, 1857; *The Atlas and Argus* (Albany, N.Y.), January 5, 1857; *Boston Daily Advertiser,* January 3, 15, 1857; *The Providence* (R.I.) *Daily Post,* January 3, 1857; *Boston Post,* January 7, 1857; *The Boston Daily Atlas,* January 20, 1857; *North American and United States Gazette* (Philadelphia), January 5, 1857; *The Weekly Chicago Times,* January 22, 1857; *Daily Missouri Democrat* (St. Louis), January 27, 1857; *The Daily Union* (Washington, D.C.), January 3, 1857; *The Daily Globe* (Washington, D.C.), January 2, 1857; *The Sun* (Baltimore), January 2, 1857; *The Charleston* (S.C.)

Mercury, January 5, 19, 1857. An example of the enlivened interest in the case was shown by the publication of Blair's brief in Boston and St. Louis newspapers and of Curtis's argument in Boston and Washington journals.

19. Catron to Buchanan, February 6, 1857, James Buchanan *Ms.*, HSPa; Minutes (1856), January 5-February 9, 1857, USSC, *Ms.*; *The Daily Union* (Washington, D.C.), January 6, 1857; *New York Daily Tribune,* January 23, February 13, 1857; *North American and United States Gazette* (Philadelphia), January 23, February 10, 1857.

20. Curtis to Ticknor, February 27, 1857, in Benjamin R. Curtis, ed., *A Memoir of Benjamin Robbins Curtis* (Boston, 1879), 1: 192.

21. Catron to Buchanan, February 10, 19, 1857, James Buchanan *Ms.*, HSPa; Curtis, *Memoir of Benjamin Robbins Curtis,* 1: 194.

22. Grier to Buchanan, February 23, 1857, James Buchanan *Ms.*, HSPa; Campbell to Tyler, November 24, 1870, in Samuel Tyler, *Memoir of Roger Brooke Taney* (Baltimore, 1872), p. 383; Nelson to Tyler, May 13, 1871, in ibid., p. 385.

23. One story is that the justices became so excited and argued so heatedly, even jumping to their feet and gesticulating wildly, that Taney rapped on the table and cried: "Brothers, this is the Supreme Court of the United States. Take your seats!" "And," according to Curtis, "we sat down like rebuked schoolboys." Bernard C. Steiner, *Life of Roger Brooke Taney* (Baltimore, 1922), p. 332. On the other hand, Campbell later declared that "there was nothing in the deliberations in that cause to distinguish it from any other." Speech of Justice John A. Campbell, October 13, 1874, cited in 20 Wallace *x* (1875).

24. Grier to Buchanan, February 23, 1857, James Buchanan *Ms.*, HSPa.

25. Nelson to Tyler, May 13, 1871, in Tyler, *Memoir of Roger Brooke Taney,* p. 385. Considering his *obiter dictum* observation in the *Strader* decision, it is very unlikely that McLean agreed with the majority that *Strader* v. *Graham* could be a precedent for *Dred Scott.*

26. Grier to Buchanan, February 23, 1857, James Buchanan *Ms.*, HSPa.

27. Clement Hugh Hill to Curtis, August 5, 1858, in Curtis, *Memoir of Benjamin Robbins Curtis,* 1: 235. Curtis had indicated to Hill, a former assistant attorney-general of the United States, that if the case had thus been disposed of, the opinions would have been devoid of all the bitterness to which the case ultimately gave rise. Ibid. He was no doubt correct.

28. A good attempt to clarify this issue is by Allan Nevins in appendix 1, "Responsibility of Curtis and McLean for the Dred Scott Decision," *The Emergence of Lincoln* (New York, 1950), 2: 473-77.

29. Catron to Buchanan, February 19, 1857, James Buchanan *Ms.*, HSPa.

30. Grier to Buchanan, February 23, 1857, ibid.

31. Campbell to Tyler, November 23, 1870, in Tyler, *Memoir of Roger Brooke Taney,* p. 384.

32. George T. Curtis, *Constitutional History of the United States* (New York, 1896), 2: 274-75. See also Hill to Curtis, August 5, 1858, in Curtis, *Memoir of Benjamin Robbins Curtis,* 1: 235.

33. Alexander A. Lawrence, *James Moore Wayne, Southern Unionist* (Chapel Hill, N.C., 1943), p. 155.

34. Ibid., pp. 148-49.

35. Stephens to Stephens, December 15, 1856, in Johnston and Browne, *Life of Alexander H. Stephens*, p. 316.

36. J. Glancy Jones to Buchanan, December 3, 1856, February 14, 1857, James Buchanan *Ms.*, HSPa.

37. Auchampaugh deals extensively with the correspondence between Buchanan and the justices. Philip Auchampaugh, "James Buchanan, the Court, and the Dred Scott Case," *Tennessee Historical Magazine* 9 (January 1926): 231-40. As to the propriety and ethics of such communication, historian Charles Warren is quoted as saying: "It was not an infrequent occurrence for the judges to impart, in confidence to an intimate friend or relative, the probable outcome of a pending case. Judge Curtis had so written to his uncle, as to this very case, during the previous year; Judge Story frequently indulged in the habit; and it seems to have been regarded as a proper practice, provided the seal of secrecy was imposed." Walter Chandler, "The Centenary of Associate Justice John Catron of the United States Supreme Court," *Tennessee Law Review* 15 (1937): 48. In a private interview with the author in the summer of 1948, Chief Justice Fred M. Vinson indicated that Supreme Court judges today would "think twice" before doing something similar.

38. Blair to Van Buren, February 5, 1857, Papers of Martin Van Buren, *Ms.*, LC.

39. Campbell to Tyler, November 24, 1870, in Tyler, *Memoir of Roger Brooke Taney*, p. 384.

40. Ibid.

41. Nelson to Tyler, May 13, 1871, in ibid., p. 385; Catron to Buchanan, February 19, 1857, James Buchanan *Ms.*, HSPa; Hill to Curtis, August 5, 1878, in Curtis, *Memoir of Benjamin Robbins Curtis*, 1: 235; Curtis, *Constitutional History of the United States*, 2: 274-75.

42. Lawrence, *James Moore Wayne, Southern Unionist*, p. 155; Curtis, *Constitutional History of the United States*, 2: 275.

43. Hodder especially argued that McLean and Curtis precipitated the change. Frank H. Hodder, "Some Phases of the Dred Scott Decision," *Mississippi Valley Historical Review* 11 (June 1929): 3-22. Others who agree include Charles Warren, *The Supreme Court in United States History* (Boston, 1922), 2: 15-16; Roy F. Nichols, *Disruption of American Democracy* (New York, 1948), pp. 65-66; and Carl Brent Swisher, *Roger B. Taney* (New York, 1936), pp. 497-98. For Nevins, see footnote 28, *supra.*

44. Catron to Buchanan, February 6, 1857, James Buchanan *Ms.*, HSPa.

45. Nevins, *Emergence of Lincoln*, 1: 103.

46. Don E. Fehrenbacher, "Roger B. Taney and the Sectional Crisis," *Journal of Southern History* 43 (November 1977): 562.

47. Nevins, *Emergence of Lincoln*, 2: 474-75.

48. The opening sentence of Wayne's opinion reads: "Concurring as I do in the opinion of the court, as it has been written and read by the Chief Justice . . . I shall neither read nor file an opinion of my own in this case *which I prepared when I*

supposed it might be necessary and proper for me to do so." 19 Howard 454. Italics mine.

49. Nathaniel G. Upham to Buchanan, November 27, 1856, James Buchanan *Ms.*, HSPa; William Bigler to Buchanan, December 29, 1856, ibid.; Jones to Buchanan, February 14, 1857, ibid.; John Appleton to Buchanan, February 21, 1857, ibid.; Nichols, *Disruption of American Democracy,* p. 60.

50. Buchanan to Grier, November 10, 1856, James Buchanan *Ms.*, HSPa; James Buchanan, *Mr. Buchanan's Administration on the Eve of the Rebellion* (New York, 1866), p. 37.

51. Catron to Buchanan, February 6, 10, 19, 1857, James Buchanan *Ms., HSPa.*

52. Ibid., February 19, 1857.

53. Grier to Buchanan, February 23, 1857, ibid. Grier's switch was a surprise to some, for up to the very end there were those who thought he would stand with McLean and Curtis. *New York Daily Tribune,* March 9, 1857.

54. Grier to Buchanan, February 23, 1857, James Buchanan *Ms.*, HSPa.

55. Washington correspondent of the *Cincinnati Enquirer,* quoted in the St. Louis *Daily Missouri Democrat,* February 17, 1857, and in *The Daily Richmond* (Va.) *Enquirer,* February 20, 1857.

56. Some critics of the decision later said that this whispered conversation was the occasion when Taney informed Buchanan of the decision so Buchanan might mention it in his inaugural address. There is no truth to this story. Buchanan already knew the principles the Court would declare—Catron and Grier had informed him.

57. Statement of James Buchanan Henry, President Buchanan's private secretary, in George T. Curtis, *Life of James Buchanan* (New York, 1883), 2: 187; John Bassett Moore, ed., *The Works of James Buchanan* (Philadelphia, 1911), 12: 324. Another important problem Buchanan still had to settle was the composition of his cabinet. Nichols, *Disruption of American Democracy,* p. 70.

58. James D. Richardson, *A Compilation of the Messages and Papers of the Presidents* (New York, 1897), 6: 2962.

59. *New York Daily Tribune,* March 5, 1857.

60. For events on the day preceding decision day, see ibid., March 6, 9, 1857; *The New York Herald,* March 6, 1857; *New York Morning Express,* March 6, 7, 1857; *The Daily Globe* (Washington, D.C.), March 6, 1857; *North American and United States Gazette* (Philadelphia), March 7, 1857; *The New York Journal of Commerce,* March 7, 1857; *The Daily Richmond Enquirer,* March 7, 1857; Curtis, *Memoir of Benjamin Robbins Curtis,* 1: 194.

CHAPTER 15
Taney: Opinion of the Court

1. They were, coincidentally, *United States* v. *Sherman Booth* and *Ableman* v. *Booth,* two fugitive slave litigations that would join *Dred Scott* as landmarks in the constitutional development of the slavery struggle.

2. Statement of Thomas C. Reynolds, n.d., T. W. Chamberlain Collection, *Ms.*, MoHS; *New York Morning Express,* March 9, 1857; *The Charleston* (S.C.) *Daily Courier,* March 11, 1857; *Daily Cincinnati Gazette,* March 17, 1857; *Daily Appeal* (Memphis), April 5, 1857. One observer described the scene as follows: "The Supreme Court, though sitting in a wretched room in the basement [of the Capitol], made a far deeper impression on me [than the House and Senate]. The judges, seated in a row, and wearing their simple silken gowns, seemed to me, in their quiet dignity, what the highest court of a great republic ought to be; though I looked at Chief Justice Taney and his pro-slavery associates much as a Hindoo regards his destructive gods." Andrew D. White, *Autobiography of Andrew Dickson White* (New York, 1905), 1: 79.

3. Lowell later became a federal district and circuit judge; Gray became chief justice of the Massachusetts Supreme Court and in 1881 was appointed by President Chester A. Arthur to the Supreme Court of the United States.

4. A full-scale bibliographic essay would be necessary to give justice to all these analyses. Several excellent ones have been written, the best being Frederick S. Allis, Jr., "The Dred Scott Labyrinth," in H. Stuart Hughes, ed., *Teachers of History: Essays in Honor of Laurence Bradford Packard* (Ithaca, 1954), pp. 341-68. Also satisfactory is Thomas B. Alexander, "Historical Treatments of the Dred Scott Case, 1889-1950," in *Proceedings of the South Carolina Historical Association,* 1953, pp. 37-59.

5. Curtis to Taney, May 13, 1857, Papers of Benjamin R. Curtis, *Ms.*, LC; B. R. Curtis, Some Observations on the Above Correspondence, n.d., ibid. The latter document is a commentary by Curtis on correspondence between him and the chief justice dealing with their differences over the publication of the individual opinions. See also Tappan to Smith, March 25, 1857, Lewis Tappan Letter Book (1856-1866), *Ms.*, LC; Harvey to McLean, April 3, 1857, Papers of John McLean, *Ms.*, LC; *Bangor* (Maine) *Daily Whig and Courier,* March 17, 1857; *The Evening Post* (New York), March 21, 1857; *Boston Daily Advertiser,* March 26, 1857; *The New York Journal of Commerce,* March 31, 1857; *Morning Courier and New-York Enquirer,* April 29, 1857.

6. Taney to Curtis, June 11, 1857, and Taney to William Carroll, April 6, 1857, Papers of Benjamin R. Curtis, *Ms.*, LC.

7. Curtis, Some Observations on the Above Correspondence, n.d., ibid. Among Supreme Court records in the National Archives are proof sheets of Taney's opinion as finally printed. Handwritten additions (that appear to be in Taney's handwriting) seemingly substantiate Curtis's contention that the chief justice added considerably to his oral opinion. Supreme Court Records, Opinions in Appellate Cases, Box 52, N.A.

8. Tappan to Smith, March 25, 1857, Lewis Tappan Letter Book (1856-1866), *Ms.*, LC; *The National Era* (Washington, D.C.), March 12, 1857; *Morning Courier and New-York Enquirer,* April 29, 1857. The original opinions were all filed with the clerk but were destroyed in a file room fire in November 1898.

9. The Washington agent for the Associated Press in 1857 was Lawrence A. Gobright, but whether he or a subordinate covered this assignment is unknown. Theodore Boyle to author, July 8, 1970 (letter in possession of author).

10. "We have . . . only the confused accounts by the telegraph of the decision in Dred Scott's case." Curtis to John J. Crittenden, 1857 [sic], in Mrs. Chapman Coleman [ed.], *The Life of John J. Crittenden* (Philadelphia, 1871), 2: 137. For similar comments about the lack of an accurate account of what Taney said, see Tappan to Smith, March 25, 1857, Lewis Tappan Letter Book (1856-1866), *Ms.*, LC; *Boston Evening Transcript,* March 7, 1857; *New York Daily Tribune,* March 9, 1857; *The National Era* (Washington, D.C.), March 12, 1857; *The Charleston* (S.C.) *Daily Courier,* April 4, 1857; *The Daily Constitutionalist* (Augusta, Ga.), April 5, 1857; *Morning Courier and New-York Enquirer,* April 29, 1857.

11. The author has carefully compared the publications of this dispatch as they appeared in numerous journals and has found them to be, with extremely minor exceptions, all the same. The dispatch can be found in the *New York Daily Tribune,* March 9, 1857, *The Daily Union* (Washington, D.C.), March 11, 1857, and the *Daily Missouri Republican* (St. Louis), March 13, 1857, among others.

12. Raoul Berger, *Government by Judiciary: The Transformation of the Fourteenth Amendment* (Cambridge, 1977), p. 8.

13. See Harold M. Hyman, *A More Perfect Union: The Impact of the Civil War and Reconstruction* (New York, 1973), chs. 1-3.

14. See Don E. Fehrenbacher, "Roger B. Taney and the Sectional Crisis," *Journal of Southern History* 43 (November 1977): 564.

15. According to the Associated Press report, Taney delved right into the citizenship question without even mentioning the differences of opinion among his colleagues over whether the Court could even discuss this subject. In the revised opinion, however, he discussed *at great length* the technical aspects of the plea in abatement and concluded that inasmuch as it was a part of the general record transmitted to the Supreme Court, it was subject to the review of the Court. 19 Howard 400-403. After more than a century of debate on this point, scholars now tend to agree with Taney.

16. Taney's reasoning was not consistent with prior decisions and interpretations, not only on the citizenship issue, but also in other portions of the opinion. See Fehrenbacher, "Roger B. Taney and the Sectional Crisis," pp. 561-64.

17. Italics mine.

18. The full Associated Press dispatch first appeared in the *New York Daily Tribune* on Monday, March 9, 1857, with the questionable phrases appearing as indicated. There were no significant editorial comments, apparently because the dispatches from Washington correspondents James E. Harvey ("Index") and James S. Pike ("J.S.P.") had not yet arrived. On March 11, the *Tribune* attacked Taney in a lengthy editorial and accused him of ruling that "Scott and his family, being Negroes, have, under the Constitution of the United States, 'no rights which white men are bound to respect.'" The words that the *Tribune* indicated as coming from the decision ("no rights which white men are bound to respect") were quoted accurately from the Associated Press dispatch. But by using the word *have* as it did, the *Tribune* inferred that that, too, was Taney's. Other Republican and abolitionist papers repeated this wording, some including the word *have* in the larger quotation, some omitting the quotation marks completely, and thus they spread a false report of what the chief justice allegedly had said.

19. 19 Howard 407.

20. Reprovers of Taney have always overlooked this sentence, which appears in both the Associated Press dispatch and in the revised printed opinion. Taney's biographers invariably stress his strong biases that white and black could not live side by side as equals. Fehrenbacher says that the way Taney stressed this racism in the *Dred Scott* decision was not merely "a discreditable intellectual performance by an upright man" or an "unfortunate aberration," but that it was actually "in harmony with Taney's entire judicial record on the issue of slavery." (Fehrenbacher, "Taney and the Sectional Crisis," p. 565.) Yet this one sentence suggests provocative speculation on Taney's racism. Did Taney, in spite of his judicial record on slavery, genuinely believe that a "life, liberty, and pursuit of happiness" document *written in 1857* really should include blacks? Or was this sentence merely a tactical sop to antislavery protagonists?

This sentence created a dilemma for supporters of the decision. They could have countered Taney's "have no rights" critics by showing that the opinion referred narrowly only to the prenational period. But that would have left them open to an unacceptable inference that the status of blacks now (in 1857) should be different. This makes it more inexplicable why Republicans did not pick up this particular sentence in Taney's opinion and exploit it.

In his revised version, the chief justice first cited supportive enactments of the colonial legislatures of Maryland and Massachusetts before he discussed the contents of the Declaration of Independence. 19 Howard 408-9. These examples did not appear, however, in the Associated Press report.

21. Taney erred in his facts. In at least two slave states, Maryland and North Carolina, free blacks had the right to vote, although that right was later taken away, in 1810 in Maryland and in 1835 in North Carolina. John Hope Franklin, *The Free Negro in North Carolina* (New York, 1971), pp. 112-13; Fletcher M. Green, *Constitutional Development in the South Atlantic States, 1776-1860* (New York, 1966), p. 193.

22. Whereas Taney apparently generalized in broad terms on these subjects according to the Associated Press dispatch, he devoted a great deal of attention to them in his revised version, citing numerous state laws as well as laws of Congress, decisions of state courts, and acts of individual federal officers. 19 Howard 412-26.

23. The contrast between Taney's narrow approach toward citizenship and his much broader approach in expanding Jacksonian democratic principles has been noted by many historians of the Supreme Court and especially by Taney's biographers. They have also noted that as far back as 1832 Attorney General Taney had held that Negroes were a degraded people never having had the status of citizens. Among others, see Carl Brent Swisher, *The Taney Period, 1836-64* (New York, 1964), p. 623.

24. One of the major weapons of those who opposed the decision was the *obiter dictum* issue. The Associated Press reports of the opinion gave them excellent ammunition, for by those accounts Taney appeared to have arrogantly flaunted lack of jurisdiction and jaundicedly gone to the merits to declare the Missouri Compromise unconstitutional.

25. 19 Howard 427-28.

26. R. Kent Newmyer, review of Bernard Schwartz, *From Confederation to Nation, 1835-1877*, in *The American Journal of Legal History* 19 (January 1975): 66. For more on the *obiter dictum* issue see ch. 18, *infra*.

27. In the revised official version, Taney elaborated: "The right of property in a slave is distinctly and expressly affirmed in the Constitution. The right to traffic in it, like an ordinary article of merchandise and property, was guaranteed to the citizens of the United States, in every State that might desire it, for twenty years. And the government in express terms is pledged to protect it in all future time, if the slave escapes from his owner. This is done in plain words—too plain to be misunderstood. And no word can be found in the Constitution which gives Congress a greater power over slave property, or which entitled property of that kind to less protection than property of any other description. The only power conferred is the power coupled with the duty of guarding and protecting the owner in his rights." 19 Howard 451-52.

28. This totally contradicted the Republican "freedom national" concept and appeared to undercut one of that party's major stances. See Eric Foner, *Free Soil, Free Labor, Free Men: The Ideology of the Republican Party before the Civil War* (New York, 1970), pp. 82-84.

29. The last word *Illinois* seems to be an error on the part of the Associated Press reporter or else a slip on Taney's part, for the chief justice undoubtedly was referring here to the Louisiana Purchase territory. In the revised version, at least, this error does not appear. It reads: "It is the opinion of the court . . . that neither Dred Scott himself, nor any of his family were made free by being carried into this territory." 19 Howard 452.

CHAPTER 16
Concurring Opinions

1. Fred Rodell, *Nine Men: A Political History of the Supreme Court from 1790 to 1955* (New York, 1955), p. 133.

2. There is a degree of painful validity to Judge Horace H. Hagan's admonition: "If the circumstances surrounding the Dred Scott case have been misconceived, the decision itself has been even more grievously mistreated. It is a shining example of the danger inherent in college professors writing on legal subjects. A degree in sociology, philosophy, or political science does not necessarily qualify even a first-rate historical mind to analyze properly a complicated legal decision or opinion." Horace H. Hagan, "The Dred Scott Decision," *Georgetown Law Journal* 15 (January 1926): 106-7, quoted in Frederick S. Allis, Jr., "The Dred Scott Labyrinth," in *Teachers of History: Essays in Honor of Laurence Brodford Packard*, ed. H. Stuart Hughes (Ithaca, N.Y., 1954), p. 366.

3. Nelson to Tyler, May 13, 1871, in Samuel Tyler, *Memoir of Roger Brooke Taney* (Baltimore, 1872), p. 385.

4. Frank O. Gatell, "Samuel Nelson," in Leon Friedman and Fred M. Israel, eds., *The Justices of the United States Supreme Court, 1789-1969: Their Lives*

and Major Decisions (New York, 1969), 2: 817-29. There is no major biography of Justice Nelson. Carl Brent Swisher, *The Taney Period, 1836-64* (New York, 1964), contains excellent biographical materials on all who sat on the Court with Taney.

5. 19 Howard 457-69.

6. Frank O. Gatell, "John Catron," in Friedman and Israel, eds., *Justices of the United States Supreme Courts,* 1: 737-45. See also Henry J. Abraham, *Justices and Presidents: A Political History of Appointments to the Supreme Court* (New York, 1974), pp. 93-95. No full biography of Catron has yet been done.

7. They appear in the Associated Press dispatch that was printed in newspapers all over the country and are mentioned by several correspondents who were present and who heard Catron read his opinion. *New York Daily Tribune,* March 7, 1857; *The New York Herald,* March 7, 1857; *Boston Evening Transcript,* March 7, 1857; *Daily National Intelligencer* (Washington, D.C.), March 7, 1857; *The Charleston* (S.C.) *Mercury,* March 11, 1857.

8. 19 Howard 518-29. See also Harvey to McLean, April 3, 1857, Papers of John McLean, Ms., Library of Congress; *New York Daily Tribune,* March 11, 1857; *Bangor* (Maine) *Daily Whig and Courier,* March 17, 1857; *Boston Daily Advertiser,* March 26, 1857.

9. *Boston Evening Transcript,* March 7, 1857. George T. Curtis was "pained to read that there was a squabble among the judges as to who shall have the last word. I suppose Daniel and Campbell anticipate flings from McLean, and wish to pay him back." Curtis to Crittenden, 1857 [*sic*], in (Mrs.) Chapman Coleman, ed., *The Life of John J. Crittenden* (Philadelphia, 1871), 2: 137.

10. *New York Daily Tribune,* March 7, 9, 1857.

11. See John C. Hogan, "The Role of Chief Justice Taney in the Decision of the Dred Scott Case," *Case and Comment* 58 (1953): 3. The only full-length biography of Wayne is Alexander A. Lawrence, *James Moore Wayne, Southern Unionist* (Chapel Hill, N.C., 1943). An excellent biographical sketch by Frank O. Gatell is in Friedman and Israel, eds., *Justices of the United States Supreme Court,* 1: 601-11.

12. 19 Howard 454.

13. Ibid., 454-55.

14. No full-length biography of Grier has been done. Frank O. Gatell provides a good biographical sketch in Friedman and Israel, eds., *Justices of the United States Supreme Court,* 1: 813-23.

15. 19 Howard 469.

16. Frank O. Gatell, "Peter V. Daniel," in Friedman and Israel, eds., *Justices of the United States Supreme Court,* 1: 804. A recent good biography of Daniel is John P. Frank, *Justice Daniel Dissenting: A Biography of Peter V. Daniel, 1784-1860* (Cambridge, 1964).

17. For Daniel's opinion see 19 Howard 469-92.

18. Ibid., p. 475.

19. Ibid., p. 483.

20. For Campbell's opinion see ibid., pp. 493-518.

21. The only scholarly biography of Campbell is Henry G. Connor, *John Archibald Campbell* (Boston, 1920). A good recent biographical sketch is William Gillette,

"John A. Campbell," in Friedman and Israel, eds., *Justices of the United States Supreme Court*, 2: 927-39.

CHAPTER 17
Dissenting Opinions

1. The standard McLean biography is Francis P. Weisenburger, *The Life of John McLean* (Columbus, 1937). A good brief sketch by Frank O. Gatell can be found in Leon Friedman and Fred M. Israel, eds., *The Justices of the United States Supreme Court, 1789-1969: Their Lives and Major Decisions* (New York, 1969), 1: 536-46. Robert Cover argues that McLean's antislavery judicial record was not as staunch as commonly portrayed. He criticizes McLean for not condoning from the bench disobedience to abhorrent slave laws as advocated by some abolitionists. Robert M. Cover, *Justice Accused* (New Haven, 1975), p. 245. Cover cites, among other examples of McLean's purported lack of resoluteness, his response in *Van Zandt* (to Salmon P. Chases's natural-law arguments) that "a proper view of conscience leads to obedience to positive law." Ibid., p. 173.

2. Because of the great demand and interest in knowing what the Court had said in *Dred Scott*, Court Reporter Howard arranged with Cornelius Wendell, printer of the Washington, D.C., *Daily Union,* to publish a special pamphlet containing just those nine opinions. Similar pamphlets were published shortly afterwards by Horace Greeley in New York and by others. *The Daily Union* (Washington, D.C.), May 19, 1857; *New York Daily Tribune,* May 20, 1857; *The Worcester* (Mass.) *Daily Spy,* May 23, 1857; *The Charleston* (S.C.) *Mercury,* June 11, 1857. Carl Brent Swisher, *The Taney Period, 1835-64* (New York, 1964), pp. 638-45, deals with the publication of these different pamphlet editions.

3. *New York Daily Tribune,* March 10, 1857; *Morning Courier and New-York Enquirer,* March 12, 1857; *Daily Missouri Republican* (St. Louis), March 14, 1857; *Daily Cincinnati Gazette,* March 16, 1857; *The National Era* (Washington, D.C.), March 19, 1857. As early as Sunday, March 8, Montgomery Blair "heard it read even in the House of God today." Blair to McLean, March 8, 1857, Papers of John McLean, *Ms.,* LC.

4. Even Taney's fellow justices could not get copies of his opinion. William Thomas Carroll to Curtis, April 6, 1857, Papers of Benjamin R. Curtis, *Ms.*, LC. This is one of almost a dozen letters between Curtis, Taney, and Carroll dealing with Curtis's unsuccessful attempt to see a copy of Taney's opinion. See Benjamin R. Curtis, ed., *A Memoir of Benjamin Robbins Curtis* (Boston, 1879), 1: 212-30; Benjamin P. Poore, *Perley's Reminiscences of Sixty Years in the National Metropolis* (Philadelphia, 1886), pp. 517-18.

5. *New York Day Book,* March 10, 1857; *New York Morning Express,* March 11, 1857; *The Daily Union* (Washington, D.C.), March 18, 1857; *The Sun* (Baltimore), March 28, 1857.

6. McLean's opinion is found in 19 Howard 529-64.

7. As already indicated, legal scholars do not support McLean on this; they believe the entire record was open to review, as Taney maintained.

8. 19 Howard 533-34.

9. See Eric Foner, *Free Soil, Free Labor, Free Men: The Ideology of the Republican Party before the Civil War* (New York, 1970), pp. 83-84.

10. 19 Howard 660. This was a very strong argument. Indeed, one of the enigmas of the *Dred Scott* case was the conflicting interpretations of *Strader* v. *Graham.*

11. See footnote 35, ch. 12, *supra.*

12. 19 Howard 549-50.

13. The best recent work on Curtis is Richard H. Leach, "Benjamin R. Curtis: Case Study of a Supreme Court Justice" (Doctoral dissertation, Princeton University, 1951). Leach has published a few scholarly articles about Curtis, but a definitive biography is yet to be published. A good brief biographical sketch is by William Gillette in Friedman and Israel, eds., *Justices of the United States Supreme Court,* 2: 859-908. Perhaps one of Curtis's most notable moments in a very distinguished career occurred when he defended impeached President Andrew Johnson before the United States Senate in 1868. Johnson was spared ignominious conviction by a mere one vote, and Curtis's brilliant arguments undoubtedly helped bring about the president's acquittal. At the same time Curtis perhaps unwittingly contributed to an untoward distortion of the constitutional removal process by arguing that impeachment and conviction must be for an indictable criminal offense only. Walter Ehrlich, *Presidential Impeachment: An American Dilemma* (St. Charles, Mo., 1974), p. 47.

14. A recent evaluation by lawyers, historians, and political scientists rates Curtis higher than all his contemporaries except Taney (whose legal reputation, in spite of *Dred Scott,* remains second only to Marshall and perhaps Story). *American Bar Association Journal* 58 (November 1972): 1183-89 (cited in Henry J. Abraham, *Justices and Presidents: A Political History of Appointments to the Supreme Court* [New York, 1974], pp. 289-90). Gillette's sketch of Curtis (footnote 13, *supra*, at 905) quotes Justice Felix Frankfurter on Curtis: "No one can have seriously studied the United States Reports and not have felt the impact of Curtis' qualities—short as was the term of his office."

15. Curtis's opinion was actually the lengthiest opinion of all, covering about seventy pages of small print in volume 19 of Howard's Reports. Taney's was fifty-four pages long; McLean's forty-seven; Campbell's twenty-five; Daniel's twenty-four; Catron's twelve; Nelson's twelve; Wayne's two; and Grier's only one paragraph.

16. "After the adjournment of the court, and on that day, the editor of a Boston newspaper, or his agent in Washington, applied to Judge Curtis for a copy of his dissenting opinion. It was given to him, because Judge Curtis supposed that all the opinions had been filed as the rule required, and that they would therefore be accessible to the press, and would be published for the information of the public, just as they had been read. The copy of his dissenting opinion was taken to Boston, and in a few days it was published." Curtis, *Memoir of Benjamin Robbins Curtis,* 1: 211.

17. *Morning Courier and New-York Enquirer,* March 17, 1857; *National Anti-Slavery Standard* (New York), March 26, 1857; *The National Era* (Washington, D.C.), March 26, 1857.

18. This premature publication of the Curtis dissent elicited a succession of bitterly worded letters between him and the chief justice that precipitated Curtis's

resignation. The episode is described in several accounts, including Swisher, *The Taney Period, 1836-64*, pp. 633-37. The letters are reproduced in Curtis, *Memoir of Benjamin Robbins Curtis*, 1: 211-30.

19. Curtis's full opinion appears in 19 Howard 564-633.

20. Ibid., pp. 565-66. It is precisely for this reason that the consensus of legal opinion has justified Taney going into the merits even after he rejected jurisdiction.

21. Ibid., p. 575. Curtis's factual data on this point was much more accurate than Taney's.

22. Curtis considered especially important the fact that the legal marriage of Dred Scott and Harriet Robinson was a contract universally recognized as made by free people only.

23. Curtis added at the very end two observations, perhaps as afterthoughts, which indicate they may not have been in his original opinion but were put in after he heard his colleagues in Court the day before. The first repudiated Taney's contention that slaves were property protected by the due process clause of the Fifth Amendment. Curtis viewed that clause much more restrictively, that due process was confined to procedural limitations. The second point tacked on was a refutation to Catron's argument that the Missouri Compromise violated the 1803 treaty that had ceded Louisiana from France to the United States.

CHAPTER 18
The Verdict

1. Perhaps the most inflammatory controversies developed over the "Negroes have no rights which white men were bound to respect" statement and the assertion that the Court had denied citizenship to all Negroes. For instance, see Joseph A. Ware to Fessenden, March 12, 1857, Correspondence of William Pitt Fessenden, *Ms.*, LC; Cushing to Taney, October 28, 1857, Caleb Cushing Papers, *Ms.*, LC; *New York Daily Tribune*, March 7, 11, May 20, 28, 1857; *The New York Herald*, March 7, 14, 1857; *Daily National Intelligencer* (Washington, D.C.), March 7, 1857; *Boston Post*, March 11, 1857; *The Charleston* (S.C.) *Mercury*, March 11, 1857; *The Lafayette* (Ind.) *Daily Journal*, March 13, 1857; *The Daily Union* (Washington, D.C.), March 24, 1857; *The Weekly Argus and Democrat* (Madison, Wisc.), June 23, 1857; *The Providence* (R.I.) *Daily Post*, July 3, 20, 1857; *Daily Pennsylvanian* (Philadelphia), July 22, 1857; Carl Brent Swisher, *Roger B. Taney* (New York, 1936), p. 505; Charles Warren, *The Supreme Court in United States History*, 3: 25; Daniel W. Howe, *Political History of Secession to the Beginning of the American Civil War* (New York, 1914), pp. 133-34; William N. Brigance, *Jeremiah Sullivan Black* (Philadelphia, 1934), p. 113; Henry Waller, *Speech of Henry Waller, Esq., on the Dred Scott Decision*, pamphlet (n.p., 1858), pp. 19-21; Hilary A. Herbert, *The Supreme Court in Politics*, pamphlet (n.p., 1883), pp. 12-13.

2. Many scholars have perhaps been overly influenced by the Republican and antislavery press and have overlooked that much of the American press actually praised the Dred Scott decision. For instance, Allan Nevins refers repeatedly to how

the "Northern" press attacked the decision. (Allan Nevins, *The Emergence of Lincoln*, 1: 96-98.) That was not so. A survey of American newspaper reaction indicates that only the Republican and abolitionist press was critical. Northern Democratic and other journals, on the other hand, ranged from joining the southern press in lauding Taney and the Court to reluctantly accepting the decision as at long last settling the divisive territorial issue.

3. "If people were to defy the decision [without defying the law] . . . they had to find a way to regard the decision as lacking in ordinary judicial force. They could do this only by categorizing the decision as a *dictum*. Such a categorization was a psychological godsend to them; it got them out of an intolerable dilemma." David M. Potter, *The Impending Crisis, 1848-1861* (New York, 1976), p. 284. For more on strategy to oppose the decision, see ibid., 279-90, and Michael F. Holt, *The Political Crisis of the 1850s* (New York, 1978), p. 202.

4. For a full discussion of this point, see Edward S. Corwin's landmark article, "The Dred Scott Decision, in the Light of Contemporary Legal Doctrines," *American Historical Review* 17 (October 1911): 52-69.

5. Some confusion arose because Curtis also endorsed the "entire record" principle. But the end product of his analysis was favorable to Republicans. Furthermore, Curtis had concluded from the citizenship issue that the Court had jurisdiction anyway. Thus Republicans could denounce Taney for using the "entire record" doctrine while upholding Curtis for following the same principle.

6. This was, of course, in addition to disagreements over substantive issues.

7. See ch. 15, p. 137, *supra*.

8. See footnote 4, *supra*.

9. See among others William B. Hesseltine, *The South in American History*, (New York, 1943), p. 350; Helen T. Catterall, *Judicial Cases Concerning American Slavery and the Negro* (Washington, 1937), 5: 121; John D. Hicks, *The Federal Union* (Boston, 1957), p. 535; Samuel E. Morison and Henry S. Commager, *The Growth of the American Republic* (New York, 1950), 1: 626; Elbert William Robert Ewing, *Legal and Historical Status of the Dred Scott Decision* (Washington, 1909), pp. 6-17; Don E. Fehrenbacher, *Prelude to Greatness: Lincoln in the 1850's* (Stanford, 1962), pp. 133-34; Frank H. Hodder, "Some Phases of the Dred Scott Case," *Mississippi Valley Historical Review* 16 (June 1929): 12; Corwin, "The Dred Scott Case, in the Light of Contemporary Legal Doctrine," p. 576; Horace H. Hagan, "The Dred Scott Decision," *Georgetown Law Journal* 15 (1926): 112-14. See also Thomas B. Alexander, "Historical Treatments of the Dred Scott Case, 1889-1950," *The Proceedings of the South Carolina Historical Association, 1953*, vol. 23, pp. 37-59, and especially Frederick S. Allis, Jr., "The Dred Scott Labyrinth," in *Teachers of History: Essays in Honor of Laurence Bradford Packard*, ed. H. Stuart Hughes (Ithaca, N.Y., 1954), pp. 341-68. The latter does the best job of unravelling all these conflicting analyses.

10. "The real problem for the historians—widely overlooked—is not whether Taney's opinion was dictum, but why the question of dictum has been blown up to such vast proportions. . . . This false focus on the question of dictum has led

historians to criticize the Court for deciding a crucial question at all, when perhaps the real criticism ought to be for deciding it incorrectly." Potter, *The Impending Crisis, 1848-1861,* pp. 283, 285.

11. Bernard Schwartz, *From Confederation to Nation, 1835-1877* (Baltimore, 1973), p. 108.

12. Ibid., pp. 114-15.

13. Wallace Mendelson, "Dred Scott's Case—Reconsidered," *Minnesota Law Review* 38 (1953): 28. See also Stanley I. Kutler, *Judicial Power and Reconstruction Politics* (Chicago, 1968), p. 9.

14. Even Justice Curtis was quoted as saying: "If you ask me what the Supreme Court of the United States decided in the case of Dred Scott, I answer that I don't know." Ben W. Palmer, *Marshall and Taney, Statesmen of the Law* (Minneapolis, 1939), p. 191.

15. Eric Foner, *Free Soil, Free Labor, Free Men: The Ideology of the Republican Party before the Civil War* (New York, 1970), p. 97. See also Potter, *The Impending Crisis, 1848-1861,* pp. 279-80, 287; Holt, *The Political Crisis of the 1850s,* p. 202, and William M. Wiecek, "Slavery and Abolition Before the United States Supreme Court, 1820-1860," *The Journal of American History* 65 (June 1978): 55.

16. Minutes (1856), March 6, 1857, USSC, *Ms.*

17. Notation by Samuel Treat dated only "1894" on Catron to Treat, May 31, 1857, Judge Samuel Treat Papers, *Ms.,* MoHS.

18. According to the Deputy Clerk of the Supreme Court of the United States, no exception has ever been made to this rule.

19. Fee Book E, p. 359, USSC, *Ms.*

20. Bailey to Morrill, May 8, 1857, Papers of Justin S. Morrill, *Ms.,* LC; Bailey to Trumbull, May 12, 1857, Papers of Lyman Trumbull, *Ms.,* LC.

21. Fee Book E, p. 359, USSC, *Ms.*; Docket (1856), ibid.

22. Certainly this was so in 1894. Notation by Samuel Treat on Catron to Treat, May 31, 1857, Judge Samuel Treat Papers, *Ms.,* MoHS. As far as the author has been able to ascertain, no change has been recorded since.

23. Permanent Records, No. 26 (1856-1857), p. 163, CCStL., *Ms.*

EPILOGUE

1. The impact of the decision is not within the scope of this monograph. For some brief generalities see preface and prologue, *supra.* The best recent works that include postdecision developments are David M. Potter, *The Impending Crisis, 1848-1861* (New York, 1976); Carl Brent Swisher, *The Taney Period, 1836-64* (New York, 1964); Allan Nevins, *The Emergence of Lincoln,* 2 vols (New York, 1950); Eric Foner, *Free Soil, Free Labor, Free Men: The Ideology of the Republican Party before the Civil War* (New York, 1970); Michael F. Holt, *The Political Crisis of the 1850s* (New York, 1978); and Joel H. Silbey, *The Transformation of American Politics, 1848-1860* (Englewood Cliffs, N.J., 1967). The definitive work may be a new study by Don E. Fehrenbacher, to whom the author has provided many primary materials.

2. Corcoran to Lawrence Riggs, February 7, 1857, Papers of William W. Cor-

coran, *Ms.*, LC; *Morning Courier and New-York Enquirer,* December 18, 1856; *New York Daily Tribune,* May 7, 1857; *The Saint Louis Daily Evening News and Intelligencer,* September 20, 1858; *Daily Missouri Democrat* (St. Louis), September 20, 1858.

3. *The Providence* (R.I.) *Daily Post,* March 17, 1857; *New York Morning Express,* June 1, 1857; *Boston Post,* June 1, 1857.

4. *Springfield* (Mass.) *Daily Republican,* March 16, 1857.

5. *New York Daily Tribune,* June 6, 1857.

6. *Springfield* (Mass.) *Daily Republican,* March 16, May 29, 1857.

7. Examples of the denunciations and other similar comments about Dr. Chaffee can be found in the following: *Cleveland Daily Plain Dealer,* March 16, 1857; *The Providence* (R.I.) *Daily Post,* March 17, 1857; *Daily Louisville* (Ky.) *Democrat,* March 19, 1857; *Daily Missouri Republican* (St. Louis), March 22, April 3, 1857; *The Daily Richmond Enquirer,* March 23, June 9, 1857; *Indianapolis Daily State Sentinel,* April 6, 1857; *New Hampshire Patriot and State Gazette* (Concord), April 29, 1857; *New York Morning Express,* June 1, 1857; *Boston Post,* June 1, 1857.

8. R. A. Chapman to Editor, n.d., in *Springfield* (Mass.) *Daily Republican,* May 29, 1857. The stepdaughter, of course, was the fourteen-year-old Henrietta, the daughter born to Mrs. Emerson shortly before Dr. Emerson died.

9. Ibid.; *Daily Missouri Republican* (St. Louis), May 27, 1857.

10. Permanent Records, No. 26 (1856-1857), p. 263, CCStL, *Ms.*; Dalton to Hill, February 22, 1907, Dred Scott Papers.

11. *The Saint Louis Daily Evening News,* April 3, June 20, 1857; *The Daily Union* (Washington, D.C.), April 23, 1857; *Saint Louis Leader,* May 18, 27, 1857; *Boston Evening Transcript,* May 28, 1857; *The Daily News* (Philadelphia), June 2, 1857; *Frank Leslie's Illustrated Newspaper* (New York), June 27, 1857; *The Savannah* (Ga.) *Daily Republican,* June 29, 1857; *Daily Missouri Republican* (St. Louis), August 4, October 4, 1857.

12. *Saint Louis Leader,* May 18, 27, 1857; *Boston Evening Transcript,* May 28, 1857.

13. *Frank Leslie's Illustrated Newspaper* (New York), June 27, 1857. The St. Louis city directory for 1854-55 (p. 173) listed him as a "white washer," and gave his address as "al. b. 10th and 11th, n. of Wash" (alley between 10th and 11th streets north of Wash Street).

14. Clipping from *St. Louis Globe Democrat,* July 3, 1927, in Dred Scott Papers.

15. J. Milton Turner, "Dred Scott Eulogy," in Dred Scott Papers; Irving Dilliard, "Dred Scott Eulogized by James Milton Turner," *Journal of Negro History* 26 (1941): 1-11. The original of this painting is in the library of the Missouri Historical Society in St. Louis. An oil copy, in somewhat poor physical condition, is in the possession of the New York Historical Society. No one there knows who painted this copy or how it happened to come into the possession of the society. The author came across it by accident, in a storage closet. Personnel of the New York Historical Society were not even aware of its existence before then. See photograph on p. 8.

16. *The Saint Louis Daily Evening News and Intelligencer,* September 20, 1858; *Daily Missouri Republican* (St. Louis), September 20, 1858; *New York Daily Tribune,* September 22, 1858; *The New York Herald,* September 22, 1858; *Daily National Intelligencer* (Washington, D.C.), September 22, 1858; *The Atlas and Argus* (Albany, N.Y.), September 22, 1858; *The Sun* (Baltimore), September 23, 1858; *The Weekly Argus and Democrat* (Madison, Wisc.), September 28, 1858.

17. J. Hugo Grimm to Charles Van Ravenswaay, October 29, 1946, Dred Scott Papers; unidentified and undated document, T. W. Chamberlain Collection, *Ms.,* MoHS; John A. Bryan, "The Blow Family and their Slave Dred Scott," Missouri Historical Society *Bulletin,* pt. 2, pp. 24-25. Harriet Scott lived for only a few years after the death of her husband. Eliza, who never married, also died shortly thereafter. The other daughter, Lizzie, married Wilson Madison of St. Louis, and they had two children, Harry and John Alexander Madison. Harry never married and had no issue. John Alexander Madison married Grace Cross, and they had seven children.

18. *St. Louis Post Dispatch,* March 7, July 25, September 17, 18, 1957; *St. Louis Globe Democrat,* March 7, July 25, September 16, 1957. Also present at the services were John Alexander Madison, Jr. (great-grandson of the former slave), Dred Scott Madison (great-grandson), and Wendell Scott Miller and Raymond Scott Miller, great-great-grandsons.

Selected Bibliography

PRIMARY SOURCES

MANUSCRIPT COLLECTIONS, DIARIES, JOURNALS

Anthony, Susan Brownell, Papers. LC.
Anti-Slavery Papers. LC.
Bailly, Alexius, Papers. WiSHS.
Barlow, Samuel Latham Mitchell, Miscellaneous Papers. New York Public Library.
Bates, Edward, Diary. MoHS.
Bates, Edward, Journal. MoHS.
Bayard, Thomas F., Papers of. LC.
Benton, Charles S., Papers. WiSHS.
Bigler, William, Papers. HSPa.
Black, Jeremiah S., Papers of. LC.
Blair, Francis Preston, Jr., Papers of. LC.
Blair, Gist, Collection. LC.
Blair, Montgomery, Papers of. LC.
Blow Family Papers. MoHS.
Breckenridge Family, Papers of. LC.
Buchanan, James, Papers. HSPa.
Buchanan-Johnston Papers. LC.
Cameron, Simon, Papers of. LC.
Carroll, Anna Ella, Letters. Maryland Historical Society, Baltimore.
Chamberlain, T. W., Collection. MoHS.
Chase, Salmon P., Papers of. LC.
Cobb, Howell, Papers. LC.
Corcoran, William W., Papers of. LC.
Crittenden, John Jordan, Papers of. LC.
Curtis, Benjamin R., Papers of. LC.
Cushing, Caleb, Papers. LC.

242   SELECTED BIBLIOGRAPHY

Darby, John F., Papers. MoHS.
Davis, John Givan, Correspondence. WiSHS.
Donelson, Andrew J., Papers of. LC.
Douglas, Stephen A., Papers. University of Chicago.
Drake, Charles D., Autobiography. State Historical Society of Missouri, Columbia, Missouri.
Ewing, Thomas, Papers of. LC.
Fessenden, William Pitt, Correspondence of. LC.
Fish, Hamilton, Correspondence of. LC.
Gamble, Hamilton R., Papers. MoHS.
Giddings-Julian Collection. LC.
Hammond, James H., Papers of. LC.
Johnson, Andrew, Papers of. LC.
Lincoln, Abraham, Collection. Chicago Historical Society.
Lincoln, Robert Todd, Collection of the Papers of Abraham Lincoln. LC.
Marcy, Lilliam Learned, Papers of. LC.
Mason, Charles, Diary. LC.
McLean, John, Letters. Ohio State Archaeological and Historical Society, Columbus, Ohio.
McLean, John, Papers of. LC.
Morrill, Justin S., Papers of. LC.
Napton, William B., Diary of. MoHS.
Pierce, Franklin, Papers of. LC.
Pierce, Franklin, Papers, Photostat Collection. LC.
Potter, John Fox, Papers. WiSHS.
Ruffin, Edmund, Diary of. LC.
Scott, Dred, Papers. MoHS.
Seward, William H., Papers. University of Rochester.
Snyder, Dr. John F., Collection. MoHS.
Stanton, Edwin M., Papers of. LC.
Stevenson, Andrew, and White, John, Papers of. LC.
Stuart, Alexander H. H., Papers. LC.
Taliaferro, Lawrence, Papers. Minnesota Historical Society, St. Paul.
Taney Papers. Maryland Historical Society, Baltimore.
Tappan, Lewis, Letter Books. LC.
Treat, Judge Samuel, Papers, MoHS.
Trumbull, Lyman, Papers of. LC.
Tyler, John, Papers. LC.
Van Buren, Martin, Papers of. LC.
Washburne, Elihu B., Papers of. LC.
Welles, Gideon, Papers of. LC.
Wright, Elizur, Papers of. LC.

COURT RECORDS

Court records encompass (1) documents of the various litigations themselves, as well as (2) other documents that provide pertinent information about litigants and others. The latter category includes especially probate files of Peter Blow (No. 976), John Emerson (No. 1914), Alexander Sanford (No. 2486), and John F. A. Sanford (No. 5328) in the St. Louis Probate Court; probate records of Peter Blow in Southampton County, Courtland, Virginia; probate records of John Emerson in Scott County, Davenport, Iowa; and probate files of John F. A. Sanford in the Surrogate's Court, New York City. Ancillary to these are General Records Y-4 (1849) and Y-5 (1850) in the Recorder of Deeds office in St. Louis, and Southampton County Deed Books, Land Books, and Personal Property Books in the Virginia State Library, Richmond.

Document files of the litigations are found in the courts where those actions transpired. *Dred Scott* v. *Irene Emerson* (Case No. 1, November Term, 1846) and *Harriet Scott* v. *Irene Emerson* (Case No. 2, November Term, 1846) are in the Circuit Court in St. Louis. Only remnants of the original documents remain. Some are reprinted in John D. Lawson, ed., *American State Trials,* vol. 13 (St. Louis, 1921). Three document files are in the Missouri Supreme Court in Jefferson City: *Irene Emerson* v. *Dred Scott* (Case No. 14, March Term, 1848); *Irene Emerson* v. *Harriet (of color)* (Case No. 16, March Term, 1848); and *Dred Scott* v. *Irene Emerson* (Case No. 137, October Term, 1851). The latter is the file lost for half a century, containing the full transcript of proceedings in the lower court. See appendix A for how I found those missing papers. The document file of *Dred Scott* v. *John F. A. Sandford* [sic] (Case No. 692, Circuit Court of the United States for the District of Missouri) is located in the United States District Court, Eastern District of Missouri, St. Louis. Finally, *Dred Scott* v. *John F. A. Sanford* (File No. 3230, Case No. 7, December Term, 1856) is in the clerk's office in the Supreme Court of the United States.

In addition to the document files, court records include dockets and proceedings entries that help one trace litigation developments. The Missouri lower court records are the Permanent Records of the Circuit Court of St. Louis County, Records 17 through 26, covering the period 1845-57. They are found in the clerk's office, Circuit Court, St. Louis. In the Missouri high court are the General Record, Jefferson City, 1847-57, and the General Record, St. Louis, 1849-54. They are in the clerk's office of the Missouri Supreme Court in Jefferson City. Corresponding records in the lower federal court litigation are the Complete Records, vol. 5 (1853-54), and Law Records B and C (1853-57) in the United States District Court in St. Louis. United States Supreme Court records include Docket G (1854-57); individual yearly Dockets (dated 1854, 1855, and 1856); Minutes (1855 and 1856); and Fee Book E (1854-57). Also in the United States Supreme Court are a printed *Transcript of Records, 1856,* vol. 1, containing a copy of lower court proceedings, and file copies of some attorneys' briefs. Additional materials are in Supreme Court Records (Record Group 267) in the National Archives.

Only the supreme court decisions were published. The first nine volumes of Missouri Reports contain Missouri decisions precedent to the *Dred Scott* case. The decision in Mrs. Emerson's unsuccessful appeal in 1848 is found in 11 Missouri Reports (1848). The decision and opinions in the final state supreme court litigation are in 15 Missouri Reports (1852). The lengthy decision and opinions of the final federal case are found in 19 Howard (1857).

NEWSPAPERS

Alabama

The Mobile Daily Advertiser
The Mobile Daily Register

Arkansas

Arkansas State Gazette and Democrat (Little Rock)

California

Evening Bulletin (San Francisco)
San Jose Pioneer
The San Francisco Herald

Connecticut

Columbian Weekly Register (New Haven)
New-London Daily Star
The Norwich Weekly Courier

Delaware

The Delaware Gazette (Wilmington)
Delaware Republican (Wilmington)
Delaware State Reporter (Dover)

District of Columbia

The Constitution
The Daily Globe
Daily National Intelligencer
The Daily Union; continued as The Washington Union
The National Era

Georgia

The Daily Constitutionalist (Augusta)
The Savannah Daily Republican; continued as The Savannah Republican

Illinois

Chicago Daily Press; continued as Chicago Daily Press and Tribune
The Daily Democratic Press (Chicago)
Daily Illinois State Journal (Springfield)
Daily Illinois State Register (Springfield)
The Ottawa Weekly Republican
The Weekly Chicago Times

Indiana

Indianapolis Daily State Sentinel
The Lafayette Daily Journal

Iowa

Daily Iowa State Democrat (Davenport)
The Davenport Gazette; continued as The Davenport Daily Gazette

Kentucky

Daily Louisville Democrat
The Kentucky Statesman (Lexington)
Presbyterian Herald (Louisville)

Louisiana

The Daily Advocate (Baton Rouge)
The Daily Picayune (New Orleans)

Maine

Bangor Daily Whig and Courier
The Eastern Argus (Portland)

Maryland

Baltimore American
Baltimore Republican
The Sun (Baltimore)

Massachusetts

Anglo-Saxon, European and Colonial Gazette (Boston)
Boston Daily Advertiser
The Boston Daily Atlas; continued as *The Boston Morning Traveller*; continued as *Boston Daily Traveller*
Boston Evening Transcript
Boston Post
Essex County Mercury (Salem)
Springfield Daily Republican
The Worcester Daily Spy

Minnesota

The Daily Pioneer and Democrat (St. Paul)

Missouri

Daily Missouri Democrat (St. Louis)
Daily Missouri Republican; continued as *The Missouri Republican*; continued as *St. Louis Republican*
The Morning Signal (St. Louis)
The Saint Louis Daily Evening News; continued as *The Saint Louis Daily Evening News and Intelligencer*; continued as *St. Louis Daily Evening News*
St. Louis Daily Morning Herald
St. Louis Daily New Era
Saint Louis Daily Union; continued as *The Saint Louis Daily Morning Union*
The St. Louis Intelligencer; continued as *St. Louis Daily Intelligencer*; continued as *Daily Saint Louis Intelligencer*; continued as *The Saint Louis Daily Evening News and Intelligencer*; continued as *St. Louis Daily Evening News*
Saint Louis Leader
Weekly Reveille (St. Louis)
The Weekly Tribune (Liberty); continued as *Liberty Weekly Tribune*
The Western Watchman (St. Louis)

Nebraska

The Nebraskian (Omaha); continued as *The Omaha Nebraskian*

New Hampshire

> *Democratic Standard* (Concord)
> *The New Hampshire Gazette* (Portsmouth)
> *New Hampshire Patriot and State Gazette* (Concord)
> *New Hampshire Statesman* (Concord)
> *The Portsmouth Journal of Literature and Politics*

New Jersey

> *Newark Daily Advertiser*

New York

> *The Atlas and Argus* (Albany)
> *The Evening Post* (New York City)
> *Frank Leslie's Illustrated Newspaper* (New York City)
> *Morning Courier and New-York Enquirer*
> *National Anti-Slavery Standard* (New York City)
> *New York Daily Tribune*
> *New York Dispatch*
> *The New York Herald*
> *The New York Journal of Commerce*
> *New York Morning Express*
> *New York Observer*

North Carolina

> *Semi-Weekly Standard* (Raleigh)

Ohio

> *Cleveland Daily Plain Dealer*
> *Daily Cincinnati Gazette*
> *The Daily Ohio Statesman* (Columbus)

Oregon

> *Oregon Statesman* (Salem)

Pennsylvania

>   *The Daily News* (Philadelphia)
>   *Daily Pennsylvanian*; continued as *Philadelphia Daily Pennsylvanian*;
>   continued as *The Philadelphian*; continued as *The Morning Pennsylvanian*
>   *Harrisburg Daily Telegraph*
>   *North American and United States Gazette* (Philadelphia)
>   *Patriot and Union* (Harrisburg)
>   *The Sun* (Philadelphia)

Rhode Island

>   *Newport Advertiser*
>   *Newport Mercury and Weekly News*
>   *The Providence Daily Post*

South Carolina

>   *The Charleston Daily Courier*
>   *The Charleston Mercury*

Tennessee

>   *Daily Eagle and Enquirer* (Memphis)
>   *The Memphis Daily Appeal*
>   *Nashville Union and American*
>   *Republican Banner* (Nashville)

Texas

>   *The San Antonio Ledger*
>   *State Gazette* (Austin)

Vermont

>   *Vermont Watchman and State Journal* (Montpelier)

Virginia

>   *The Daily Richmond Enquirer*

Wisconsin

The Weekly Argus and Democrat (Madison)

MILITARY RECORDS

Dred Scott's travels with Dr. Emerson are traced by following the latter's military career, which is well documented by records in the Adjutant General's Office, Record Group 94, War Records Division, National Archives. Two document files pertain specifically to Emerson: file of Emerson, John, Asst. Surg., U.S.A., Letters and Reports, 1835-42; and file of Emerson, John, Asst. Surg., U.S.A., 1832-42. Other AGO files with valuable information are: Army Letters of Appointment, 1829-45, vol. 1; General Orders, 1841-42; Letters Received, Adjutant General's Office, 1833-43; Letters Sent, Adjutant General's Office, 1833-43; and muster rolls and post returns of appropriate outfits and military posts.

Records of the Office of the Secretary of War, Record Group 107, War Records Division, National Archives, include: Letters Received, Secretary of War, 1833-43; and Letters Sent, Secretary of War, 1833-43.

Records of the Surgeon General's Office, Record Group 112, War Records Division, National Archives, contain: Letter Book, Surgeon General's Office, 1833-43; Letters Received, Surgeon General's Office, 1833-43; and Medical and Hospital Accounts, Register B.

Two more collections in the National Archives contain valuable information, records of the Veterans' Administration (Record Group 15) and records of the Office of Indian Affairs (Natural Resources Records Division, Record Group 75). The latter include Letters Received, Indian Office, 1830-36; and Letters Sent, Indian Office, 1830-36. These are particularly valuable in following Lawrence Taliaferro's travels, and with him, Harriet Robinson Scott.

MISCELLANEOUS PRIMARY SOURCE MATERIALS

Any careful study of this period must include the tedious but necessary perusal of the *Congressional Globe* and *Appendix* for the 33rd, 34th, and 35th Congresses. Heated discussions took place also in many state legislatures, where some passed resolutions endorsing or denouncing the Supreme Court's action. Such deliberations are recorded in legislative journals of the states of Connecticut, Illinois, Iowa, Maine, Massachusetts, Michigan, Missouri, New Hampshire, New York, Ohio, Pennsylvania, Vermont, and Wisconsin and of the Territory of Washington. The following state legislatures apparently took no official action on the decision: Alabama, Arkansas, Georgia, Kentucky, Louisiana, Minnesota, Mississippi, Nebraska, New Jersey, Oregon, Rhode Island, South Carolina, Tennessee, Texas, Utah, and Virginia.

A number of important materials appeared in printed pamphlet form. Montgomery Blair's and Henry S. Geyer's Supreme Court briefs are indispensable. (Apparently

Reverdy Johnson did not make a separate brief; at least there are neither copies to be found nor even references to a brief.) George T. Curtis's argument was widely distributed in pamphlet form (George T. Curtis, *The Constitutional Power of Congress over the Territories. An Argument delivered in the Supreme Court of the United States, December 18, 1856, in the Case of Dred Scott, Plaintiff in error, v. John F. A. Sanford* [Boston, 1857].) The nine opinions appeared in several forms once they were published officially. The latter was in volume 19 of Court Reporter Benjamin C. Howard's *Reports*. The Senate authorized publication of twenty thousand copies of a separate pamphlet containing the opinions. Horace Greeley's *Tribune* printed its own pamphlet, as did others. Carl Brent Swisher, *The Taney Period, 1836-64* (New York, 1974), pp. 640-45, deals with the different pamphlet publications.

Contemporary reviews of the decision give an insight into reactions. These reviews appeared either in journals or in pamphlet form. The first important one was by Horace Gray and John Lowell, "The Case of Dred Scott," in *The Law Reporter* 20 (June 1857): 61-118. It soon appeared as a pamphlet, *A Legal Review of the Dred Scott Case, as Decided by the Supreme Court of the United States* (Boston, 1857). Other useful contemporary reviews of the decision include Timothy Farrar, "Benjamin F. Howard, 'A Report of the Decision of the Supreme Court of the United States . . . in the Case of Dred Scott versus John F. A. Sanford,'" *North American Review* 85 (October 1857): 392-415; [A Kentucky Lawyer], *A Review of the Decision of the Supreme Court of the United States in the Dred Scott Case* (Louisville, 1857); Samuel Nott, *Slavery and the Remedy; or, Principles and Suggestions for a Remedial Code* (New York, 1857); *Kansas-Utah-Dred Scott Decision: Speech of Hon. S. A. Douglas, delivered at Springfield, Illinois, June 12, 1857* (Springfield, 1857); [Frederick Douglass], *Two Speeches, by Frederick Douglass: one on . . . the Dred Scott Decision, Delivered in New York, on the Occasion of the Anniversary of the American Abolition Society, May, 1857* (Rochester, 1857); Thomas Hart Benton, *Historical and Legal Examination of That Part of the Decision of the Supreme Court of the United States in the Dred Scott Case, which Declares the Unconstitutionality of the Missouri Compromise Act* (New York, 1858); Henry Waller, *Speech of Henry Waller, Esq., on the Dred Scott Decision* (Chicago, 1858); Samuel A. Foot, *An Examination of the Case of Dred Scott against Sanford, in the Supreme Court of the United States* (New York, 1859); [A Southern Citizen], *Remarks on Popular Sovereignty, as Maintained and Denied Respectively by Judge Douglas and Attorney-General Black* (Baltimore, 1859); J. H. Van Evrie, *The Dred Scott Decision: Opinion of Chief Justice Taney, with an Introduction by Dr. J. H. Van Evrie* (New York, 1860); Daniel W. Gooch, *The Supreme Court and Dred Scott* (Washington, 1860); William S. Holman, *Party Issues and the Dred Scott Decision* (Washington, 1860); and Israel Washburn, *The Issues; the Dred Scott Decision; the Parties* (Washington, 1860).

SECONDARY WORKS

Vincent Hopkins, *Dred Scott's Case* (New York, 1951) is the only published monograph dealing with the history of this litigation. Standard constitutional histories contain accounts of the case, but they emphasize the decision and its ramifications. Among these are Charles Warren, *The Supreme Court in United States History*, vol. 3 (Boston, 1922); Carl Brent Swisher, *American Constitutional Development* (Boston, 1954); Alfred H. Kelly and Winfred A. Harbison, *The American Constitution* ((New York, 1963); Charles G. Haines and Foster H. Sherwood, *The Role of the Supreme Court in American Government and Politics, 1835-1865* (Berkeley, 1957); Hermann von Holst, *The Constitutional and Political History of the United States*, vol. 6 (Chicago, 1889); George T. Curtis, *Constitutional History of the United States*, vol. 2 (New York, 1896); Francis N. Thorpe, *The Constitutional History of the United States*, vol. 2 (Chicago, 1901); Westel W. Willoughby, *The Constitutional Law of the United States*, vol. 1 (New York, 1910); Andrew C. McLaughlin, *A Constitutional History of the United States* (New York, 1935); Homer C. Hockett, *The Constitutional History of the United States*, vol. 2 (New York, 1939); Robert G. McCloskey, *The American Supreme Court* (Chicago, 1960); Broadus and Louise Mitchell, *A Biography of the Constitution of the United States* (New York, 1964); Bernard Schwartz, *The Reins of Power* (New York, 1963).

Many general studies of American constitutionalism and the judiciary identify the *Dred Scott* decision as the nadir of judicial imprudence. These include: Charles Evans Hughes, *The Supreme Court of the United States: Its Foundations, Methods and Achievements* (New York, 1928); Alexander M. Bickel, *The Least Dangerous Branch: The Supreme Court at the Bar of Politics* (New York, 1962); Arthur E. Sutherland, *Constitutionalism in America* (New York, 1965); Wallace Mendelson, *Capitalism, Democracy, and the Supreme Court* (New York, 1960); Herbert A. Hillary, *The Supreme Court in Politics* (n.p., 1883); Blaine F. Moore, *The Supreme Court and Unconstitutional Legislation* (New York, 1913); Louis B. Boudin, *Government by Judiciary* (New York, 1932); Charles G. Haines, *The American Doctrine of Judicial Supremacy* (New York, 1932); Robert H. Jackson, *The Struggle for Judicial Supremacy* (New York, 1941); John R. Schmidhauser, *The Supreme Court as Final Arbiter in Federal-State Relations, 1789-1957* (Chapel Hill, N.C., 1958); Alpheus T. Mason, *The Supreme Court: Palladium of Freedom* (Ann Arbor, 1962); Henry J. Abraham, *Freedom and the Court* (New York, 1967).

Several excellent works deal with laws of slavery. Helen T. Catterall, "Some Antecedents of the Dred Scott Case," *American Historical Review* 30 (October 1924): 56-71, identifies Missouri precedents. Also valuable for a background of slavery in Missouri are Harrison A. Trexler, *Slavery in Missouri, 1804-1865* (Baltimore, 1914), and Benjamin Merkel, "The Antislavery Movement in Missouri, 1819-1865" (Doctoral dissertation, Washington University, St. Louis, 1939). The legal status of slaves in Illinois is described in N. Dwight Harris, *The History of Negro Servitude in Illinois and of the Slavery Agitation in That State, 1819-1864* (Chicago, 1904). Other studies involving slavery in the courts in various states are Fletcher M. Green, *Constitutional Development in the South Atlantic States, 1776-1860* (New York, 1966); John Hope Franklin, *The Free Negro in North Carolina, 1790-1860* (New York, 1971); Leon F. Litwack, *North of Slavery: The Negro in the Free States, 1790-1860* (Chicago, 1961). Exceedingly valuable for a nationwide overview of the legal status of slavery are John C. Hurd, *The Law of Freedom and Bondage in the United States*, 2 vols. (Boston, 1858 and 1862); J. Willard Hurst, *Law and the*

Condition of Freedom in the Nineteenth-Century United States (Madison, 1956); and Helen T. Catterall's comprehensive *Judicial Cases Concerning American Slavery and the Negro,* 5 vols. (Washington, 1937). Also useful are Henry Wilson, *History of the Rise and Fall of the Slave Power in America,* vol. 2 (Boston, 1874), and Theodore C. Smith, *Parties and Slavery, 1850-1859* (New York, 1906). William M. Wiecek, *"Somerset:* Lord Mansfield and the Legitimacy of Slavery in the Anglo-American World," *The University of Chicago Law Review* 42 (Fall 1974): 86-146, is a penetrating study of the English background of American slave law. The same author demonstrates the growing role of the Court in interpreting slave law in "Slavery and Abolition Before the United States Supreme Court, 1820-1860," *The Journal of American History* 65 (June 1978): 34-59.

Many secondary works provide valuable background information related to the lives and travels of Dred and Harriet Scott. For important data on military personnel see George W. Cullum, *Biographical Register of the Officers and Graduates of the U. S. Military Academy, . . . from its Establishment, March 16, 1802, to the Army Re-Organization of 1866-67,* vol. 1, 1802-1840 (New York, 1868), and Francis B. Heitman, *Historical Register and Dictionary of the United States Army, from Its Organization, September 29, 1789, to March 2, 1903,* 2 vols. (Washington, 1903). Helen L. C. Heideman, "The History of the United States Army during the Administration of Andrew Jackson, 1829-1837" (Master's thesis, Washington University, St. Louis, 1948), is a good study of military problems on the frontier when Dred Scott was at Forts Armstrong, Jesup, and Snelling.

Frontier problems during the 1830s in the upper Mississippi valley are covered in standard frontier history texts, including Frederick L. Paxson, *History of the American Frontier, 1763-1893* (Cambridge, 1924), and LeRoy R. Hafen and Carl C. Rister, *Western America* (New York, 1941). Specialized studies that focus on the upper Mississippi include E. W. Gould, *Fifty Years on the Mississippi; or Gould's History of River Navigation* (St. Louis, 1889); William J. Peterson, *Steamboating on the Upper Mississippi* (Iowa City, 1937); Wesley F. Diem, "Steamboating on the Upper Mississippi" (Master's thesis, Washington University, St. Louis, 1932); and Stephen R. Riggs, "Protestant Missions In the Northwest," *Collections of the Minnesota Historical Society* 6 (1894): 117-88. Living conditions at Fort Armstrong are vividly described in John H. Hauberg, "U. S. Surgeons at Fort Armstrong," *Journal of the Illinois State Historical Society* 24 (January 1932): 609-29; and Gladys E. Hamlin, "Mural Painting in Iowa," *The Iowa Journal of History and Politics* 37 (July 1939): 227-307. Conditions at Fort Snelling are described in William W. Folwell, *A History of Minnesota,* vol. 1 (St. Paul, 1921), and Edward D. Neill, "Occurrences In and Around Fort Snelling, From 1819 to 1840," *Collections of the Minnesota Historical Society* 2 (1860-67): 102-42. Biographical information on Lawrence Taliaferro is in "Autobiography of Maj. Lawrence Taliaferro: Written in 1864," *Collections of the Minnesota Historical Society* 6 (1894): 189-225; Willoughby M. Babcock, Jr., "Major Larence Taliaferro, Indian Agent," *Mississippi Valley Historical Review* 11 (December 1924): 358-75; and Grace L. Nute's sketch, "Lawrence Taliaferro," in the *Dictionary of American Biography,* vol. 13, 1936 ed.

Information about participants in the state phase of the litigation comes mostly from primary sources, but is augmented considerably by secondary materials. Invaluable for data about St. Louis and St. Louisans are: Richard Edwards and M. Hopewell, *Edwards's Great West and her Commercial Metropolis* (St. Louis, 1860); L. U. Reavis, *Saint Louis: The Future Great City of the World* (St. Louis, 1875); J. Thomas Scharf, *History of Saint Louis City and County,* 2 vols. (Philadelphia, 1883); William Hyde and Howard L. Conard, eds., *Encyclopedia of the History of St. Louis,* 4 vols. (New York, 1899); Walter B. Stevens, *St. Louis, The Fourth City, 1764-1909,* 2 vols. (St. Louis, 1909); and Floyd C. Shoemaker, ed., *Missouri and Missourians,* 5 vols. (Chicago, 1943).

The best account of the Blow family is a two-part article by John A. Bryan, "The Blow Family and Their Slave Dred Scott," in the Missouri Historical Society *Bulletin.* Part 1 appears in volume 4 (July 1948): 223-31; part 2 is in volume 5 (October 1948): 19-33. The only biographical sketch of Dr. Emerson is Charles E. Snyder, "John Emerson, Owner of Dred Scott," *Annals of Iowa* 21 (October 1938): 441-61. For biographical information about others associated with the case, see John F. Darby, *Personal Recollections* (St. Louis, 1880); Paul Beckwith, *Creoles of St. Louis* (St. Louis, 1893); Theodore H. Bingham, *Genealogy of the Bingham Family* (Harrisburg, 1898); H. D. Pittman, ed., *Americans of Gentle Birth and Their Ancestors* (St. Louis, 1903); William H. Chaffee, *The Chaffee Genealogy* (New York, 1909); George W. Stevens, *The History of the Central Baptist Church* (St. Louis, 1927); James M. Breckenridge, *William Clark Breckenridge, His Life, Lineage, and Writings* (St. Louis, 1932); Alexander N. DeMenil, "A Century of Missouri Literature," *Missouri Historical Review* 15 (October 1920): 74-125; Jensen, (Mrs. Dana O.), ed., "Stephen Hempstead, 'I at Home,'" Missouri Historical Society *Bulletin* 20 (July 1966): 410-45; Stella M. Drumm and Charles Van Ravenswaay, "The Old Courthouse," *Glimpses of the Past* 7 (1940): 3-41; Edmund P. Walsh, "The Story of an Old Clerk. Address before the Circuit Clerks and Recorders' Convention, St. Louis, July 14, 1908," ibid., 1 (July 1934): 63-70; and Irving Dilliard, "Dred Scott Eulogized by James Milton Turner," *Journal of Negro History* 26 (1941): 1-11. For the struggle to unseat Thomas Hart Benton and its association with the case, see William M. Meigs, *The Life of Thomas Hart Benton* (Philadelphia, 1904); William N. Chambers, *Old Bullion Benton: Senator from the New West* (Boston, 1956); P. Orman Ray, "The Retirement of Thomas Hart Benton from the Senate and Its Significance," *Missouri Historical Review* 2 (January 1908): 97-111; Clarence H. McClure, "Opposition in Missouri to Thomas Hart Benton," *Bulletin of Central Missouri State Teachers College* 27 (December 1926): 1-234; and Benjamin Merkel, "The Slavery Issue and the Political Decline of Thomas Hart Benton, 1846-1856," *Missouri Historical Review* 38 (July 1944): 388-407.

The role attorneys play in litigations is vital; yet often their motives may be obscured by their professional adversary role. This is especially true of the lawyers in the state case. The Reavis, Scharf, Stevens, Shoemaker, and Hyde and Conard compendia give some background on some lawyers in the state case, as do W. V. N. Bay, *Reminiscences of the Bench and Bar of Missouri* (St. Louis, 1878), and Alexander J. D. Stewart, ed., *The History of the Bench and Bar of Missouri* (St.

Louis, 1898). See also Frank E. Stevens, "Alexander Pope Field," *Journal of the Illinois State Historical Society* 4 (April 1911): 7-37; and David D. March, "The Life and Times of Charles D. Drake" (Doctoral dissertation, University of Missouri-Columbia, 1949). As to attorneys in the federal case, for Roswell M. Field see Frederick C. Pierce, *Field Genealogy* (Chicago, 1901), and Frank L. Fish, "Roswell M. Field," *Virginia Historical Society Proceedings,* 1923, pp. 229-47. No biographies exist on Hugh A. Garland or Henry S. Geyer. Montgomery Blair's career is included in William E. Smith, *The Francis Preston Blair Family in Politics,* 2 vols. (New York, 1933). The best biographical materials on Reverdy Johnson are Bernard C. Steiner, *Life of Reverdy Johnson* (Baltimore, 1914), and *Proceedings of the Bench and Bar of the Supreme Court of the United States in Memoriam of Reverdy Johnson* (Washington, 1876).

Valuable biographical materials are available for members of the Taney Court, especially for the famous chief justice. Samuel Tyler, *Memoir of Roger Brooke Taney, LL.D.* (Baltimore, 1872), contains Taney's sketchy autobiography. Others are Bernard C. Steiner, *Life of Roger Brooke Taney* (Baltimore, 1922); Charles W. Smith, *Roger B. Taney: Jacksonian Jurist* (Chapel Hill, 1936); and Walker Lewis, *Without Fear or Favor: A Biography of Chief Justice Roger Brooke Taney* (Boston, 1965). But the best is still Carl Brent Swisher, *Roger B. Taney* (New York, 1936). Ben W. Palmer, *Marshall and Taney, Statesmen of the Law* (Minneapolis, 1939), compares the Marshall and Taney records, but it is done in more detail and with better interpretive analysis by R. Kent Newmyer, *The Supreme Court under Marshall and Taney* (New York, 1968).

Conflicting appraisals of Taney by his contemporaries are in *Proceedings of the Bench and Bar of the Supreme Court of the United States, on the Occasion of the Death of Roger Brooke Taney, Fifth Chief Justice of the Said Court, at the December Term, 1864* (Washington, 1865); *Proceedings of the Bench and Bar of Baltimore, upon the Occasion of the Death of the Hon. Roger B. Taney, Chief Justice of the Supreme Court of the United States* (Baltimore, 1864); [Anonymous], "Roger Brooke Taney," *The Atlantic Monthly* 15 (February 1865): 151-61; [Charles Sumner], *The Unjust Judge: A Memorial of Roger Brooke Taney, Late Chief Justice of the United States* (New York, 1865); *The Taney Fund: Proceedings of the Meeting of the Bar of the Supreme Court of the United States* (Washington, 1871). Equally conflicting appraisals by later analysts are Charles N. Gregory, "A Great Judicial Character, Roger Brooke Taney," *Yale Law Journal* 18 (November 1908): 10-27; Thomas Z. Lee, "Chief Justice Taney and the Dred Scott Decision," *The Journal of the American Irish Historical Society* 22 (1923): 142-44; Charles Evans Hughes, "Roger Brooke Taney," *American Bar Association Journal* 17 (1931): 785-90; and William L. Ransom, "Roger Brooke Taney," *Georgetown Law Journal* 24 (1936): 809-47.

Biographical materials are available on all other members of the Court, although in varying quality and quantity. The only full-length biography of Campbell is Henry G. Connor, *John Archibald Campbell* (Boston, 1920). It is supplemented by George W. Duncan, "John Archibald Campbell," *Alabama Historical Society Transactions* 5 (1904): 107-51; Eugene I. McCormac, "Justice Campbell and the Dred Scott Decision," *Mississippi Valley Historical Review* 19 (March 1933): 565-71; and *Proceedings of the Bench and Bar of the Supreme Court of the United States in Memo-*

riam of John Archibald Campbell (Washington, 1889). No full-scale biography has been done on Catron, but briefer sketches are found in Boutwell Dunlap, "Judge John Catron of the United States Supreme Court," *Virginia Magazine of History* 28 (April 1920): 171-74; Edmund C. Gass, "The Constitutional Opinions of Justice John Catron," *East Tennessee Historical Society's Publications*, no. 8 (1936): 54-73; and Walter Chandler, "The Centenary of Associate Justice John Catron of the United States Supreme Court," *Tennessee Law Review* 15 (1937): 32-51. Alexander A. Lawrence, *James Moore Wayne, Southern Unionist* (Chapel Hill, 1943), and John P. Frank, *Justice Daniel Dissenting: A Biography of Peter V. Daniel, 1784-1860* (Cambridge, 1964), are the only biographies of those two jurists and present their contrasting philosophies toward the sectional crisis. Francis P. Weisenburger, *The Life of John McLean* (Columbus, 1937), is the standard biography of that Ohio jurist. Robert M. Cover, *Justice Accused: Antislavery and the Judicial Process* (New Haven, 1975), presents a revisionist view that McLean's judicial record was not as avidly antislavery as traditionally presented. Although Curtis is rated (next to Taney) as the outstanding person on that Court, no scholarly biography has been published. Curtis's son and namesake produced a two-volume memoir, *A Memoir of Benjamin Robbins Curtis, LL. D., with Some of his Professional and Miscellaneous Writings* (Boston, 1879). Volume 1 is a biography written by George Ticknor Curtis (the judge's brother); volume 2 consists of correspondence, including Curtis's heated exchange with Taney over the controversial publication of the *Dred Scott* opinions. The only modern work is Richard H. Leach, "Benjamin R. Curtis: Case Study of a Supreme Court Justice" (Doctoral dissertation, Princeton University, 1951). Leach's Benjamin Robbins Curtis: Judicial Misfit," *New England Quarterly* 25 (December 1952): 507-23, justifies Curtis's reasons for resigning from the Bench; and his "Justice Curtis and the Dred Scott Case," *Essex Institute Historical Collections* 94 (January 1958): 37-56, defends Curtis's strong dissent. See also *Proceedings of the Bench and Bar of the Circuit Court of the United States, District of Massachusetts, upon the Decease of Hon. Benjamin Robbins Curtis, September and October, 1874* (Boston, 1875), and Frank W. Grinnell, *Glimpses of the Life of Benjamin Robbins Curtis* (Boston, 1932), reprinted from *Proceedings of the Massachusetts Historical Society* 64 (March 1931).

Biographical sketches of all justices are in the *Dictionary of American Biography*. Far better and much more useful are the sketches in the appropriate volumes of Leon Friedman and Fred M. Israel, eds., *The Justices of the United States Supreme Court, 1789-1969: Their Lives and Major Decisions* (New York, 1969). The sketches of the careers of Campbell and Curtis are done by William Gillette; Frank O. Gatell authors the others. See also Henry J. Abraham, *Justices and Presidents: A Political History of Appointments to the Supreme Court* (New York, 1974).

President James Buchanan's association with the case is inadequately described in George T. Curtis, *Life of James Buchanan*, 2 vols. (New York, 1883), and [Anonymous], "The Collusion Between the Supreme Court and Buchanan," *The Independent* 71 (August 1911): 428-30. Philip Auchampaugh, "James Buchanan, the Court, and the Dred Scott Case," *Tennessee Historical Magazine* 9 (January 1926): 231-40, is the first scholarly analysis of Buchanan's correspondence with Grier and Catron. It is augmented by Philip S. Klein's excellent scholarship in *President James Buchanan: A Biography* (University Park, Pa., 1962).

Biographies of contemporaries provide insight and fuller understanding of the events of the time. Many contributed to this study, including Albert J. Beveridge, *Abraham Lincoln, 1809-1858,* 2 vols. (Boston, 1928); John G. Nicolay and John Hay, *Abraham Lincoln,* vol. 2 (New York, 1917); M. A. DeWolfe Howe, *The Life and Letters of George Bancroft* (New York, 1908); William N. Brigance, *Jeremiah Sullivan Black* (Philadelphia, 1934); (Mrs.) Chapman Coleman, ed., *The Life of John J. Crittenden* (Philadelphia, 1871); Claude M. Fuess, *The Life of Caleb Cushing,* vol. 2 (New York, 1923); George F. Milton, *The Eve of Conflict: Stephen A. Douglas and the Needless War* (Boston, 1934); George W. Julian, *The Life of Joshua R. Giddings* (Chicago, 1892); Bliss Perry, *Life and Letters of Henry Lee Higginson* (Boston, 1921); Charles Henry Jones, *The Life and Public Service of J. Glancy Jones,* 2 vols. (Philadelphia, 1910); Ralph V. Harlow, *Gerritt Smith* (New York, 1939); Richard M. Johnston and William H. Browne, *Life of Alexander H. Stephens* (Philadelphia, 1883); Henry Cleveland, *Alexander H. Stephens, in Public and Private* (Philadelphia, 1866); Rudolph von Abele, *Alexander H. Stephens* (New York, 1946); Horace Greeley, *The Autobiography of Horace Greeley, or Recollections of a Busy Life* (New York, 1872); James G. Blaine, *Twenty Years in Congress,* 2 vols. (Norwich, Conn., 1884); Edward L. Pierce, *Memoir and Letters of Charles Sumner,* vol. 3 (Boston, 1894); George S. Hillard, ed., *Life, Letters, and Journals of George Ticknor,* vol. 2 (Boston, 1876); Pleasant A. Stovall, *Robert Toombs* (New York, 1892); Ulrich B. Phillips, *The Life of Robert Toombs* (New York, 1913); Horace White, *The Life of Lyman Trumbull* (Boston, 1913); Denis T. Lynch, *An Epoch and a Man: Martin Van Buren and his Times* (New York, 1929).

Most studies of the decision have focused on one or both of two major topics: (1) what the Court decided and whether some of it was *obiter dictum*; and (2) the ramifications of the decision and especially how it contributed to the polarization that resulted in the Civil War. Contemporary analyses (identified under "Primary Sources" *supra*) fall in the first category and tend to be harsh on Taney by stressing *obiter dictum.* As nineteenth-century sectionalism gave way to twentieth-century revisionism, newer interpretations saw Taney in a different light. The ground was broken by Elbert W. R. Ewing, *Legal and Historical Status of the Dred Scott Decision* (Washington, 1909), who reflected more a prosouthern defense of sectionalism than a scholarly analysis. Nevertheless, he paved the way for the landmark work by Edward S. Corwin, "The Dred Scott Decision, in the Light of Contemporary Legal Doctrines," *American Historical Review* 17 (October 1911): 52-69, a scholarly analysis concluding that the decision was not *obiter dictum.* Complemented by Horace H. Hagan, "The Dred Scott Decision," *Georgetown Law Journal* 15 (January 1926): 95-114, which fortified the Corwin interpretation, the stage was set for a running conflict between Taney's defenders and detractors. Foremost among the former is Carl Brent Swisher, probably the twentieth century's leading Taney scholar, in his *Roger B. Taney* (New York, 1935) and his constitutional history text, *American Constitutional Development* (Boston, 1954). Arguing *obiter dictum* are Charles Warren, *The Supreme Court in United States History* (Boston, 1922); Frank H. Hodder, "Some Phases of the Dred Scott Case," *Mississippi Valley Historical Review* 16 (June 1929): 3-22; and Richard R. Stenberg, "Some Political Aspects of the Dred Scott Case," ibid., 19 (March 1933): 571-77. Two indispensable historiographical essays

unravel the complexities of these conflicting interpretations. The best is Frederick
S. Allis, Jr., "The Dred Scott Labyrinth," in *Teachers of History: Essays in Honor
of Laurence Bradford Packard*, ed. H. Stuart Hughes (Ithaca, N.Y., 1954), pp. 341-
68. Also useful is Thomas B. Alexander, "Historical Treatments of the Dred Scott
Case, 1889-1950," *The Proceedings of the South Carolina Historical Association,
1953*, vol. 23, pp. 37-59. See also Stanley I. Kutler, *The Dred Scott Decision: Law
or Politics?* (Boston, 1967), for a fine bibliographical essay.

Other analytic studies focus on different issues. Morris M. Cohn, "The Dred
Scott Case in Light of Later Events," *American Law Review* 46 (1912): 548-77,
sees the *Dred Scott* decision as the basis for the later *Insular Cases*. Isabel Paterson,
"The Riddle of Chief Justice Taney in the Dred Scott Case," *Georgia Review* 3
(Summer 1949): 192-203, posits an illogical and unconvincing theory that Taney
denied citizenship to Negroes as a step to shipping them back to Africa. John C.
Hogan, "The Role of Chief Justice Taney in the Decision of the Dred Scott Case,"
Case and Comment 58 (1953): 3-8, suggests unpersuasively that Wayne wrote most
of Taney's opinion. Of much more import are the provocative analyses of Robert
J. Harris, "Chief Justice Taney: Prophet of Reform and Reaction," *Vanderbilt Law
Review* 10 (February 1957): 227-57, and Don E. Fehrenbacher, "Roger B. Taney
and the Sectional Crisis," *Journal of Southern History* 43 (November 1977): 555-
66, who see Taney's racism deliberately injected into the decision as a forerunner
of events to come.

The role of the decision in the polarization that then resulted in civil war receives
appropriate attention in the abundant literature on the sectional controversy. James
F. Rhodes, *History of the United States from the Compromise of 1850*, vol. 2, 1854-
1860 (New York, 1904), stresses the prominence of the decision in contributing to
the slavery agitation. Others include John W. Burgess, *The Middle Period, 1817-
1858* (New York, 1904); Daniel W. Howe, *Political History of Secession to the
Beginning of the American Civil War* (New York, 1914); Roy F. Nichols, *The Dis-
ruption of American Democracy* (New York, 1948); Bernard Schwartz, *From
Confederation to Nation, 1835-1877* (Baltimore, 1973). Analytic and provocative
interpretations are found in Henry A. Forster, "Did the Decision in the Dred Scott
Case Lead to the Civil War?" *The American Law Review* 52 (1918): 875-84; Harry
V. Jaffa, *Crisis of the House Divided: An Interpretation of the Issues in the Lincoln-
Douglas Debates* (New York, 1959); Don E. Fehrenbacher, *Prelude to Greatness:
Lincoln in the 1850's* (Stanford, 1962); and John R. Schmidhauser, "Judicial Be-
havior and the Sectional Crisis of 1837-1860," *The Journal of Politics*, 23 (November
1961): 615-40. The constitutional implications are developed in two penetrating
articles by Arthur Bestor, "State Sovereignty and Slavery: A Reinterpretation of
Proslavery Constitutional Doctrine," *Journal of the Illinois Historical Society* 54
(Summer 1961): 117-80, and "The American Civil War as a Constitutional Crisis,"
American Historical Review 69 (January 1964): 327-52.

Several works deal with the motivation behind the case. Frederick Trevor Hill,
Decisive Battles of the Law (New York, 1907), suggests the case originated for
monetary reasons, so that Scott could acquire back wages. Walter Ehrlich shows
that the case originated instead only to secure freedom for Scott and his family,
with no financial or political overtones, but that these became involved in the

case later. See his "Was the Dred Scott Case Valid?" *The Journal of American History* 55 (September 1968): 256-65 (reprinted in *Missouri Historical Review* 62 [April 1969] : 317-28), and "Origins of the Dred Scott Case," *The Journal of Negro History* 59 (April 1974): 132-42.

Traditional scholarship holds with Charles Evans Hughes that the *Dred Scott* decision was a "self-inflicted wound" that diminished the Court's prestige at this critical period in history, forcing it into a relatively minor role until well after Reconstruction. Recent scholarship claims otherwise, that Republicans attacked not the institution of the Court, but its members, and that once Lincoln "Republicanized" the Court it exercised as much authority and influence as ever. See Stanley I. Kutler, *Judicial Power and Reconstruction Politics* (Chicago, 1968); William M. Wiecek, "The Reconstruction of Federal Judicial Power, 1867-1875," *The American Journal of Legal History* 12 (October 1969): 333-59; and Harold M. Hyman, *A More Perfect Union: The Impact of the Civil War and Reconstruction on the Constitution* (New York, 1973). Wallace Mendelson, "Dred Scott's Case—Reconsidered," *Minnesota Law Review* 38 (1953): 16-28, points out that Congress for a long time had been trying to get the Court to decide on the vexing issue of slavery in the territories.

Recent studies point out that Republicans and abolitionists used two basic tactics to discredit the Court without at the same time undermining its institutional integrity: (1) attack the decision as a procedural *obiter dictum* abomination; and (2) accuse Taney of being part of a broader proslavery conspiracy. See especially Joel H. Silbey, *The Transformation of American Politics, 1848-1860* (Englewood Cliffs, N.J., 1967); Michael F. Holt, *Forging a Majority: The Formation of the Republican Party in Pittsburg, 1848-1860* (New Haven, 1969), and *The Political Crisis of the 1850s* (New York, 1978); Eric Foner, *Free Soil, Free Labor, Free Men: The Ideology of the Republican Party before the Civil War* (New York, 1970); and Ronald P. Formisano, *The Birth of Mass Political Parties, 1827-1861* (Princeton, 1971). For more traditional views of Republican party attitudes toward the *Dred Scott* decision, see Winfield J. Davis, *History of Political Conventions in California, 1849-1892* (Sacramento, 1893); Ernest W. Winkler, ed., *Platforms of Political Parties in Texas, Bulletin of the University of Texas, 1916,* no. 53 (Austin, 1916); Walter C. Woodward, *The Rise and Early History of Political Parties in Oregon, 1843-1868* (Portland, 1913); William S. Myers, *The Republican Party* (New York, 1928); and Jeter A. Isely, *Horace Greeley and the Republican Party, 1853-1861* (Princeton, 1947).

Finally, the most comprehensive modern accounts and those absolutely indispensable to anyone wanting a brief but scholarly account of the place of the *Dred Scott* decision in American history are the appropriate chapters in Allan Nevins, *The Emergence of Lincoln,* vol. 1 (New York, 1950), and the appendix in volume 2; Carl Brent Swisher, *The Taney Period, 1836-64* (New York, 1964), which is volume 5 of the massive Oliver Wendell Holmes Devise *History of the Supreme Court of the United States;* David M. Potter, *The Impending Crisis, 1848-1861* (New York, 1976), completed and edited after Professor Potter's death by Don E. Fehrenbacher; and the latter's new book, *The Dred Scott Case: Its Significance in American Law and Politics* (New York, 1978).

Index

Contributions in Legal Studies
Series Editor: *Paul L. Murphy*

About the Author
Walter Ehrlich is associate professor of history and education at the University of Missouri—St. Louis. He is the author of *Presidential Impeachment: An American Dilemma* and has had articles published in *Journal of American History* and *Journal of Negro History.*

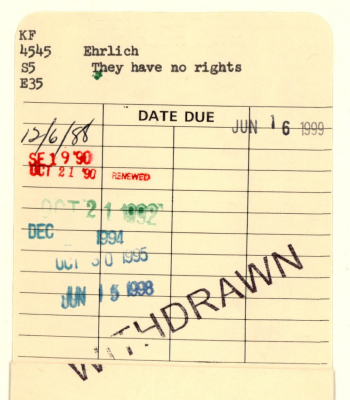